THE COMPREHENSION EXPERIENCE

Engaging Readers Through Effective Inquiry and Discussion

W. Dorsey Hammond
&
Denise D. Nessel

Heinemann
Portsmouth, NH

Heinemann
361 Hanover Street
Portsmouth, NH 03801–3912
www.heinemann.com

Offices and agents throughout the world

The authors and publisher wish to thank those who have generously given permission to reprint borrowed material:

Figure 6.1: From *Lost!* by David McPhail. Copyright © 1990 by David McPhail. Used by permission of Little, Brown and Company.

Figures 6.2, 6.3, and 6.4: From *Frog, Where Are You?* by Mercer Mayer. Copyright © 1969 by Mercer Mayer. Used by permission of Dial Books for Young Readers, a division of Penguin Young Readers Group, a member of Penguin Group (USA) Inc., www.penguin.com. All rights reserved.

Figure 6.5 and text: From *Elephant Families* by Arthur Dorros. Copyright © 1994 by Arthur Dorros. Reprinted by permission of HarperCollins Publishers.

Library of Congress Cataloging-in-Publication Data
Hammond, W. Dorsey.
   The comprehension experience : engaging readers through effective inquiry and discussion / W. Dorsey Hammond, Denise D. Nessel.
      p. cm.
   Includes bibliographical references.
   ISBN-13: 978-0-325-03041-8
   ISBN-10: 0-325-03041-3
   1. Reading comprehension—Study and teaching. I. Nessel, Denise D. II. Title.
LB1050.45.H35 2011
372.47—dc23   2011019980

Acquisitions Editor: Wendy M. Murray
Developmental Editor: Margaret LaRaia
Production: Victoria Merecki
Typesetter: Kim Arney
Cover design: Monica Crigler
Interior design: Bernadette Skok
Manufacturing: Steve Bernier

Printed in the United States of America on acid-free paper
15   14   13   12   11   VP   1   2   3   4   5

We dedicate this book to

Samantha, Alex, Madison, and Mason
and to
Joan and Ford

Contents

Foreword

Once in a great while, a book comes along that radically changes how we perceive and process crucial understandings. *The Comprehension Experience*, seamlessly written and meticulously researched, is that rare book that causes us to rethink much of what we thought we knew about meaningful comprehension instruction and learning. Dorsey Hammond and Denise Nessel—respected scholars who are also highly skilled in the classroom—have written a masterpiece of a book, one that needs to be carefully read by all K–12 teachers of reading and teacher educators.

This is a serious book with an uncommon depth of thinking, yet the text is clear, easy to read, and full of practical suggestions that you will immediately want to put into practice. Most of all, and a cause for celebration, *The Comprehension Experience* is about teaching and empowering all students to think and deliberate at high levels while giving us educators the language and examples of exemplary teaching to make that happen. The authors state:

> What we have proposed in this book is a rethinking of how we go about teaching children to read. Whether we can teach reading comprehension directly or explicitly is not a question that particularly interests us because we believe it to be the wrong question. Rather, the central question is: "What can teachers do on a day-to-day basis to enhance students' existing propensity for comprehension and high-level thinking?"

To that end, the authors give us myriad examples and workable ideas along with the supportive language and specific daily actions that help us to guide students to think deeply about text and to develop the habits of highly skilled readers. In reconsidering common practices and ingrained approaches, the teacher-reader explicitly learns why and how to:

- use guided reading primarily to enhance comprehension and enjoyment of the text
- introduce a story—without the traditional picture walk and the prereading questioning and vocabulary teaching
- do more silent reading, even with young readers
- effectively use prediction and hypothesizing to help students reason their way through stories and informational text

- probe, through asking authentic questions, to stimulate students to ask their own important questions and carefully examine their own ideas
- orchestrate rich discussions and debate across the curriculum
- have students independently collaborate in small groups to productively converse about texts
- use writing to support, improve, and deepen comprehension
- understand the important difference between being a strategic reader and merely applying strategies
- teach all necessary skills and strategies in the course of meaningful reading and writing
- create a respectful classroom culture where all learners "feel honored as thinkers and contributors"

This text could not be timelier. We are teaching in a culture of high anxiety and accountability where standardized test scores define student achievement. Reading instruction overfocuses on skills without sufficient attention to rich discussion around notable fiction and nonfiction texts. The authors state: "The idea of skills or subskills to be mastered needs to be replaced with the idea that reading skillfully is a complex process that is heavily context-dependent." The authors believe that today, and they believed it thirty years ago.

I first met Dorsey Hammond in Chicago in 1981 at the annual conference of the International Reading Association when I attended a session he presented on beginning reading. As a reading specialist who was pulling out small groups of students struggling to learn to read, I knew that my skills-in-isolation approach with its overemphasis on phonics was not serving my students well. Dorsey Hammond was the first educator I heard speak whose words about teaching reading completely resonated with me. He put phonics in perspective, put meaning first, and focused on high-level thinking by asking students inferential questions about worthwhile texts. And he did all of this with even our youngest readers!

After his presentation, I approached him and said, "This was the most in-depth and sensible presentation I've ever heard on teaching reading. I need to learn more. Do you ever come to Cleveland, Ohio?" He graciously invited me to come as his guest to an upcoming presentation at Baldwin-Wallace College, in the Cleveland area where I lived at the time. He later told me he was surprised and delighted when he looked out into the audience and saw me sitting front and center. I was hanging on to his every word and thought. I've been hanging on to his every word and thought ever since and am thrilled that he has teamed up with Denise Nessel to write the book on reading comprehension that we have all needed for a very long time.

Denise Nessel and Dorsey Hammond each studied at the University of Delaware, where they were both highly influenced by the brilliant work and thinking of their most important mentor, Russell Stauffer. Stauffer was one of the first researchers to fully utilize readers' prior knowledge by asking probing questions that guided readers to think more deeply about what they were going to learn through their reading. Stauffer's work and text, *Teaching Reading as a Thinking Process* (1969), became a jumping-off point for Nessel and Hammond's own ground-breaking work and teaching.

Denise has worked for many years as a mentor to teachers, giving particular attention to helping them work more effectively with their underachieving students. One of her primary interests has been engaging students in rich conversations that lead them to deeper, more thoughtful comprehension, knowing that all learners are capable of high-level thinking and substantive learning. One of the delights of this text is that we get to eavesdrop on the conversations these two educators and like-minded teachers have had with students around texts—from the primary grades through high school. Those rich discussions can serve as models for the kinds of conversations we can have with our own students.

It is noteworthy that *The Comprehension Experience* is one of the most thoroughly researched books I've ever read, and this is a good thing. As educators, we often hear "Recent research suggests. . ." or "Research says. . ." without fully understanding what the research actually says and means. Some readers may be tempted to skip Chapter 1, "What We Know About Reading Comprehension: A Century of Research and Thinking." Do not skip it! Knowing and understanding the research is empowering and crucial for being able to wisely problem solve and make the moment-to-moment instructional decisions that are the hallmark of all excellent teaching. Not only that, but it is only through understanding a wide body of relevant research that we can effectively advocate for sane, sensible, exemplary practices for our students and not swing every time the political pendulum moves. Although you can read the chapters in any order that suits you, for example, beginning with Chapter 6, "The Importance of Comprehension Instruction in the Primary Grades," or Chapter 7, "Reading and Thinking Without the Teacher," my strong recommendation is you read the book straight through, in its logical order.

One of my favorite chapters is Chapter 2, "The Power of Story: Supporting Students' Reading of Narrative Texts." It's the first time I've seen such beautifully detailed examples of how to help a story unfold through rich and probing dialogue with students. Such dialogue is not easy to orchestrate but it can be done, and the authors guide us through this journey. As well, Chapter 3, "The Power of Inquiry: Supporting Students' Reading of Informational Texts," also provides rich examples of what it looks like and sounds like to put rich questioning and dialogue at the center of all teaching and learning. Notice how the authors' recommended postreading questions promote genuine inquiry and learning:

- Which of our questions did we answer?
- What questions have we not answered and what new questions have we raised?
- What else did we learn that we didn't talk about or didn't have questions about?
- What was the most surprising or interesting thing you learned from reading?
- What was the most important thing we learned today?
- What do we know now that we didn't know before?

Perhaps most important of all, the power of talk and arousing the readers' curiosity and desire to read are at the heart and soul of *The Comprehension Experience*. The reader comes away with how to use dialogue with students, that is, the specific questions to ask—and the follow-up responses to give—all with the end purpose of leading students to raise their own questions and construct meaning as they read. It is through talking and meaningful conversation, initially guided by the teacher as skillful communicator, that students learn at the highest levels. The authors write:

What the teacher says and does determines how students think about the experience of reading and what they aim to do when they read. Effective instructional language helps students acquire a sense of agency about their reading and thinking.

Hammond and Nessel's text is a winning combination of practical, research-based approaches and ideas that always put respect for the learner's intelligence first. I still remember an anecdote Dorsey told many years ago. He and a colleague were visiting a kindergarten classroom and doing research to learn more about segmentation and blending. Dorsey's colleague made a request to a kindergartner: "Divide these words into as many sounds as you can." The student replied, "Why would I want to do that?"

Children are natural constructors of meaning, but we educators often take the sense out of reading and make the whole process more difficult for them. *The Comprehension Experience* forces us to confront the way we have been teaching reading—to go beyond the current over-emphasis on skills, strategies, and test prep—and to constantly reflect on our practices and ask ourselves, "Why would I want to do that?" Dorsey Hammond and Denise Nessel provide everything we need to know and do to turn the complex process of reading into a deeply meaningful, successful, and satisfying experience. What a magnificent gift to our students and us teachers!

Regie Routman
May 2011

Preface

As graduate students, we each had experiences as learners under the mentorship of Russell Stauffer at the University of Delaware that opened our eyes to the pleasure and depth of learning that's possible when students are guided by a true master teacher. Those unforgettable comprehension experiences led us to refine our own teaching so that we could arouse the same kind of interest and excitement in other learners. We have been focused on this for many years, teaching and guest teaching in elementary, secondary, and university classrooms and conducting workshops for educators. Our years of practical experience, coupled with study and research, have honed our understanding of what works best to develop learners' reading comprehension.

With this book, we invite you to look at comprehension through our eyes and to think with us about what makes comprehension experiences most effective. We discuss basic principles and share what we know about the psychology of learning. We also include extensive lesson dialogues to show the kinds of teacher–student interactions that are particularly effective when comprehension is the goal. These dialogues showcase instruction that is not commonplace in today's classrooms but is highly effective when it forms the core of the reading program. They help tell our story in important ways.

Some of our perspectives diverge from current conventional wisdom. This is because we are not easily swayed by what happens to be popular when it goes against what we know to be effective. We are concerned with some recent trends in instruction and assessment that do not reflect what the most skillful readers do and that at times may even work against students' attempts to comprehend. We think it's time to decrease the emphasis on skills and strategies and turn our attention to increasing learners' capacity to construct meaning. Our priority is developing students who think critically when they read, who are primarily and consistently attentive to meanings, who proceed as well independently as when guided by a teacher, who are genuinely enthused about reading, and who experience joy in learning and discovery.

What we say in this book is relevant to reading instruction for all students at all grade levels, from those who learned to read before they came to school and would read well without much help from us to those who are struggling and suspect that they may not have what it takes to read well. In our minds, these students all share important characteristics: intelligence, curiosity, useful prior knowledge and life experiences, a natural inclination to make sense of things, and a genuine desire to learn. We think it's up to us, as teachers, to make good use of these considerable strengths that all learners bring to the classroom and to design comprehension experiences that will help them all flourish as readers and learners.

We have sequenced the chapters in the book in the way that makes the most sense to us, but readers may choose to read them in a different order.

In Chapter 1, we take a look at the people who have shaped our views of reading comprehension, beginning with the scholars of the early twentieth century and ending with those who are today making useful contributions. We are especially interested in one strong, unbroken thread that is evident through the decades: the view that reading is, at heart, a dynamic meaning-making process and that instruction is most effective when the priority at all grade levels is helping students construct meaning as they read.

With meaning making in mind, we focus in Chapters 2 and 3 on guiding the reading of narrative and informational text, respectively. We see these categories of text, and the comprehension experiences associated with them, as different enough to warrant substantially different instructional approaches. Similarities do exist, but the pathways to success are different. The more the differences are appreciated, the better the teaching and learning.

We devote Chapter 4 to an examination of how talking nurtures and enhances comprehension. We elaborate on the guided discussions described in Chapters 2 and 3 to consider a wider range of classroom interactions. We note how the quantity and quality of student talk strongly influences the nature and depth of students' comprehension, calling attention to general principles and giving examples of effective classroom interactions.

We focus in Chapter 5 on reading–writing connections, especially noting how writing supports and extends comprehension. We make a distinction between writing in conjunction with narrative text and informational text, highlighting important principles and suggesting specific activities. We also suggest how students can explore different forms of discourse in ways that enhance their comprehension abilities and how they can most easily develop the disposition to write in order to communicate their own meanings.

In Chapter 6, we describe the kind of early literacy instruction that is most useful in orienting students to reading as a meaning-construction process. We think the discussions in this chapter are most meaningful when read with the first five chapters as background, but those who are particularly interested in emergent literacy may want to read this chapter first.

Chapter 7 rounds out our perspective with a discussion of the ultimate goal of reading instruction: students' effective functioning as readers when they are not under the direct supervision of teachers. This is a critical measure of an instructional program's success.

We would like to express our gratitude to the many friends and colleagues who contributed one way or another to the final product. We thank George and Gerry Coon for reading selected manuscript chapters and providing good advice and encouragement, and we give special recognition to colleague Ron Cramer for his friendship and inspiration and for being a model of scholarship and diligence. We also thank Joan Buffone for her sage advice on numerous questions we raised and Ford Newbold for his response to key points that helped further our thinking. Their intellectual and emotional support and encouragement were vital to the completion of this project.

In addition, we thank our university students, the educators with whom we have worked in so many schools, the participants in our many workshops, and the valued colleagues with whom we have had so many enriching discussions. Their response to our ideas has helped us understand how to explain our thinking to a wider audience. We also particularly thank Darlene Wade, Shirley Oleinick, Sylvia Nagel, and Linda Dickieson from Ferndale, Michigan, and Sue Case from Waterford, Michigan, whose skill as teachers and rapport with learners are especially admirable. With their permission, we used lessons they conducted as the basis for several of the dialogues in this book. We also warmly acknowledge the many young people in classrooms across the country who respond with such enthusiasm to our pedagogy and to the texts we and their classroom teachers read and discuss with them. Their amazing responses again and again sustain our faith in the thinking capacities of school-aged learners.

In the Heinemann family, we thank Regie Routman for putting us in touch with the editorial team, initiating what has become such a positive relationship, and for giving us such useful feedback. We are grateful to Wendy Murray, who gave us invaluable guidance as we began to prepare our final manuscript, and to Margaret LaRaia, who diligently and enthusiastically saw the project through still more revisions. And we appreciate the fine support of the rest of the in-house team, including Victoria Merecki, Eric Chalek, Monica Crigler, and Steve Bernier. We especially thank our friends at Heinemann for understanding and believing in our ideas. In short, they get it. We are grateful that they have been so interested in helping us get our message out to a wider audience.

We have been thinking about this project for more than a decade, having realized how often we responded in the same ways to what was going on in the world of reading, but we were too busy to turn the thoughts into a book. We are glad we finally found the time. The endeavor has been exceedingly pleasurable and rewarding. We hope you find as much satisfaction in reading the book as we did in writing it.

Dorsey Hammond
Denise Nessel
2011

What Do You Think?

An Invitation to Our Readers

Here are some statements related to reading comprehension. We did not design them to be tricky or to make you wonder about "right" or "wrong" answers. This is just our way of inviting you to think about some of the issues we explore in this book.

Based on your experiences, decide if you agree or disagree with each statement. Put an *A* or *D* on the line to indicate what you think or the direction in which you are leaning.

You may wish to respond to all the statements at once or think about them chapter by chapter, as they are arranged here. If you are reading and discussing the book with colleagues, we encourage you to share your views about the statements related to each chapter before reading the chapter. We are confident that such professional reflection and discussion will enhance your reading.

At the end of the book we will invite you to think again about the statements.

Chapter 1

____ 1.   Much of what we know about reading comprehension has been discovered within the past two or three decades.

____ 2.   Classroom observation studies indicate that teachers in grades 1–6 spend a significant amount of time teaching students how to comprehend texts.

____ 3.   Young children are predisposed to make sense of their world, including understanding the texts they read in school.

Chapter 2

____ 4.   The anticipation or prediction of upcoming story events motivates students and enhances their comprehension.

____ 5.   It is normal for several students to read the same story and generate different interpretations.

____ 6. Extensive preparation before reading enhances students' understanding of a narrative text.

____ 7. It is a good technique to teach a skill or strategy before reading a story so that students can immediately practice it as they read.

____ 8. A strong emphasis on explicit instruction in skills and strategies is a major priority when the goal is developing critical and thoughtful readers.

Chapter 3

____ 9. Prior knowledge is a critical factor in the successful reading of informational texts.

____ 10. A student's misconceptions about a topic should be minimized or corrected before the student reads an informational text about the topic.

____ 11. Allowing students to share their misconceptions with peers may inhibit the comprehension and learning of the other students.

____ 12. The process of reading informational texts tends to be similar across the various subject areas (e.g., science, social studies, math, health).

Chapter 4

____ 13. Talking is a primary vehicle for constructing meaning.

____ 14. One of the most effective ways to improve the quality of student talk is to change the nature of teacher talk.

Chapter 5

____ 15. Writing is a major means of fostering comprehension and learning.

____ 16. First students learn to write, and then they write to learn.

____ 17. Writing models and frames can develop student dependency.

____ 18. At any grade level, the primary focus of writing should be on the quality of the content.

Chapter 6

____ 19. The long-held view that first children learn to read and then read to learn is still viable in today's schools.

____ 20. Word recognition must be accurate and rapid before sufficient attention can be directed to comprehension.

____ 21. When students read text orally to a teacher or classmates, their comprehension is usually enhanced.

Chapter 7

____ 22. An effective way of enhancing vocabulary growth is to address vocabulary after the reading of the text.

____ 23. Effective comprehension instruction usually begins with teacher modeling.

____ 24. Thinking about one's own thinking is critical to effective independent reading.

____ 25. An important measure of effective literacy instruction is how readers perform when the teacher is not present.

Now that you have completed some or all of the statements, check (√) the ones you feel confident about. If you feel ambivalent about any, indicate that with a question mark (?).

CHAPTER 1

What We Know About Reading Comprehension

A Century of Research and Thinking

Each year, scores of articles appear in professional journals suggesting strategies and techniques for improving reading comprehension. Teachers' manuals provide step-by-step directions, and professional books offer yet other perspectives. The advice in one source, however, all too often conflicts with that in others, leaving the practitioner without clear and consistent guidelines. Educators understandably wonder how to make the best decisions about instruction when they are faced with so many options, competing theories, and practices.

A logical first step is to examine what is known about how humans learn, concentrating on those aspects of learning that are especially relevant to text comprehension. Fortunately, investigations into the process of comprehending text have a long and rich history, dating back more than one hundred years. As a body of work, the research provides an excellent foundation for understanding the process of comprehension and is of great value to teachers today.

Why Knowing About the History of Reading Research Is So Important

To engage readers with texts effectively, sustain motivation for reading, and ensure that the learners retain and use what they read, it isn't enough to have a repertoire of instructional strategies and techniques. Understanding the comprehension experience from the student's perspective is essential, and that's what the most fruitful research has always focused on.

What does it mean for students to genuinely comprehend what they are reading? What do excellent teachers do and say to enhance comprehension? How does the reader's prior knowledge affect comprehension? Does prior knowledge serve different functions for narrative versus informational texts? How is it possible for two skilled readers to construct different interpretations when reading the same text, and how should we deal with this phenomenon? Does it help young readers to think about their own thinking? If so, what can teachers do to facilitate this? Eminent scholars through the years have given thought to such questions. Their research has clear implications for classroom teachers, but many are unaware of the useful findings. Certain practices are in widespread use today, even though reading experts have raised cautions about them for years. Other effective practices are often overlooked, although knowledgeable scholars have long encouraged teachers to use them. It's time we all became more conversant with this important body of knowledge.

Without the critical knowledge about comprehension that has been developed and refined through the years, teachers end up basing instructional decisions on what others say is appropriate, or perhaps they just follow the latest trends. With this knowledge, however, they can make sound decisions, from the important thinking involved in lesson planning to the moment-to-moment shifts during lessons and discussions that expert teachers make every day. Knowing what is known about comprehension is thus critical for those who want to teach effectively.

Our purpose here is not to provide an exhaustive review of comprehension research through the years. We want only to highlight the scholarly work that we consider most important for understanding the comprehension experience and most useful for improving classroom practice.

Early Twentieth-Century Scholarship

In the early twentieth century, five seminal thinkers gave careful thought and research attention to reading comprehension, laying foundations on which the profession is still building. These scholars are not sufficiently cited today, but their influence remains significant.

Huey: Reading for Meaning

In 1908, Edmund Burke Huey published one of the most enlightening and important books ever written about reading: *The Psychology and Pedagogy of Reading*. The book balances overarching principles and practical pedagogy, drawing upon the scientific and scholarly work of the time. Huey (1908) indicates unequivocally that reading is not the serial recognition of individual words, stressing that the sentence is "a unitary expression of thought" (123). He asserts that reading is an active, meaning-seeking process, equates reading with thinking, and points out that meaning cues help readers recognize and process words.

Huey emphasizes the importance of reading silently, even for young readers, so that learners can focus on meaning. He points out that reading orally places undue emphasis on performance, to the detriment of comprehension, and that outside of school, people read silently much more frequently than they do orally. He advocates a focus on "thought getting" (comprehension) from the beginning of reading instruction, advising that correspondingly less attention be paid to pronouncing words and engaging in isolated drills to learn letter–sound correspondences. These ideas were revolutionary. At the time, many scholars were focused on eye movement studies and recognition of individual words, and teachers were focused primarily on oral reading.

Thorndike: Reading as Reasoning

Just a few years later, in 1917, Edward Thorndike published his classic "Reading as Reasoning." In this study, approximately five hundred students in grades 5–8 read a fifty-seven-word, one-sentence paragraph and answered questions about the contents. In his analysis of the results, Thorndike notes that the students' responses did not fall into a few clearly defined categories, as might be expected, but showed a variety that "threatens to baffle any explanation" (1917, 327). He concludes that in order to read effectively, readers must give more attention to certain words and less attention to others, referring to the "over-potency and under-potency of words." He argues that individual words make differential contributions to the reader's overall comprehension and that the reader determines their relative importance by using the surrounding words.

Thorndike stresses the cognitive complexity involved in understanding a sentence or a paragraph. He agrees with Huey that readers do not simply identify words one by one but instead consider word connotations, note different units of information, decide on their relative significance, and put all the pieces together to make sense of the whole. He compares comprehending a

> *Reading is primarily about comprehension and thinking. Oral reading of the round-robin type interferes with this complex, meaning-oriented process.*

paragraph to solving a mathematical problem, stressing that the reader "must select, repress, soften, emphasize, correlate and organize" in the context of "the right mental set or purpose or demand" (1917, 330).

Thorndike, like Huey, asserts that reading is not primarily a process of decoding but rather one of interpreting and reasoning. He also argues for more silent reading in classrooms, noting that readers do not usually attend to meanings when they read aloud. He strengthens Huey's argument that reading is primarily about comprehension and thinking and that oral reading of the round-robin type interferes with this complex, meaning-oriented process.

Bartlett: Reading as a Constructive Process

Several years later, Sir Frederic Bartlett published the influential *Remembering* (1932) that is the genesis of the constructivist perspective. His best-known experiment involved a passage titled "The War of the Ghosts." He chose this Native American tale because it was quite different from the stories of his British subjects' culture. The passage required subjects to make many inferences because the information is not organized, sequenced, or connected in ways that are clear to most European minds. In response to the passage, each of the twenty subjects wrote individual recalls. They were subsequently asked to produce additional written recalls days, months, and even years later. Bartlett analyzed the recalls, comparing them to the original text, and observed several phenomena.

Over time the subjects condensed the story. Unexpectedly, however, their remembering was not simply verbatim or detail-by-detail recall; rather, they changed the story, a process Bartlett refers to as "transformation." Although they recalled some elements quite well, they added others to create causal links or explain events, making the story more comprehensible (to them) and adjusting the elements to conform to their own cultural experiences. This was a consistent finding across Bartlett's studies. For example, in another passage he used in his research, a young boy decides to hide from his father. Some subjects recalled that the boy wished to play a trick on his father, others that he was hiding because he was afraid of his father. Some subjects even constructed a moral for the story. However, the original text made no reference to tricks or the boy's fear and contained no moral.

Bartlett's findings suggest that individuals actively build or create their own meaning through the generative and selective processing of information. The meaning does not reside in the text, waiting to be plucked out. The text provides information; the reader, interacting with the text, generates the meaning. This accounts for how individuals can read the same text and arrive at different but equally legitimate interpretations or can watch the same film and draw different conclusions about the characters, theme, and even the plot. Ogden and Richards (1923) suggest a similar idea: that the concept of a text's objective meaning is elusive because individuals generate different interpretations when they read.

Bartlett's work demonstrates also that humans are strongly disposed to make sense of what they experience and are uncomfortable when things do not make sense. When his subjects did not see connections between events in a story, they constructed scenarios that made sense to them and "re-membered" those rather than the originals. Many scholars since Bartlett have noted similar cognitive maneuvers aimed at meaning making. Indeed, the drive to make sense of experience is a powerful impetus for human growth and development.

> *The meaning does not reside in the text, waiting to be plucked out. The text provides information; the reader, interacting with the text, generates the meaning.*

Dewey and Kelley: Reading as a Subjective Process

Others of Bartlett's generation drew similar conclusions. John Dewey believed that individuals expect things to make sense and will actively imbue experiences with meaning if they do not appear to be meaningful. In presenting this idea, Dewey (1910) posits the existence of two kinds of understanding. The first is "apprehension," the immediate, direct understanding that individuals have when what they perceive is highly familiar; the second is "comprehension," understanding that involves interpretations, inferences, and other mental efforts to make sense of perceptions (120). An example from our own experience will illustrate. Two beach walkers apprehend pebbly sand, but only one comprehends that small crabs have been at work. The meaning is not inherent in the sand's appearance; the more knowledgeable individual has prior knowledge of crab behavior and uses it to generate the meaning. Dewey also stresses that curiosity must be nurtured if students are to develop inquiring minds and sustain motivation for learning.

John Dewey believed that individuals expect things to make sense and will actively imbue experiences with meaning if they do not appear to be meaningful.

Earl Kelley, a friend and colleague of Dewey's, was strongly influenced by groundbreaking visual perception experiments he witnessed at Dartmouth College. He concluded from these studies that meaning does not lie in external reality but is constructed by the individual who perceives the phenomenon. He further argued that individuals are selective in their perceptions and that comprehension is thus "doubly personal and subjective" because of the combined effects of the individual's experiences and purposes (Kelley 1947, 67). Thus, beach walkers who are interested in the crabs will notice the pebbly sand, while surfers may not even attend to the sand, intent instead on the appearance of the waves. The situation with readers is analogous. Each attends to details in the text that relate to specific past experiences, interests, and current purposes. What one individual considers vitally important to the overall meaning may be downplayed or even ignored by another. This phenomenon does not suggest careless reading; it simply reveals the influence of individual perspectives on the reading process.

Mid-Twentieth-Century Scholarship

The middle of the twentieth century saw expanded attention to the psychology of reading and changes in classroom practice. Scholars explored a range of issues, from analyzing the reading process to devising specific pedagogical techniques. Key contributors during this period had far-reaching effects on educators' belief systems and instructional practices.

Frederick Davis: Comprehension Skills Identified and Analyzed

Frederick Davis (1944) used factor analysis to determine if comprehension could be defined in terms of components. He named several, including understanding word meaning, grasping author's purpose, identifying the main idea, and making inferences. His statistical analysis led to a belief that the factors he named are the building blocks of comprehension and that instruction in these "subskills" would improve students' comprehension. Because of Davis' work, an entire industry emerged in the 1950s and 1960s to publish workbooks and exercises designed to give students practice in comprehension subskills. The focus continued in the 1970s, when subskills were more and more seen as the "basics" of comprehension. This orientation is evident today in many instructional materials, in the standards that state governments set for student performance, and in the standardized tests and other assessments that are used to measure reading achievement.

Although measures of comprehension can be factored statistically into components, whether or not the process should be broken down for instructional purposes is highly questionable. Learners who comprehend text can understand word meanings, make inferences, and state the main idea. However, that doesn't mean that the reverse holds true. In fact, little evidence exists that the common classroom practice of assigning isolated comprehension skill exercises improves comprehension of stories, articles, and other texts. Also, the view of comprehension as a collection of subskills is contrary to all that Huey, Thorndike, Bartlett, Dewey, and Kelley noted about the reading process and all that we have later come to understand.

Betts: The Directed Reading Activity (A Teacher-Centered Approach)

While Davis was popularizing the idea of subskills, Emmett Betts emerged as a major influence on reading pedagogy. Though grounded in psychology and learning theory, Betts was also interested in the instruction he saw in classroom and clinical settings. Like Huey and Thorndike, Betts understood the importance of silent reading. He recognized that students need to apply background knowledge, learn vocabulary, and have clear reading purposes. He also noted that reading aloud expressively is a characteristic of skilled readers, and he believed that students should use reading to extend, enrich, and apply their knowledge. Like Davis, he thought that explicit skill instruction was important, at least to some degree, but usually in the context of the guided reading of a text. His beliefs led him to devise the Directed Reading Activity, or DRA, for guiding students through a text (Betts 1946). He advised organizing students into small groups according to their reading levels and following these steps:

1. Prepare students by building their background knowledge, teaching relevant concepts and/or vocabulary, and setting purposes for reading.
2. Have students read silently to accomplish these purposes.
3. Have students review the purposes after reading to determine if they have been addressed. In addition, develop word recognition, comprehension, and language conventions through specific skill instruction and the use of practice exercises.

4. Have students take turns rereading the selection orally, usually on a subsequent day, in order to develop their fluency and expressiveness.

5. Provide story-related enrichment or extension activities.

Betts' DRA appears to be the first formal plan offered to teachers for guided reading, and its straightforward, orderly steps made it quite popular. In fact, with few variations, the DRA has been used in the teachers' manuals of almost every major reading series published since the 1950s and has had a profound effect on classroom reading instruction and on the models of guided reading that have emerged since then. Notably, the DRA is a teacher-centered approach to reading. The teacher introduces vocabulary, provides background knowledge, sets the reading purposes, decides what will be read aloud, determines how well students have understood the text, and devises the follow-up activities.

Stauffer: The Directed Reading-Thinking Activity (A Learner-Centered Approach)

Russell Stauffer was a student of Emmett Betts. He was well acquainted with the work of Huey, Thorndike, Bartlett, and others, and he was greatly interested in the cognitive aspects of the reading process. Influenced by Dewey, he also recognized the importance of the reader's personal involvement and the value of curiosity as a motivator. In addition to his scholarly interests, Stauffer was also informed by his teaching experiences. He founded and directed the Reading-Study Center at the University of Delaware, where children with reading difficulties came four days a week for instruction. He observed them closely, analyzing the effect that interactions with their teachers had on their motivation and learning. When he was not at the Reading-Study Center, he was in classrooms, teaching, observing, and analyzing learners' behavior. He repeatedly tested theory against classroom pedagogy; what made sense theoretically had to have positive effects on real learners.

The combination of theory and practice, along with intuitive insights, led Stauffer in the 1950s to view reading as an active process of constructing meaning, driven by the reader's interests and levels of motivation. He was convinced that even the youngest children have a great capacity to think critically. He concluded that the core of reading must be thinking, and he realized that Betts' DRA did not sufficiently encourage high-level thinking. In response, he devised the Directed Reading-Thinking Activity (DRTA). This fundamentally different way of teaching stemmed from significantly different assumptions about learners and learning than those dominating Betts' views. Stauffer disseminated the new approach in a series of classroom materials for children (Stauffer and Burrows 1960) and in professional books for teachers (Stauffer 1969, 1975). He also taught it to his university students, who have honored his efforts by sharing and building on his perspectives.

Stauffer understood the importance of prior knowledge, but he rejected the didactic approach to building background that Betts advocated. Rather, he elicited learners' existing knowledge through probing questions and guided them to apply that knowledge in thinking about what they were going to learn. This way of tapping and using prior knowledge is a hallmark of the DRTA and stands in contrast to the prereading instruction that occurs in a DRA. Furthermore, although Stauffer agreed with Betts that learners must read purposefully, he objected to the use of teacher-declared purposes. He believed that learners must set their own purposes for reading, pointing out that "self declared purposes . . . make the reader a student of what he is reading rather than a servant" (1969, 12). Rather than telling students what to look for, he used predicting (with narrative texts) and hypothesizing (with informational texts) to stimulate their curiosity so that their own unanswered questions would motivate them to read. In these ways, Stauffer moved the student to the front and center of the act of reading, which he saw as a problem-solving process.

When Stauffer spoke of self-declared purposes, he wasn't suggesting that students should have carte blanche to read for whatever purposes they happened to generate. He thought their purposes should reflect their own preconceptions and follow directly from the predictions or hypotheses that would most naturally arise in the context of the lesson. He believed that students do not need necessarily to declare their purposes explicitly or publicly; they must simply know in their own minds why they are reading and what they hope to find out, and they should be able to articulate their purposes when queried. For example, when reading *Sarah, Plain and Tall* (MacLachlan 1985), a reader might say, if queried, *I'm reading to find out if Sarah is coming back after she goes to town or if is she going back to Maine instead*. Or when reading an informational text about ladybugs, a reader might say, *I'm reading to find out what ladybugs eat and if they all have the same number of spots*. Both examples illustrate an important point about self-declared purposes, namely that they are specific to the text and to the individual reader's interests and questions. They are thus more useful than vague purposes such as reading for pleasure or reading for information, more substantive than reading to complete a certain number of pages, and more engaging than reading to fulfill teacher purposes.

Stauffer's focus on effective use of prior knowledge, prediction or hypothesizing, self-generated purposes, and intellectual engagement revealed him to be a constructivist before the term was commonly used in education. We will return to his perspective in succeeding chapters as we examine more closely the nature and nurture of comprehension.

Rosenblatt, Britton, and Moffett: Reader–Text Interactions

Other scholars also espoused constructivist views of learning. Three whose work we find particularly relevant are Louise Rosenblatt, James Britton, and James Moffett. All helped to illuminate the dynamics of reader–text interactions.

Rosenblatt laid the foundations for reader response theory with *Literature as Exploration* (1938) and focused on eliciting response to literature in *The Reader, the Text, the Poem* (1978). Between these two major books, she published scores of articles about teaching literature from a student-centered perspective. A constructivist, she believed that reading involves a back-and-forth exchange between the text and the reader, a transaction that results in the generation of meaning. In her *transactional theory,* the reader's prior knowledge, cultural perspectives, and feelings as well as the specific time and place of the reading experience are as significant to comprehension as the words on the page. Thus, different individuals can read the same text and arrive at different interpretations, and the same individual can read a text at different times in life and have different interpretations and reactions.

Rosenblatt also argued that students should have the opportunity to discuss what they read because sharing ideas in a group leads to deeper understanding. In fact, the collaborative construction of understanding is at the heart of many human endeavors. Teachers hold faculty meetings to solve problems; business partners work together on a course of action; physicians confer with colleagues about patients. Negotiating meaning with others and seeking clarification through interaction are very common in the adult world outside of school and should be common in the classroom, especially when comprehension is the goal.

One of Rosenblatt's best-known distinctions is between efferent and aesthetic reading (Rosenblatt 1978). Reading aesthetically is the "joy of the journey," the pure pleasure of interacting with a text, savoring the language, or appreciating the author's craft. Efferent reading, in contrast, is aimed at finding information (from the Greek *effere*, to take or carry away). Reading directions to assemble a toy or to identify an antidote for poison are oft-cited examples of efferent reading. Individuals also engage in efferent reading to learn new skills, answer questions, satisfy curiosity, and acquire more knowledge. Some contrast the two as stark either-or stances. However, readers may shift fluidly from one to the other as they read or may sustain both simultaneously. For example, a child with a keen interest in dinosaurs can find useful information about dinosaurs and at the same time savor the attractive pictures or enjoy the simple act of discovery. Similarly, an adult may appreciate a beautifully written historical novel while simultaneously making note of important information about the era.

James Britton, perhaps best known for his work on language development and his influence on writing instruction, has also contributed useful insights about the reading process. Britton (1982) cites early-twentieth-century studies in which London researcher Daniel Jones played unclear recordings of a conversation. At first, the subjects were unable to make any sense of what they heard. Jones then described the setting and the people involved. When the subjects listened again, they were now able to follow much of the conversation. Britton uses this study, and other observations, to contend that a reader's expectations have a strong influence on the meanings the reader generates. He asserts that reading should not be seen as a word-by-word building up of meaning but a process in which readers combine their expectations with the information in the text to generate meaning. He stresses that expectations are as critical as the text, pointing out that when readers are focused on meaning, they don't so much look at the words as see beyond the words to the meaning. Britton further asserts that reading comprehension is one manifestation of the more general process individuals use to understand the world around them.

James Moffett (1968b) agrees that reading comprehension is a text-oriented instance of the broader process of understanding that includes comprehension of speech and of experience in general. This is a useful point of view, especially when considering students who have difficulty comprehending a specific text. The problem, seen from Moffett's perspective, is one of grappling with meanings, not of decoding the message. The implication is that in most cases comprehension difficulties should not be addressed by providing additional instruction in word processing because the critical issue is understanding the concepts to which words refer, not pronouncing the words.

Moffett (1968a) presents a framework for instruction that puts the student at the center of learning and makes discourse processing the focus of teaching. He argues that reading and writing—and the various thinking processes associated with each—are central to learning in all disciplines. In addition, he outlines a curriculum that coordinates discourse processing with students' cognitive development, advocating language and thinking activities that begin with the highly personal and concrete (e.g., first-person narratives) and move gradually to the more remote and abstract (e.g., argumentative essays or scientific theories). Such an approach to instruction gives special emphasis on how students think, see the world, and make use of experience. In the classroom, texts are thus used for developing students' thinking and their use of language rather than entities to be learned about or to be mastered; the content is subordinate to the students' growing capacity to comprehend and compose. The resulting "student-centered curriculum" focuses on integrating reading and writing, on engaging students in activities that best match their current levels of cognition, and on keeping classroom activities as authentic as possible and reflective of students' genuine interests and purposes. Refined and extended through the years (Moffett and Wagner 1991), this framework for language learning remains highly useful for practitioners.

Rosenblatt, Britton, and Moffett all noted the value of whole-class discussions, small-group collaborations, and conversations with a partner as means for developing comprehension. A major implication of their work is that students must have opportunities to talk things through. From their perspectives, giving brief answers to teacher questions does not adequately develop learners' understanding.

> *Students must have opportunities to talk things through. Giving brief answers to teacher questions does not adequately develop learners' understanding.*

The Critical Thinking Movement

Other mid-twentieth-century scholars were intent on positioning critical thinking and problem solving as vital goals of schooling. This emphasis may have stemmed in part from Cold War politics, which placed a new premium on rigorous academics, although the scholars themselves seem to have been apolitical. Highlights of this development included David Russell's publication in 1956 of *Children's Thinking* and the appearance in the same year of *A Study of Thinking*, the classic work by Bruner, Goodnow, and Austin. Then Hullfish and Smith (1961) published *Reflective Thinking*, and Louis Raths (1961) articulated his design for a cognition-oriented curriculum in *Teaching for Thinking*. Soon thereafter, Hilda Taba (1962) published a social studies curriculum that placed problem solving and critical thinking at its core. Substantive discussions of classic works of literature also received considerable attention during this period. The Great Books movement, begun by Mortimer Adler and Robert Maynard Hutchins in 1947, was extended in 1960 to school-aged children. The purpose of the program was to encourage the kind of critical reading described by Adler (1940) in his influential publication *How to Read a Book*.

The emphasis on critical thinking and problem solving became an increasingly important part of the dialogue on reading comprehension.

The Goodmans: A Closer Look at Reading as a Language and Thinking Process

Another group of scholars, led by Ken and Yetta Goodman, have conducted several hundred studies on the nature of the reading process. See, for example, Goodman (1969), Goodman and Burke (1973), and Brown, Goodman, and Marek (1996). The research methodology was simple and straightforward: listen to individuals read extended text orally, record their performance, and analyze it. The Goodmans were particularly interested in the qualitative nature of the act of reading and the reader's departures from text, which they called "miscues." Before their studies, these departures were thought of as errors, but Ken Goodman (1967) notes that many of these departures show the strengths of the reader and upon closer examination reveal what might be going on in the reader's head. In addition, Goodman points out that many miscues have no deleterious impact on the reader's understanding.

From this research, several patterns emerged. First, the findings indicated that good readers usually generate fewer miscues than poor readers and their miscues are less costly. That is, their deviations from the text seldom detract from comprehension. Good readers are also far more likely to correct a miscue to preserve meaning. In the vast majority of cases, when miscues are at the word level, the substituted word has the same grammatical function as the word in the text; for example, *happy* for *funny* or *slowly* for *carefully*, suggesting a strong knowledge-of-syntax influence on reading performance. In addition, some readers, especially young children, add words that are not in the text, reflecting language patterns they have heard; for example, if the text reads *the tiny baby* the child may read *the tiny little baby*. The miscue research also strongly suggested that readers anticipate some words in the text before their eyes perceive the words and that dialect-influenced pronunciations of words almost never affect the reader's comprehension of the text. Overall, the findings demonstrated that merely counting the number of an oral reader's deviations from the text is seldom an indication of the reader's strengths or weaknesses.

Goodman generated his constructivist theory of the reading process from his extensive observations, asserting that readers use three kinds of cues: semantic, syntactic, and visual/auditory. These cues operate interactively and redundantly not only in the construction of meaning but also in the actual processing of text. In brief, a reader's knowledge of language and knowledge of the world facilitate word recognition as well as comprehension. The most important implications are:

- The process of reading cannot be adequately analyzed or studied at the word level.
- Reading is both a cognitive and a language process. Miscues consistently indicate the inner workings of readers' thinking as they process text.
- Readers of all ages are disposed to generate meaning as they process texts. Even the youngest children will go to great lengths to produce utterances that are meaningful to them when they read.
- Readers' attention to meaning, along with their intuitive knowledge of language, facilitates word recognition, but pronouncing words accurately does not necessarily facilitate comprehension, either for novice readers or for mature readers.
- The construction of meaning is not merely the goal of reading; it is a major contributor to the actual process of learning to read.

The Impact of Cognitive Psychology on Conceptions of Comprehension

While the Goodmans studied the constructivist and linguistic tendencies of individual readers, three scholars on the world stage were making an impact from a cognitive perspective: Jean Piaget in Switzerland, Lev Vygotsky in Russia, and Jerome Bruner in England and the United States. These cognitive psychologists contributed additional critical elements to the constructivist view of reading comprehension.

Jean Piaget: Using Cognitive Disequilibration to Motivate Learning

Jean Piaget first published his ideas in the 1930s, but his work began to influence the English-speaking world only in the 1950s and 1960s as he extended his research and as more of his works were translated into English. Two of his concepts are critical to our exploration of the process of comprehension: assimilation/accommodation and disequilibration. Piaget (1953, 1973) considered assimilation and accommodation the essence of learning. Simply put, individuals take in (assimilate) new information and adjust (accommodate) to the new information by modifying their existing perspectives and/or behavior. They are not passive in this process but are actively engaged in incorporating new information and adjusting their conceptual frameworks accordingly.

Originally a biologist, Piaget understood that organisms are ordinarily in a state of equilibrium; homeostasis is the rule. When a disruption occurs (disequilibration), the organism adjusts to restore homeostasis. For example, physical exertion generates heat and raises internal body temperature. Sweat glands then begin the cooling process, which brings the temperature back to normal. Cognitive disequilibration results in similar adjustments. As an example, you may see someone familiar in a social situation but draw a blank. Your forgetting bothers you, and you ask someone for help. Reminded of the name, your uncertainty disappears and you are again at ease, back to a state of cognitive equilibrium. The phenomenon of cognitive dissonance (Festinger 1957) is another example of this kind of disequilibration: You become uncomfortably aware that two ideas contradict one another and are motivated to reduce the dissonance and restore cognitive equilibrium by accepting one idea and rejecting the other, rejecting both and looking for third, or perhaps simply ignoring some of the information.

Although Piaget did not address the connection between curiosity and cognition, his concept of disequilibration accounts for the manner in which curiosity motivates learning. For example, uncertainty about the outcome of a novel propels readers through the text, and when they have questions they want to answer, they are eager to seek relevant information. In both situations, the awareness of not knowing is a form of disequilibration that demands attention and resolution.

Teachers do not need to teach students to assimilate, accommodate, and respond to a state of cognitive disequilibration: these are natural mental processes. However, teachers can capitalize on them. They can, for example, design learning activities that make students conscious of taking in new information and changing their thinking as a result, and they can motivate students by creating learning situations that lead to cognitive disequilibration.

Lev Vygotsky: The Importance of Social Culture on Students' Learning

Vygotsky's work, like Piaget's, gained popularity in the United States in the 1960s and 1970s when English translations made it more widely accessible. He is perhaps best known for his focus on the close relation between language and thought, his interest in the social dimensions of learning, and his use of the concept of the zone of proximal development (ZPD).

Vygotsky (1962, 1978) asserts that cognition is enhanced by language and language is influenced by thought. Children use language not only to communicate with others but also to mediate their own thinking and responding. When young children at play talk to themselves, for example, they are not primarily announcing what they are doing to anyone who may be watching but are most likely vocalizing what they are doing in order to process it and understand it. In fact, for learners of all ages, talk serves a critical function in helping to shape and clarify

> *Classroom interactions, which are part of the culture of the classroom, have as much impact on student learning as the content of the curriculum.*

thought. The implication is that learners must talk in order to learn: to the teacher, to each other, and to themselves. Britton (1970) draws the same conclusions.

Vygotsky was especially interested in the individual as a member of society, noting that individuals' language, thinking, and learning are heavily influenced by the social contexts within which they grow and develop. As he pointed out, individuals learn language in social settings, interacting with others to negotiate and construct meaning. Furthermore, these interactions have subtexts: what is allowed, what is expected, what should be avoided, what is valued, and so on. Thus, classroom interactions, which are part of the culture of the classroom, have as much impact on student learning as the content of the curriculum.

According to Vygotsky (1978), the ZPD is the interval between the individual's actual level of development, as determined by unassisted performance, and the potential level of development, as determined by the individual's performance under adult guidance or in collaboration with more capable peers. This gap between current performance and potential performance is breached with scaffolding: The teacher adjusts instructional language and activities to move learners to new levels that they could not attain on their own, or the teacher leads them to develop understandings that they would not attain unassisted.

From the Vygotskian perspective, the teacher is not simply a transmitter of knowledge but rather a mediator or guide who enables learners to discover things for themselves. The teacher must be a keen listener, observer, and skilled communicator to frame the learning and adjust instruction at a moment's notice. From this perspective, effective teaching is seen as a skilled orchestration. The teacher designs instruction that stretches learners' thinking and arranges peer interactions that help learners effectively construct meanings.

Jerome Bruner: Learning as a Process of Inquiry and Discovery

Jerome Bruner emerged as one of the most influential cognitive psychologists of the second half of the twentieth century. A professor at Harvard and Oxford, he led the cognitive revolution that has dominated the profession's thinking about learning for several decades. He was particularly interested in translating his theories into practical advice for teachers. To Bruner, learning is not a product; it is a process that involves inquiry and discovery, even for the youngest learners, and is best initiated by stimulating the learner's interests. *The Process of Education* (1960) continues to be regarded as a seminal work and a major resource for educational reform. In it, Bruner describes the process of learning as one of selecting, transforming, hypothesizing, and constructing, stating that learners build new understandings on the base of their current knowledge.

To fully appreciate Bruner, it is important to consider the context within which he presented his ideas. From the 1950s through the 1970s, the behaviorist school of thought dominated much of the discourse in psychology and education. Watson (1925), Skinner (1938), Gagne (1965), and other behaviorists were interested only in how to elicit desired responses by employing various stimuli and reinforcements; they took little or no interest in what might be going on in the learner's mind. What mattered, for example, were the responses students made, not their level of motivation or curiosity or the thinking that led to the responses. Behaviorist views led to programmed instruction, behavioral objectives, and other specific classroom practices that focused on observable and measurable responses. The continued emphasis on comprehension subskills, noted earlier, was bolstered by the behaviorist perspective: Observable and measurable responses to skill exercises were deemed by many to be the most useful evidence of learning if not the only evidence.

Bruner's perspective on learning directly challenged the stimulus-response view of behaviorists. In fact, in many circles he was considered a maverick because he persisted in his focus on the internal workings of the mind and on how humans make sense of their world and themselves. His emphases on concept development, inquiry and discovery, hypothesis testing, intellectual risk taking, and the impact of learners' interests on motivation contributed to the constructivist school of thought and remain highly useful in understanding how readers construct meaning from text.

Late Twentieth Century: The Center for the Study of Reading

Although behaviorist perspectives continued to be voiced in the last quarter of the twentieth century and skills-based instruction remained popular, the thread of constructivism remained and was given renewed strength when The Center for the Study of Reading (CSR) at the University of Illinois was funded in 1976. Under the able leadership of learning theorist and cognitive psychologist Richard C. Anderson, the new center established an ambitious research agenda devoted to reading in general and the process of comprehension specifically. Anderson assembled a high-powered team of literacy specialists, cognitive psychologists, learning theorists, linguists, and other scholars. Over two decades, the CSR team produced numerous monographs and more than six hundred technical reports on all aspects of reading comprehension. Many of these publications drew on the work of the constructivists, going as far back as Bartlett, and provided educators with a growing body of theories and research-based instructional frameworks to support the teaching of reading. (For more information, see http://csr.ed.uiuc.edu.) Five CSR research emphases are of particular interest: the characteristics of skilled readers, the status of comprehension instruction, the critical influence of prior knowledge on learning, the complexity of the comprehension process, and the role of metacognition in learning.

The Characteristics of Skilled Readers

Anderson, Hiebert, Scott, and Wilkinson (1985) coauthored the highly influential *Becoming a Nation of Readers*, which summarizes the research and thinking of the CSR faculty and invited scholars from other institutions. The authors conclude that skilled readers are constructive, fluent, strategic, motivated, and lifelong. Each descriptor reflects important research findings that are supported by informed classroom observations and that echo the research and thinking of the scholars cited previously in this chapter. Briefly:

- **Skilled readers are constructive.** They use their existing knowledge along with information in the text to construct new meanings. At all levels of age and skill, reading is more than extracting meaning from text; it is an active process of meaning making.
- **Skilled readers are fluent and efficient.** They have learned to decode written symbols so adeptly that the process is almost effortless.
- **Skilled readers are strategic.** They understand what to do before, during, and after reading. Aware of their thinking and their reading behavior, they adjust their actions as needed so that the result is the construction of meaning.
- **Skilled readers are motivated.** They are eager to engage with text, sustain themselves for long stretches, and tend to persevere if the text is challenging.
- **Reading is a lifelong process.** Learning to read is not something done only in kindergarten, first, and second grade. Throughout life, readers continue to develop their capacities to process and comprehend text and to use reading as a way of learning about themselves and their world.

From these conclusions, the authors derived important implications for classroom instruction and suggested how to develop and nurture these characteristics from the earliest years of childhood through adulthood.

Classroom Comprehension Instruction: Assessing Is Not Teaching

Delores Durkin, a CSR scholar, was interested in the extent to which classroom instruction matched the growing body of research findings about comprehension. Durkin (1978–1979) conducted a series of illuminating studies that showed teachers were giving far less instruction in comprehension than was generally assumed. In one investigation, twenty-four classrooms representing thirteen different school districts in central Illinois were observed during reading/language arts classes for approximately seventy-five hours. Durkin selected fourth grade for observation because she reasoned that at this level, instruction would have shifted from phonics and word recognition to comprehension. Amazingly, she found only forty-five minutes devoted to comprehension instruction, or 1 percent of the total. In observing approximately forty-six hours of social studies instruction, she found no evidence of comprehension instruction whatsoever.

What was happening in these classrooms? One major finding was that more than 17 percent of the time was devoted to assessment—for example, asking students questions to check their comprehension. Durkin rightfully pointed out that assessing comprehension was not the same as teaching students how to comprehend. She also found little evidence of students making predictions, accessing their prior knowledge before reading, or discussing with each other what they were reading. Her observations called attention to what appeared to be a clear disconnect between classroom practice and the best theory and research of the day. The most sobering realization was that prior to Durkin's studies, classroom teachers and other educators believed that comprehension actually was being taught. Durkin's work and the ongoing efforts of the CSR put reading comprehension front and center on the literacy landscape and led to concentrated attention on comprehension instruction.

How Prior Knowledge Influences Comprehension

CSR researchers noted that existing knowledge structures, often called *schemas*, are critical components of comprehension. This was not a new idea. The term *schema* had appeared in the literature before the 1970s, notably in relation to the work of Piaget and in Bartlett (1932), but the CSR faculty conducted numerous studies to explore schema theory in depth, particularly the impact of prior knowledge on new learning. These scholars took a new look at Bartlett's constructivist perspective, and their research extended Bartlett's research in ways that would surely have intrigued him.

The CSR researchers envisioned schemas as networks of information. Any given network is not merely a collection of events or details stored serially. Rather it is a complex and interconnected system of memories, facts, beliefs, assumptions, and feelings that together form a holistic mental construct. Consider these scenarios:

Scenario 1: Brad and Marie studied the menu. The specials looked wonderful, as did several of the appetizers. First they would have drinks and think about ordering. Dessert was a definite possibility.

Scenario 2: Sam and Sara looked at the menu. Would it be #2 for both or possibly #2 for Sam and #6 for Sara? They should decide soon. Already cars were backed up behind them.

Most readers create a reality around Brad and Marie that involves a leisurely evening meal in a nice restaurant, whereas they infer that Sam and Sara are in a car ordering at a fast-food establishment. Readers' existing schemas lead them not only to construct meaning that goes beyond the words but also to visualize each scene in some detail. Readers are also confident of the conclusions they draw, although the first text does not mention the time of day or the establishment and the second makes no mention of fast food. Responses to these texts demonstrate once again that meaning does not lie solely in the text. Both the text and the reader's schemas are essential for the construction of meaning. This focus on prior knowledge, led by the CSR, has widespread significance for the profession in terms of research and classroom practice.

> *Both the text and the reader's schemas are essential for the construction of meaning.*

The Complexity of the Comprehension Process

Research by cognitive psychologists in the 1970s further refined the view of reading as a constructive, relative, and selective process. Studies during this period led to an even greater appreciation for the complexity of the comprehension process.

Pichert and Anderson (1977) asked two student groups to read about two boys visiting one of their homes after school. One group was asked to read the text from a home buyer's viewpoint, the other from a burglar's perspective. The text describes a well-appointed, air-conditioned home in a secluded area. A gun collection, a coin collection, and jewelry are noted as well as a ceiling under repair. When readers retold the story, those who read with the home buyer's view focused on the features of the property that would appeal to a buyer. Those reading from the burglar's point of view focused on the guns and jewelry and other details attractive to thieves. Each group noted the secluded location, an important consideration for both buyers and burglars, though for different reasons. The researchers' directions clearly influenced the subjects' recall, revealing the importance of the perspective that readers bring to a text.

A similar investigation was conducted by Anderson, Reynolds, Schallert, and Goetz (1977). Subjects read a purposely ambiguous passage about a man in a predicament. He is described as being "on a mat," being "held against his will," and getting "ready to make his move." When university music majors read the text, they tended to construct a scenario involving a prisoner about to escape. Physical education majors were more likely to envision a wrestler about to break free from the grip of his opponent. Replications in a variety of situations found that the interpretation of the text varied depending upon the subjects and even the physical context in which the research was conducted.

These two studies vividly illustrate the point that Thorndike made in 1917: Some words or phrases are more important than others in a given text, and the background, experiences, perspectives, and purposes of the reader determine their relative importance. Given the relative importance the reader assigns to information, the reader's recall is selective. Good readers usually select more to remember than poor readers. But it is also probably true that good readers tend to select what other readers or teachers generally deem as important and pay less attention to what others consider less important. Additionally it appears that individuals who have difficulty with comprehension tend not only to select less but also select relatively less of the important information.

A third important study extends our understanding of how schemas can influence comprehension and problem solving in new situations. Gick and Holyoak (1980) had college students read and memorize a passage about an army general planning to attack a fortress. The text stated that the many approaches to the fortress were mined, precluding the use of heavy equipment but allowing small groups of foot soldiers. The general sent in foot soldiers from multiple directions, having them converge on the fort. Later, the students who read this were given a description of a tumor that was deemed inoperable because the necessary laser treatment would destroy too many healthy cells. The instructor asked how the patient might be treated. Few students were able to suggest a procedure, but when they were reminded of the information about the general attacking the fortress, more than 90 percent speculated that the cancer might be treated by using multiple weaker lasers converging on the tumor from different directions. This is a classic example of transfer of learning: using information from one situation to solve a problem in a new situation. Interestingly, the students actually possessed useful prior knowledge but were unaware that they had it until the researchers provided the reminder as a scaffold.

> *Comprehension is complex not only because of the nature of the reader–text interaction but also because the process is influenced by the context in which the reading occurs and the actions of whoever guides the reader.*

These studies show that comprehension is complex not only because of the nature of the reader–text interaction but also because the process is influenced by the context in which the reading occurs and the actions of whoever guides the reader. The directions, questions, and comments that teachers use before, during, and after reading have a considerable influence on students' comprehension.

Metacognition: Readers' Awareness of Their Reading and Thinking Processes

The CSR also gave close attention to metacognition. This term was first used by Flavell (1976), who described it as "one's knowledge concerning one's own cognitive processes or anything related to them" (232). Although scholars have different views of what constitutes metacognitive behavior, widespread agreement seems to exist that metacognitive learners think about their own thinking, are aware of when they are learning effectively, and take action if their learning falters.

It appears that skilled readers can be distinguished from unskilled readers by their metacognitive awareness. Skilled readers tend to monitor their comprehension and change tactics when something doesn't make sense. For example, they might reread a passage or paraphrase the ideas. They also tend to raise questions when they read, think ahead, visualize, adjust their rate of reading to their purpose, and reflect on what they are reading. Less skilled readers tend not to engage in these actions—see, for example, Brown (1980) and Paris and Jacobs (1984).

Pendulum Swings

CSR's work had a profound impact on the profession's thinking by responding to limited, skills-oriented perspectives with evidence that reading is a complex, constructive process. The center's work throughout the 1970s and 1980s did much not only to uncover the essential nature of comprehension but also to suggest fruitful implications for classroom instruction. Unfortunately, CSR's meaning-oriented perspective lost its priority status several years later. As Pearson (2010) observed, "For a host of reasons, much of the momentum toward reading as a meaning-making process dissipated in the last few years of the 20th century and the first few years of the 21st. . . . Several forces conspired to create [another] movement that took us back to the basics—a sort of "first things first" reform movement . . . [and] while there is nothing in this reform movement that suggests that comprehension instruction should be suspended, there is a subtle repositioning" (312). A key element of this new movement was the designation of phonics as a top priority. Attention to comprehension, it was argued, should come later, after children are decoding words accurately and rapidly. Another key element was an emphasis on objectively measurable responses. Test scores became the dominant means of assessing student performance, and instruction in specific skills to raise test scores became another priority. These views, though inadequate, influenced the national literacy agenda, the contents of state standards, the design of instructional materials, and the emphasis of many professional books and articles.

However, the reading pendulum seems to be reversing direction, with comprehension and thinking once again receiving substantive attention. For example, the RAND Reading Study Group (Snow 2002) calls for a renewed emphasis on comprehension research. Another notable event has been the publication of *How People Learn* (Bransford, Brown, and Cocking 2000), which describes comprehension as a complex cognitive process. In this important work, the authors argue that because students learn little or nothing unless they build on their initial preconceptions, effective strategies for accessing these preconceptions are of critical importance. They also stress that rigorous, in-depth learning is far more important than broad coverage of a subject because it helps students learn to think and inquire instead of simply memorize (and soon forget) collections of facts. The authors further assert the importance of an emphasis on metacognition, pointing out that students need to become aware of themselves as learners if they are to take control of their own learning. Both publications point the way to continued research into the process of comprehension that will build on the important work done earlier by the CSR.

From Theory to Practice: Seven Essential Ideas to Inform Reading Instruction

The giants in psychology and education described in this chapter have given us their shoulders to stand on. From their research and scholarship, we have distilled seven principles that we think create the most effective framework for comprehension instruction. Together, they form the constructivist perspective that has guided our own work for decades and that we continue to refine as we work with students and teachers.

1. **Comprehension is a process of constructing meaning.** The meaning is a new creation that results from the interplay of the information in the text and the existing schemas of the active and thoughtful reader.

2. **The learner's prior knowledge is an essential component of comprehension.** What readers understand and remember is heavily influenced by what they already know. The extent to which they realize that they have relevant prior knowledge and use it makes a great difference in what they comprehend, how much they comprehend, and how enjoyable and satisfying they find the reading and learning.

3. **The learner's purposes and expectations are critical elements of comprehension.** What readers take away from a reading experience is heavily influenced by the intentions and mind-sets that they bring to the experience.

4. **Comprehension is a dynamic process.** Effective readers are not like clams, stationary in the muddy bottom of the bay, waiting for the currents to bring them sustenance. They move eagerly toward the text, dive inside it, interact with it, and are changed by the process. They do so to the extent that they are allowed and encouraged to be active participants and are made to feel comfortable in their attempts at personal discovery.

5. **Collaboration enhances comprehension.** Comprehension is deeper and often more satisfying when readers share interpretations and insights in skillfully mediated conversations. When readers discuss their responses with full appreciation for the differences that arise, they deepen their understanding of the text, of themselves, and of the reading process.

6. **Effective readers are metacognitive.** They read attentively, monitor their own thinking, and critically evaluate their performance. They adjust their reading behaviors to optimize understanding and have an ever-growing command of what they know and what they don't know. In learning something new, they are not discouraged by their initial

ignorance but welcome the chance to acquire more knowledge. They evaluate their own thinking and learning with an eye to improving their performance.

7. **Learners are disposed to make sense of their world.** The human inclination to search for meaning includes making sense of texts. Readers' disposition to comprehend when they enter school is a huge advantage for teachers. This does not mean that teachers can simply get out of the way and let comprehension happen. The process requires nurturing if it is to remain viable, and it is best nurtured by an effective orchestration of teaching and learning activities.

The extent to which instructional practices reflect these principles will, to a significant degree, define the quality of the reading comprehension instructional program. A word of caution is in order, however. In some instances, advocates of particular practices or strategies may appear to embrace what is known about reading comprehension, but closer examination of the practices sometimes reveals that they are not aligned with these principles. It is incumbent upon the discerning educator to determine how well specific practices actually reflect these principles.

A Century of Scholarship as a Guide to Contemporary Thinking

For many years, scholars have been giving substantive attention to how humans learn, building on one another's theories and research or coming from different perspectives to draw similar conclusions. We have provided only highlights of this rich history. Many scholars, too numerous to mention here, have made useful contributions. We hope our brief review will spark further interest in the insights of past thinkers. Current research and theory in reading are important but are best interpreted and evaluated in the context of history.

Although meaning making is a natural cognitive process, comprehension of text is not necessarily easy. Skillful instruction is essential and is most effective when it builds upon and nurtures the students' existing dispositions to make sense of their world. In the following chapters, we describe useful and effective ways of applying constructivist principles to classroom reading instruction. What we suggest involves a skillful blend of rigor and sensitivity, of intentional teaching and incidental learning, of high-level thinking and high-level emotional satisfaction, of art as well as science. The right combination of these elements leads to memorable comprehension experiences for students.

CHAPTER 2

The Power of Story
Supporting Students' Reading of Narrative Texts

uriosity about an unfolding narrative propels a reader through the text: Will the protagonist survive? How will the dilemma be resolved? Who will prevail? The pleasure of an absorbing narrative arises from interacting intellectually and emotionally with an author-created fictional world or an artful retelling of actual events. Teachers can capitalize on the narrative's power to draw readers in and lead them to wonder what will happen next. Here is an example to illustrate. The text is a folktale from the oral tradition; this version is our own rendition of the story.*

Reading Narrative Text: An Example

This lesson was conducted with eight sixth-grade students while the rest of the class were involved with independent activities. The teacher invited predictions at the outset to encourage divergent thinking and engage students immediately.

> *Teacher:* As we read, we'll pause occasionally to talk about what we've read and think about what might happen next. I'm sure you'll have different ideas, and it will be interesting to discuss them. The title of the story is "The Wager." What do you think might happen in the story, considering just the title?

---

*Two other versions of the tale are "The Fire on the Mountain" (Courlander and Leslau 1950) and "Cooking by Candle" (Shah 1972).

(Some students speculated that the story might have to do with horse racing; others thought one person bet another person; a few thought a dare might be involved.)

Teacher: Let's read a bit and talk again. Read the first page to yourself. When you finish, think about whether or not you want to change your first ideas and what you might use from the story to support your thinking.

(Students read the following text.)

The Wager

There was once a prosperous merchant whose caravans transported costly goods to and from India, Persia, and China. With his profits, he surrounded himself with luxury on a magnificent estate.

Among the merchant's servants was a man named Hakim who had grown up on a small farm near the estate. As a child, Hakim took pleasure in tending the crops and animals, but when he was still a boy, his parents died and he lost everything. To survive, he became a servant in the merchant's household. Though he accepted his fate cheerfully, he dreamed of his childhood when he had worked contentedly close to nature.

One winter's evening twenty guests sat at the merchant's dining table, enjoying fine delicacies. As Hakim refilled the crystal wine goblets, the talk was of the unusually cold weather.

"I pity the farmers," remarked Ali, a neighboring landowner and the merchant's close friend. "How uncomfortable they must be in this cold!"

"Yes," mused another. "Yet they have some shelter, poor as it may be. Just think of the beggars and others who have none at all. It cannot be possible to survive in this weather without protection of any kind."

"Let us ask Hakim," replied the merchant. "He has had some experience with outdoor life. Hakim! What do you say? Can a man survive unprotected in weather like this?"

"I don't know, sir," said Hakim. "It would be difficult without shelter, but with a good enough reason, it would be possible."

"No!" exclaimed another guest. "Ordinary cold is one thing, but this bitter cold simply cannot be endured!"

"I agree with you," said the merchant. "Still, Hakim thinks it's possible—if there's a good enough reason. And what would motivate *you* to do such a thing, Hakim?"

Teacher: What have we learned so far? (*Students related details about Hakim, the guests' discussion, the merchant's question, and so on. Their responses showed that they understood the key events.*)

Teacher: What do you think will happen next in the story?

Justin: I think Hakim will say what would make him stay out in the cold. Because right at the end the merchant says, "And what would motivate *you* to do such a thing?"

Teacher: What do you think Hakim will say?

Bobbie: Maybe he'll say he'd do it if someone paid him enough money. Because then he wouldn't have to be a servant.

Serena: Maybe he'll say something about doing it for a farm.

Teacher: Why do you think that?

Serena: It says that he liked growing food and having animals but that he lost the farm when his parents died.

Marty: He still dreams about it, though.

Teacher: So what do you think will happen?

Mario: Maybe that's what the wager is!

Teacher: What do you mean?

Mario: The title is "The Wager," so somebody has to bet somebody else. Maybe the merchant will bet Hakim that he can't stay out in the cold.

Bobbie: That makes sense. The merchant says, "Hakim thinks it can be done if there's a good enough reason."

Thomas: But they're saying it's really, really cold. That one guy says no one can survive in weather like they're having. What kind of a bet would that be? I think they'll bet on something else.

Teacher: What else?

(*Several students suggested the story could still be about a horse race, pointing out that the merchant transported goods by caravan and reasoning that he and the guests probably had horses. Others sided with Mario's idea, noting that the beginning had included a lot of information about Hakim. One student said that perhaps Hakim would ride the merchant's horse in a race because Hakim had said he could stay out in the cold if there was a good reason. The teacher encouraged discussion with prompts such as "Talk about that" and "What makes you think that?"*)

Teacher: We have some interesting ideas. Each one could possibly happen, given what we've read so far. Let's read the next part. When you finish, consider whether or not the new information changes your thinking.

(In the next part, students read that the merchant proposes a wager: He will give Hakim five acres of his land if the servant can survive a night out of doors, from sunset until dawn, "without protection of any kind." Hakim accepts; the guests are shocked. The merchant says to them: "If he fails, the land remains mine, and he will have to revise his belief in the power of motivation—if he is still with us, that is!")

Teacher: Did this part of the story develop as you expected?

Ravi: Mario's idea was right. The merchant bet the servant that he can't stay outdoors overnight.

Thomas: Yeah. They could still have a horse race, but I think the rest of the story is about the servant trying to win the bet.

Bobbie: I agree. I think he'll make it all the way through the night and win.

Teacher: Why is that?

Bobbie: I can't think of a good reason, except I want him to! It would be like someone winning the lottery. He lost everything, and this is his chance to have a farm again and everything he wants.

Serena: Yes, but it's going to be really, really hard. I think he might die.

Teacher: Why do you think that?

Serena: The merchant says at the end here *(reading aloud)*, "if he's still with us, that is."

Leroy: I don't think he'll make it. Our car broke down last month, and we got really cold while we waited for help. I don't think we would have made it if we had to stay there all night.

Teacher: How can you use that to think about Hakim?

Leroy: I don't know. Someone came to help us, but no one is going to help him.

Serena: Yes, but he's really motivated. I think he'll make it. He'll just wear really warm clothes.

Mario: But it says, "without protection of any kind." That means no warm clothes, doesn't it?

Justin: I thought "no protection" meant just being out in the open, like not having a building to be in or a tent or something like that.

(Students discussed their various interpretations of "no protection." Most thought Hakim could wear warm clothes but could not construct a shelter. When all had had their say, the teacher invited them to read the next section and again think ahead to what might happen next.

In the next part, students read that Hakim is anxious, especially when the temperature drops still further the next day. Ali takes him aside and suggests that he reconsider, pointing out that he has nothing to prove. But Hakim is determined. At sunset, he leaves the house, dressed only in his usual indoor clothing, and goes to the agreed-upon place in the open. From a pouch, he takes a candle and a book of tales. He lights the candle and begins reading, forcing himself to concentrate on the book despite his discomfort. In the morning, he returns, numb and exhausted. The household marvels, but the merchant discovers the candle, declares it a violation of the agreement, and says that Hakim has lost. Ali, the neighboring landowner, begins to speak, but the merchant leads him into breakfast, showing by his manner that he considers the matter closed. Hakim does not argue with the merchant and resigns himself to his loss.)

Serena: We were right! He made it. And all he had was a book to read. That was really interesting. It was just a book of stories.

Mario: We also thought that he couldn't have a tent or anything like that.

Justin: But it's not fair!

Teacher: What's not fair?

Ravi: The merchant said he lost because he had a candle, but the candle didn't protect him. He just used it to read. That's like one time when someone said I was cheating on a math test because I had my calculator on my desk. I used it to hold the paper down, not to figure out the answers. So it was unfair to say I was cheating.

Teacher: That's an interesting comparison between you and Hakim. Do you all agree that Hakim was treated unfairly?

Students: *(in unison)* Yes!

Justin: And that other guy doesn't think it's fair either.

Teacher: What other guy?

Justin: *(reading)* "Ali opened his mouth as if to speak. . . ." He didn't say anything, but you can tell he thinks it's not fair either.

Ravi: I agree. Ali didn't like what the merchant did, but he didn't feel like he could say anything.

Teacher: What do you think will happen next?

Leroy: I think Hakim will get back at the merchant somehow. He knows he won, so he'll be watching for a chance.

Thomas: But what can he do? He's just a slave. And it says, "He was resigned." That means he gives up, doesn't it?

Bobbie: *(having looked back)* It doesn't say Hakim was a slave; it says he was a *servant.* There's a difference. He can do something about this. I just don't know what. Anyway, the story can't just end here. Something has to happen to make it right!

Teacher: Does anyone have any other ideas?

Ravi: Maybe Ali does something.

Teacher: What can he do if he feels he can't even say anything?

Ravi: I don't know, but I think it's going to keep bothering him, and maybe he'll do something. Maybe he'll talk the merchant into giving the guy the land.

Bobbie: But it says the whole thing is over, *(reading)* "showing by his businesslike manner that the matter was, as far as he was concerned, closed."

(The group discussed these ideas further, agreeing that something else had to happen but disagreeing on what that might be. When no new ideas were forthcoming, the teacher invited the group to read the next part, which they were eager to do. They read that Ali has invited the community to a great feast. They arrive early in the day and stand about for some hours, talking and waiting expectantly for food to be served. At last, the merchant asks Ali how much longer they must wait for something to eat.)

"Perhaps we should find out about the food," said Ali amiably. "Shall we see how things are progressing in the kitchen?"

The entire company followed Ali through the house to the great kitchen at the back. There, a servant was busily stirring the contents of a large cauldron that was suspended over a single candle.

The merchant pressed forward and peered into the pot. "Ali," he said with irritation, "this food is not even warm. And no wonder! Your foolish servant apparently thinks that he can cook with a candle. Now I ask you, what amount of heat can be obtained from a wretched candle?"

"As much heat," said Ali, "as your servant, Hakim, obtained from the candle he took with him one night this past winter."

Teacher: Now what do you think?

Ravi: That's cool. We didn't think of that!

Teacher: What's cool?

Ravi: Ali planned the whole thing to prove that a candle isn't any protection at all. But no one figured it out until they all went into the kitchen to see what had happened to the food. I knew he didn't like what the merchant did, but I couldn't figure out what he was going to do.

(Students were unanimous in their praise for Ali's action. They also agreed that the merchant had been shamed in front of everyone and ought to admit that Hakim had won, but they were not sure how he would react. They made their final predictions and read the last part with great interest: The merchant admits his error, thanks Ali for his intervention, apologizes, and declares that Hakim won the wager. Ali then has his servants bring out food that had been prepared the day before, and all enjoy a celebratory feast.)

Teacher: Let's talk for a minute. Turn to the person next to you and discuss what you're thinking right now. Then we will talk as a group.

With this prompt, the teacher capitalized on students' obvious enthusiasm for the ending. Partners eagerly talked about Ali's cleverness, his support of Hakim, and the merchant's change of heart. Some reflected on how they didn't even think about the candle at first but later realized its importance. Others discussed how their thinking changed from the beginning of the story to the end.

To deepen students' understanding and appreciation of the story and encourage metacognitive reflections, the teacher posed several questions. Any of these can also be used to stimulate writing, as discussed in Chapter 5. This teacher chose to use them in discussion to bring closure to the reading experience:

What was the most interesting or memorable part of this story to you? Why did you find that part especially interesting? Not surprisingly, students had different ideas. Leroy talked about Hakim's endurance, again comparing the servant's ordeal to his own. Bobbie said she had almost given up hope and so thought Hakim's winning in the end was significant. Serena mentioned Hakim's reading, reflecting on how books also distracted her. Ravi cited the kitchen scene, saying he realized what was going on when he connected the single kitchen candle to Hakim's candle. Justin and Mario thought the merchant was too mean to ever admit he had been wrong, so to them his admission was a memorable moment that made them change their perspectives about him.

What is this story really all about? Students first said the story was all about what was fair, noting that they didn't want the merchant to get away with what he had done. The teacher acknowledged the response, then said that stories seldom have just one meaning or theme and asked for other ideas. Students then mentioned how Hakim had taken a chance, yet remained physically and mentally strong. They talked about Ali waiting for the right moment, agreeing that was more effective than an immediate show of indignation. Through their discussion, they thus uncovered the themes of risk, endurance, and patience as well as justice.

What part of the story can you visualize most clearly? What part is most vivid to you? Students spoke of how they imagined the outdoor location, the interior of the merchant's home, and details of the kitchen. The shared visualizations led them to reflect on aspects of the story they had not discussed previously. For example, they had talked about what went on in the kitchen but not about its appearance and were interested to find that they visualized the room quite differently.

What did you notice about how the author told this story? One student brought up the author's use of dialogue, saying conversations always made stories more interesting. Two liked the description of Hakim leaving the house, citing the depiction of the dark sky and the words *icy stillness*. One wondered why the author did not give the merchant a name. Another cited the hints the author gave to Ali's character throughout, saying these helped her know that Ali would do something even though she didn't know what until the very end.

Finally, the teacher asked which interesting words or phrases from the story the students wanted to talk about. Several brought up *wretched candle*, *prosperous merchant*, and *impulsive gesture*. The context helped them understand enough to continue reading, but they weren't sure they fully understood these terms. With the teacher's guidance, dictionary checks, and further discussion, they refined their understandings of these. The teacher then brought *cauldron* into the discussion. One student said she'd seen the word in folktales; another associated it with witches. The teacher guided the group to find synonyms and asked why the author might have used *cauldron* instead of another word. The group decided that it sounded old and that only a very large pot would be appropriate for what Ali aimed to do.

Reflecting on the Example

To the students, this activity seemed to be simply an engaging discussion about a good story, but it was actually a carefully orchestrated experience for which the teacher prepared carefully. She chose as stopping points the critical junctures that would most likely spark different ideas,

> *Pauses during reading are like the pauses painters or writers take: Stepping back to reflect is part of the process of constructing meaning.*

and she thought about how students' thinking might change as the story progressed. She anticipated vocabulary they might want to discuss after reading and words she might bring up. She identified themes that would be worth discussing.

Some teachers do not like to break stories up, thinking learners should read a narrative all the way through and then discuss it. Talking only after reading may be appropriate if students are experienced, mature, or highly motivated, but for most, a few pauses, handled effectively, lead to more careful analysis of the text, reveal issues with comprehension that may need to be addressed, and slow the pace of reading so that meanings can sink in. Pauses during reading are like the pauses painters or writers take: Stepping back to reflect is part of the process of constructing meaning.

Before Reading: Thinking Ahead

The teacher did not provide background information, engage students in talking about their experiences, introduce vocabulary, teach a skill, or present them with a strategy to use when reading. She wanted students get into the story right away and stay focused on it, so she invited predictions. On another occasion, she might have asked students to read a page or two before stopping to predict. This time, she used the title alone, confident that it would generate different ideas.

The teacher repeatedly invited students to use their unique views and experiences in predicting upcoming events but did not expect students to make accurate predictions and did not steer them in that direction. By encouraging divergent ideas and not hinting at who was correct, she showed students that she valued their thinking. Her neutral stance also discouraged the readers from seeking clues in her voice, facial expressions, or body language as to which predictions were correct, and that also kept them focused on thinking instead of on trying to guess correctly. She also periodically asked students to explain their reasoning (*Why do you think that?*) to encourage thoughtful, extended responses. She was especially interested in seeing how students would change their initial thoughts as they obtained more information, knowing this is an excellent measure of comprehension. For example, she noted that although some thought early on about a horse race, they abandoned this idea when it was clear the story was taking a different direction.

In a thinking-ahead discussion, the teacher listens carefully, takes students' responses seriously, and questions or gently challenges ideas when opportunities arise for deepening thinking. Students in any grade respond well to the intellectual engagement. They realize that their ideas will be heard and honored. They learn that stimulating conversation with their teacher and peers is enjoyable. They get used to saying what they think without fear of being criticized or laughed at, knowing that all predictions must be considered tentative, subject to change as more information is revealed.

Orchestrating discussions like this takes considerable skill. Our teacher's pacing was sensitive. She allowed enough time in the discussion to involve the students cognitively and emotionally but knew just when to shift the discussion or resume reading. Also, she invited students to extend their responses (*Talk about that!* or *Why is that?*) and explain them (*What makes you think that?*) while skillfully keeping them focused on the story. When one student related a personal experience, she deftly steered him back to the story (*How can you use that to think about Hakim?*). Throughout, her guidance seemed natural and effortless to an observer, but she was fully aware of what she was doing and of the effect that her facilitation was having on the students' thinking.

During Reading: Satisfying Curiosity

With specific predictions in mind, students read purposefully to satisfy their curiosity. The story came to life not just because of the content but because of their thinking about the content. Discussing possible outcomes generated suspense that heightened their attention and kept them actively involved. They nodded excitedly, shook their heads, and caught each other's eyes, indicating their comprehension with comments such as *He made it* and *It's not fair!*

Because the students read silently, they gave their full attention to constructing meaning. This teacher knows that beyond the earliest stages of emergent literacy, silent reading takes the attention off performance and places it on comprehension. Thus, she has students read aloud without preparation only when she occasionally assesses their reading fluency. When the purpose is comprehension, they read silently.

> *Beyond the earliest stages of emergent literacy, silent reading takes the attention off performance and places it on comprehension.*

After Reading: Reflecting and Responding

The teacher stimulated reflective thinking after the story to enhance comprehension, leading students to make personal connections with the story and ponder meanings more deeply. Her questions invited students to respond on these dimensions:

- **Interpretive:** Students talk about the most memorable events, sharing their interpretations of motivations and actions. Their disparate views enrich meanings and help them realize that stories elicit different perspectives and responses.

- **Thematic:** Students discuss the generalizations about life that are illustrated by the particulars of the narrative. Asking for the theme usually suggests that a right answer is expected. Asking instead to consider what the story is really all about encourages learners to make multiple generalizations. As Moffett (1968b) notes, thinking about "what happens" in general, given the specifics of a text, is at a higher level of abstraction than simple recall of "what happened."

- **Visual/Imaginative:** Students talk about the scenes that were most vivid to them. This brings the story to life and develops a fuller appreciation for what the author may have been imagining—or possibly looking at—when writing the story. Readers also see that individuals imagine different things when reading the same words. This can lead to interesting conversations and greater appreciation for the process of constructing meaning. As Naughton (2008) and Parsons (2006) maintain, visualization is a critical component of meaning construction.

- **Writer's Craft:** Students reflect on the author's use of words and phrases or other features of the author's approach to telling the story. Doing so, they read and think like writers. This enhances their appreciation for the story and builds awareness of how authors use language and structure stories.

The teacher might have invited students to respond on these other dimensions, as well:

- **Analogical:** Students talk about how characters and events are similar to people and events in their own lives. They may compare speech, actions, motivations, or any other aspect of the story that sparks meaningful connections.

- **Metacognitive:** Students talk about what they were thinking at different points in the story, reflecting on when and why they changed their predictions, when they realized something they hadn't thought of before, or when they became aware of a shift in the way they were feeling about a character or an event.

- **Moral/Ethical:** Students talk about moral or ethical issues that are raised by the story and may also evaluate characters' actions. For example, the sixth graders judged the merchant to be unfair when he declared Hakim had lost the wager.
- **Intertextual:** Students talk about other texts, films, or television dramas that they find similar to the story in some way. This is similar to what Keene and Zimmerman (1997) call a text-to-text connection. Such responses can include simple comparisons between plots, scenes, or characters' actions. More sophisticated readers might note allusions in the literary work to other works or might discuss themes or stylistic features that are similar across texts.
- **Elaborative:** Students elaborate on one or more aspects of the story. For example, most readers of "The Wager" agree that Ali's tactic is a key event, but they want to discuss why it was so effective and so satisfying as an ending. Similarly, most readers identify endurance as a major theme of "The Wager," but that is only a starting point. How does Hakim's endurance compare with, for example, what happened to the crew of the *Endurance* when that ship became trapped in Antarctica in 1915? What enables some people to endure while others give up? Many such unique questions suggest themselves when the other questions are used as springboards.

It is important that postreading responses do not become routine or formulaic as can happen when students are asked to think about each new text in the same way. In fact, different texts provide different opportunities for response. The key is to choose one or two of these dimensions and let the students' responses take the discussion in other directions. The dimensions described here can also be the basis of engaging writing activities.

After Reading: Discussing Vocabulary

Although occasionally a word might need to be discussed before reading a story, most vocabulary is best discussed after the story. Doing so has significant benefits:

- Students engage immediately with the story. Because that is what most interests them, they read the text when they are most enthused about getting into it.
- The experience of reading is the priority. Students read to engage with the story, not to practice recognizing new words.
- The story itself provides the ideal context for discussing unfamiliar or interesting words the author may have used, but students have to read the story for this context to be useful.

- Students have a chance to figure out unfamiliar words on their own. This builds their capacity as independent readers and encourages them to make use of the skills they have learned from previous instruction.

Most vocabulary is best discussed after the story. Doing so has significant benefits.

If a word is critical to the meaning of the story, students' uncertainty about it will come to light during reading, and its meaning can be clarified through discussion. If its meaning is not critical, then it will do no harm to talk about it after reading. We discuss this point and other vocabulary issues at greater length in Chapter 7.

Refining Teacher Language and Action

When this approach to guiding the comprehension experience is at its best, the students do most of the talking, but the teacher's words and actions are critical to initiating and sustaining the discussion and to helping the students see themselves as capable, thinking readers. In fact, this way of teaching illustrates particularly well how important the teacher's language and actions are. What the teacher says and does determines how students think about the experience of reading and what they aim to do when they read. Effective instructional language helps students acquire a sense of agency about their reading and thinking, develop an inquiring mind-set, and learn to play active roles as readers and thinkers, all of which Johnston (2004) points out are important if the goal is a classroom climate conducive to high-level thinking and satisfying discourse.

Like most expert actions, the process described here looks natural and easy but ordinarily emerges only after months and perhaps years of repeatedly reflecting on and adjusting one's performance. Expert facilitation involves posing questions at the right times, wording them astutely, giving effective feedback, raising challenges in the right way, ensuring

What the teacher says and does determines how students think about the experience of reading and what they aim to do when they read.

that students are listening to and responding to each other, and so on. Facial expressions and gestures are also critical; for example, it is important to appear neutral when students are discussing predictions so as not to give away who may be on the right track and not to discourage students by making them think they have said something wrong or silly.

Studying scripts or recordings of lessons is one good way to examine one's language and actions and grapple with the question Johnston (2004) considers so important: "What do you think you're doing?" Videos are especially useful tools for considering the effect of one's questions, responses, gestures, and facial expressions. They make it possible to see the instruction more objectively. Working with a trusted colleague makes the process of self-analysis and reflection easier because of the second set of eyes and the camaraderie of working on shared goals. The key is to stay open to the idea that improvement in one's teaching is possible and may actually be necessary if student performance is to improve.

Grouping and Logistics

The previous example represents one group of students with one teacher on one day. A different story, different students, or a different day would yield different discussions, but the core components would remain the same: thinking ahead, reading purposefully, pausing to discuss and rethink at strategic points, and engaging in rich conversation after reading. These are as relevant to the reading of narratives in first grade as they are in high school. The texts change with the age and grade level of the students, but the process remains the same.

Tactics may vary from story to story or from occasion to occasion with the same story, depending on purpose and need. For example, if students agree with each other too readily, a teacher may have them read only a small amount at the beginning so that their predictions will diverge and provoke debate. If students need experience synthesizing details, the teacher may have them read several pages before making their first predictions.

It is best to vary the number and position of stopping points from story to story so that reading experiences do not become monotonous over time. One day, students may generate predictions from the title alone; the next time, they may read a few pages before they stop to predict; the next time, they may read all but the last page before discussing possible endings. Decisions about stopping points are best made by considering the structure of the story, the particular group about to read it, and the teacher's goals for that group in that lesson. Different teachers may use different stopping points for the same story and give their students equally effective reading/thinking experiences.

Grouping may also vary across grade levels, lessons, or stories. In the earlier grades, group size probably should be small, whereas in secondary classes, teachers might choose to guide the entire class through a story, maximizing dialogue by having students discuss first in small groups, then as a whole class. A critical factor in deciding on grouping is the reading level of the students: All the members of the group need to be able to read the text comfortably.

The Role of Prediction in Reading Narrative Text

Although prediction is routinely recommended as an instructional strategy, its use is too often cursory. Students give predictions, but they do not discuss their ideas or refer to them later. It is as if predicting is one of several things to do with the story and once done can be checked off the to-do list. Ineffective use of prediction also stems from concern about accuracy. Thus, some teachers invite predictions only when they are sure students will predict the actual outcome. Many are reluctant to have students predict on the basis of the title, saying readers cannot be expected to predict accurately when they have so little information. Others are concerned that students will remember incorrect predictions instead of the actual story events.

From our perspective, predicting is a natural thought process. Readers become immersed in the lives of the characters and respond to story events as participant-observers in those lives, including thinking ahead to what might happen next. They may make inaccurate predictions when reading just as they may forecast events incorrectly in their own lives, but the unfolding story events lead them to revise their thinking. Of course, some readers may want something to happen in the story so badly that they continue to maintain that it will, against all the evidence, just as people in real life are sometimes swept up in wishful thinking. Some may have trouble revising their predictions even when the story takes an unmistakable turn away from their initial ideas. However, if such inflexible responses arise, they work themselves out as the group continues weighing the evidence and eventually finishes the story.

Predictions reflect readers' reasoning. If the thinking is sound, a prediction can be considered of good quality even if it turns out to be incorrect. If the thinking is not sound, the reader will see the value of learning to think more carefully in the future. From this perspective, students can profitably be asked to make predictions on the basis of the title, a few pages, or most of the story. Each provides opportunities to use information effectively to think ahead, thereby improving thinking capacities.

Although it takes time to discuss predictions and to accept predictions that are incorrect or based on faulty reasoning, we think doing so is essential if predicting is to have the following important effects.

Prediction Arouses Curiosity and Motivation to Read

Television serial dramas end each episode at a cliff-hanger point to entice viewers to tune in next week; joke tellers build suspense so that punch lines have maximum impact; gift givers heighten anticipation by wrapping their presents. Curiosity is equally relevant to learning. As Dewey (1910) notes, curiosity is a "powerful intellectual force" that teachers need to nurture with artful instruction (33–34).

Predictions generate curiosity; curiosity raises motivation. Students are invariably interested in an outcome once they have declared what they think it will be. In fact, predictions can arouse interest in texts that students would ordinarily declare boring. For example, we once guided the reading of a story with a group of fourth graders who showed little interest in reading. The very short story in their easy-to-read textbook had little literary merit, but the plot lent itself to prediction. A man stopped by the roadside to dig up a bush for his garden. Someone appeared behind him. (Who could it be?) It was a ranger, who pointed out that the man was in a national park and could not help himself to bushes. "Come with me!" said the ranger. (What was he going to do to the man?) The students made predictions at these and subsequent stopping points, discussing possibilities at length and devising scenarios that were more complex and inventive than the original. Their comprehension was high, and they unanimously declared the lesson to have been great fun, asking when they would be able to read more stories "as good as that one." As important as excellent literature is, the process of prediction is equally important for arousing curiosity and motivation to read.

> **P**redictions generate curiosity; curiosity raises motivation.

Prediction Activates and Applies Prior Knowledge

When students use prior knowledge to support a prediction as illustrated here, the use is pointed and purposeful. The prior knowledge may come from a just-read part of the text, or the story may remind them of something that has happened to them or what they know about the world. The teacher does not decide in advance which prior knowledge should be brought into play; the students decide, based on what they consider relevant, so the discussion remains student-centered in the best sense of that word. As they read, the learners pool their experience, contributing their unique perspectives as they try to figure out the direction the story is taking.

This use of prior knowledge runs counter to current practices. Ordinarily, teachers ask students before reading if they have ever had an experience like the one portrayed in the story. For example, the sixth-grade teacher might have asked at the outset if students had ever undergone a challenging ordeal or found themselves treated unfairly, and students would have talked about their own experiences. However, such tale telling is counterproductive. First, it does not do much to arouse students' curiosity about the story nor motivate them to read it. Also, learners' attention is diverted from the story as they relate anecdotes. In addition, because the anecdotes are almost always only tangentially related to story events, the connections between the experiences and the story are tenuous. Furthermore, learners are steered toward egocentric thinking at a time when they are about to engage in collaborative thinking. Then, too, the teacher's leading questions may give away too much of the story, reducing the pleasure students could have in discovering the outcome for themselves. Finally, the transition between personal anecdotes and the story is likely to be awkward and uninspiring. For example, after hearing stories about challenges or unfair treatment, the sixth-grade teacher would have had to inform the students that they would now be reading about a challenging ordeal and unfair treatment. This would not have been the best way of arousing students' interest or giving them a compelling purpose for reading.

In fact, students may not need to make any explicit use of their own firsthand experiences when making predictions. They can think about a story by considering only their general knowledge of human behavior. They may also use their knowledge of books, television dramas, or films to figure out what might happen next. For example, they may express optimism about the ending of a narrative that has taken a negative turn, claiming that story characters usually live happily ever after. The key is to let the students make the connections between what they know and the developing story. They are the ones who best know which prior knowledge, general or specific, explicit or implicit, might help them think about the story they are reading and at what point in the story it seems relevant.

What's the Best Way to Introduce a Story?

When activating prior knowledge for reading a narrative, two kinds of memory can be tapped: semantic memory (general or conceptual knowledge) and episodic memory (recollections of personal experience). For example, readers use their semantic memories when thinking about the concept of a wager and their episodic memories in recalling their own wagering experiences. Invitations to predict tap primarily semantic memory; invitations to reminisce tap primarily episodic memory. Consider these examples that illustrate the different ways of introducing a story:

Invitation to Reminisce (Episodic Memory)	Invitation to Predict (Semantic Memory)
T: What is the title of our story? **Ss:** "The Wager."	**T:** What is the title of our story? **Ss:** "The Wager."
T: Have you ever made a wager or a bet with somebody? **S1:** I bet my brother all the time that he can't do something, and then he does it. **S2:** One time I bet my sister she couldn't get in the doghouse, and she got in there and then couldn't get out, and my mom had to get her out and she was crying and she blamed me and I got grounded.	**T:** What do you think might happen in the story? **S1:** Maybe two people bet on something. **T:** Such as?
T: Have you ever been tricked by someone? **S3:** I was once.	**S2:** Maybe a bet on sports, like a game or a race. **S3:** It could be like a dare, where you bet someone they can't do something.
T: How did that make you feel? **S3:** I didn't like it, so I tricked them. **S4:** My cousin tries to trick me all the time. He thinks it's funny, but I don't like it.	**T:** Any other possibilities? **S4:** Maybe somebody makes a bet and then he won't pay off. **S5:** Or somebody could win a lot of money from making some kind of bet.
T: Anybody else? **S5:** My mother used to trick me by putting my medicine in orange juice, but I could always taste it. So now I don't usually drink orange juice.	**T:** Any other ideas? **S4:** It's probably a really important wager because it's the title of the story.
T: Well, today, we are going to read a story about a bet and how one person tried to trick another. Let's read to find out what happens.	**T:** That's also a possibility. Let's find out more by reading the first part.

Example A is the more common. This approach is widely recommended in professional texts and commercial reading programs. In fact, prereading "have-you-ever" questions are so engrained in the collective thinking of the profession as the way to activate prior knowledge that teachers may have difficulty seeing the benefits of an alternative approach. However, the prediction-oriented approach in Example B is far more effective.

Have-you-ever questions are most effective *after* reading, when they create rich opportunities for response: "Have you ever found yourself in a similar situation? Tell us all about it." The question now leads to substantive discussing or writing as students make meaningful personal connections to the story, seeing their experience in light of the story and vice versa.

Prediction Enhances Comprehension of the Text

As readers proceed through the story, they look for details that support or contradict their predictions and thus tend to read closely with heightened attention. As Wolf (1987) observes, predictions make students "actively aware of their expectations" (3). At all grade levels, discussions can become deep and complex because students are genuinely interested in sharing interpretations and possibilities. However, regardless of the depth of the discussion, at all grade levels and skill levels, predictions prime students to comprehend. This has an especially positive effect on word callers (i.e., students who recognize the words but understand little).

During the first reading of a story, some details relate directly to the developing plot and thus are useful clues; others are of secondary importance. As Nessel (1987) points out, many questions typically used to check comprehension are ineffective because they are about secondary information. Such questioning can even seem unfair to students because, focused as they are on the plot, they don't attend to secondary details. This is a good example of what Ritchhart describes as an activity that "may even lower comprehension by interrupting a natural process" (2002, 45).

For example, in guiding the reading of "The Wager," the teacher might have asked any of these questions at the first stopping point to check students' recall: *Where did the merchant live? Where did his caravans carry goods? How many guests attended the dinner? Would you have enjoyed being a guest that evening? What happened to Hakim in his early life? How did he probably feel at that time?* However, all of these questions are of secondary importance at this point in the story. The primary questions are whether or not it is possible to survive in extreme cold and what might motivate Hakim to try, and that's what readers focus on when stopped at this point. Questions about secondary details divert attention and interfere with comprehension. However, these details may become important later. For example, Bobbie recalled at the second stopping point that Hakim had lost everything. At that point, the detail related directly to Hakim's motivation for agreeing to the wager, whereas at the first stopping point it was simply one of several details given about him.

Facilitating a discussion that allows details to come up naturally, when they seem most relevant to the readers, takes considerable skill. The teacher must be familiar with the story so as to know which details are important, given the selected stopping points, but must not call attention to them and thus give away the plot or stifle discussion of other details. For example, at the first stopping point in "The Wager," the teacher knew that Mario was right but avoided saying *Good thinking!* or *Excellent!* Such enthusiasm might have signaled that he had correctly predicted the outcome and would have brought the discussion to a quick halt. Instead, the teacher replied with a neutral request for clarification (*What do you mean?*). Because she did not seem to favor Mario's response, he and the others continued to think.

The nature of predictions changes as readers move through a narrative. Initial thoughts are based on limited information, perhaps a title or a few pages. Students' predictions may not be especially profound but do serve an important function of launching them into the story and stimulating their thinking. Subsequent predictions are more robust and astute because the readers have more text information to use. As they move through the story, they narrow the set of plausible outcomes, but their thinking about those outcomes becomes more nuanced and finely tuned. By understanding this changing nature of predictions, teachers can more effectively observe students' comprehension as they read and guide their thinking in ways that enhance comprehension.

Prediction Builds Critical Thinking Capacity

Some predictions are more plausible than others, given the available evidence. Therefore, it's important for readers to examine their predictions critically at each stopping point: Of the various possible outcomes, which are most likely and why? Regular assessment of predictions builds critical thinking capacities, yet it is too often left out of the process of prediction. Here, for example, is the approach to prediction that is frequently seen in classrooms, using "The Wager" to illustrate:

Teacher: What do you think will happen when Hakim goes outside?

Rory: I think he's going to die.

Teacher: That's interesting, Rory. Hattie, what do you think?

Hattie: I think he'll get sick.

Teacher: Really? OK. Will?

Will: I'm not sure.

Teacher: Melanie?

Melanie: I think he'll survive and win the bet.

Teacher: All right, let's read to find out.

It's important for readers to examine their predictions critically at each stopping point: Of the various possible outcomes, which are most likely and why?

The focus here is simply on generating predictions, but the reasoning underlying predictions is also important. *What do you think?* is best followed by *Why do you think that?* Of course, as Frank Smith (1998) points out, readers making predictions do not ordinarily offer capricious guesses; they select judiciously from a fairly narrow range of choices that they, themselves, consider to be reasonable in the context (163). Asking students to justify their predictions thus encourages them to articulate their thinking so that they and others can consider it. Without discussing the reasoning, predicting can degenerate into mere guessing. Figure 2.1 shows the questions that engage critical thinking when students are making predictions.

Sometimes a brief response (*What else? And so?*) is enough to prod students to extend their thinking. If a group is large and not everyone has spoken, asking for a show of hands to indicate agreement or disagreement can keep everyone involved and may prompt new contributions. Sometimes it makes sense to ask students to justify their ideas; at other times, acknowledging a response with a nod is enough. Sometimes it's best to allow differences of opinion to arise without comment; sometimes it's useful to stimulate extended debate of opposing ideas. In sum, the suggested questions can be used flexibly. They are given here not to indicate a sequence that must be followed but simply to show how to stimulate critical thinking when discussing predictions.

The questions in Figure 2.1 can be used to engage the class as a whole, initiate small-group discussions, or give pairs a chance to talk briefly. Varying these tactics will avoid monotony. The key is to have students discuss their thinking as they move through the story in ways that support close reading and thoughtful response. Reading critically doesn't mean taking the joy out of reading; it means infusing the reading experience with lively thought and enthusiastic sharing of responses.

Figure 2.1

How Predicting Engages Critical Thinking

Initial Engagement	Purpose of Question
What do you think will happen in this story?	Invites reasoned speculation and arouses curiosity.
What makes you think so?	Invites students to verbalize their thinking about the title, illustrations, or other details.

Before Reading a Text Segment	Purpose of Question
What do you think will happen next? *What could possibly happen?*	Invites students to predict outcomes. Invites divergent and creative thinking.
Why do you think that? *Share your thinking with us.* *Tell us what makes you think that.* *Talk about that.*	Asks students to explain their reasoning, as much as possible, with evidence from the story, relevant firsthand experience, or what they remember from similar narratives.
How many of you tend to agree with this idea? *Who else thinks this is a good possibility?*	Makes a quick check of the group's thinking and invites critical evaluation.
What is another possibility? *Who has a different idea?* *Is there another way of looking at this?*	Invites multiple perspectives and encourages flexible thinking.
What else do we need to talk about? *Are there any other ideas you would like to share?* *Is there anything we haven't discussed that might be important?*	Invites students to examine story events more carefully and plants in their minds the idea that they may have missed something.

After Reading a Text Segment	Purpose of Question
What have we learned so far? *Now what do we know?* *What is happening in our story?*	Invites students to reflect on what they have read so far in preparation for thinking ahead to the next section.
Now what do you think? *How are our ideas changing?* *Based on what we have read, what are you thinking now about what might happen?*	Invites reexamination of earlier predictions in light of new evidence from the text and encourages new predictions.
Why do you think that? *Talk about what you are thinking.*	Asks students to justify their thinking with evidence, if possible.
What do you think about the new ideas that we have just shared? *What thoughts do you have about these new ideas?*	Invites critical evaluation of new predictions.

Prediction Establishes Useful Dispositions

Predicting has multiple impacts on learners' dispositions. First, the sharing of different ideas and interpretations helps students develop flexibility and learn to value different points of view. A good example occurred when a class read a Japanese folktale. In the story, an old man sets fire to his neighbors' rice fields, seemingly without reason. One student reasoned that the man was probably using the fire to warn people and predicted a tidal wave, an idea that seemed unlikely to the group. The student explained his reasoning but did not persuade the others. When his prediction turned out to be accurate, the group congratulated him for having thought of the idea, which they now realized was insightful. Such incidents help students learn to respect and seek multiple perspectives when interpreting texts and, very possibly, when engaging in other endeavors. They are also more likely to question their own thinking, aware that they could be overlooking something.

Also, students develop a think-ahead mind-set that serves them well when reading other narratives. Instead of passively taking in a story, they think actively about the developing plot and the characters' motivations. Over time, reading alertly in this way becomes a disposition that transfers to reading other narratives, hearing stories, or viewing television dramas or films. This active involvement enhances students' quality of thinking.

In addition, because predicting is highly engaging, students learn to perceive reading narratives as an agreeable activity. The repeated pleasure, even exhilaration, that students experience leads them to associate narratives with enjoyment and develops in them the desire and tendency to read more.

Finally, as students sharpen their capacity to perceive and use information in narrative texts, they become more alert to details around them that can help them solve problems, make decisions, and prepare for the future. By getting better at predicting events in narratives, they enhance their skill in "reading" real-life situations.

The Issue of Comprehension Skills and Strategies

Current reading curricula and state standards detail specific kinds of responses that students are expected to make when reading: recall explicitly stated information, make inferences, remember sequences of events, or draw conclusions, to name a few. These are presented as skills to be mastered, reflecting the skills-oriented mind-set that, as discussed in Chapter 1, has strongly influenced reading instruction for decades. Teachers devise lessons to teach these skills in conjunction with text selections and give students exercises to practice them. This approach merits serious reconsideration for several reasons.

When story reading routinely begins with a skill lesson, the message appears to be that the purpose for reading is to practice the skill rather than to comprehend and enjoy the story. Also, transfer is always an issue. Even if students do well with skill instruction and practice, they do not necessarily apply that learning on other occasions. For example, they may be able to draw the expected conclusions in a workbook exercise and yet have difficulty drawing conclusions about the characters in the stories they read. In too many reading curricula, the numerous skills to be taught tend to take precedence over reading and discussing texts (Dewitz, Jones, and Leahy 2009). Concerned about doing a good job, many teachers spend more time on skill instruction and assign many more practice exercises than the students actually need. Furthermore, when skill work is divorced from the experience of reading actual texts, students are not likely to perceive it as meaningful and useful. For example, a group of students read and discussed a story that they enjoyed and readily connected to their own life experiences. The teacher then sent them off to complete worksheets that involved putting sentences in the correct order, matching meanings to words, and doing a crossword puzzle. The practice work didn't do the students any harm, but following the story with the exercises wasn't the best instructional choice when writing, dramatizing, or other activities could easily have been used instead (see Chapter 5). Expert practitioners agree that it is best to avoid skill instruction or skill practice in such isolation; see, for example, Routman (2002).

For these reasons, we question the common assumption that students need extensive instruction and practice in comprehension subskills. The idea of skills or subskills to be mastered needs to be replaced with the idea that reading skillfully is a complex process that is heavily context-dependent. For example, following a sequence of events in a given narrative depends on the reader's prior knowledge and expectations and the complexity of the sequence. An individual with experience reading mysteries will be more attentive than a novice to the way a new mystery unfolds and will weigh each detail carefully, leery of red herrings. Then, too, for most readers, a short story that relates a handful of events in chronological

The idea of skills or subskills to be mastered needs to be replaced with the idea that reading skillfully is a complex process that is heavily context-dependent.

order will be easier to follow than a novel with a main story line, several subplots, and numerous flashbacks. Even experienced readers may be confused by the plots of some novels, real-life news stories, or other narratives. In fact, each narrative presents a reader with a new opportunity to follow a sequence and perhaps a new intellectual challenge.

All of the other comprehension skills that young readers are expected to master have similar degrees of complexity and context-dependence. Some main ideas and themes can be determined with ease; others are elusive. Information implied by the author may or may not be inferred. Even when the reader shares the author's background of experience and frame of reference, the author's implications are not always clear. The same kind of complexity exists in the processes of drawing conclusions, making generalizations, and other comprehension skills. As Paris (2005) points out, such skills are "unconstrained" in that they do not have finite numbers of elements to be mastered. (In contrast, naming the letters of the alphabet is a "constrained" skill that can be mastered.) Giving students exercises to help them supposedly master these complex "unconstrained" skills thus misses the mark.

More important than skill building are regular experiences with ever more complex and sophisticated texts, each with its own challenges and opportunities. Reading and discussing should occupy the large majority of classroom time because this is what students must learn to do well. As students read, the teacher has many opportunities to observe how well they are reading closely and thinking about texts. Their abilities to make inferences, draw conclusions, follow sequences, note cause–effect relationships, discern main ideas, and so on are readily evident when the teacher engages them in substantive discussions about texts. Over time, with adept guidance, students increase their capacities with all of these thinking processes. By doing so in the context of actual reading, they become skillful readers, not students who have simply mastered skills in narrow contexts. The difference is profound.

In recent years, some comprehension skills have been recast as cognitive strategies: actions that good readers regularly employ in the process of comprehending. For example, reference is commonly made to such strategies as inferring and determining importance, and many teachers present a strategy lesson before having students read a story. However, this kind of strategy instruction does not necessarily result in the kind of thoughtful, deep comprehension that we are discussing here. That's because the instruction involves *teaching about reading* more than *engaging in reading* and for that reason does not always have a positive effect on students' comprehension.

Students increase their capacity for comprehension more readily when they are focused on the story, not on learning or practicing a so-called reading skill or comprehension strategy. In fact, if students are asked to attend to a skill or strategy as they are reading, it is likely that their attention will be diverted away from constructing meaning, and their comprehension will thereby be diminished. We cannot stress too strongly that any guided reading experience should be done for the purpose of enhancing comprehension and enjoyment of the text, not to teach or practice a skill or strategy!

Students increase their capacity for comprehension more readily when they are focused on the story, not on learning or practicing a so-called reading skill or comprehension strategy.

Although reading and discussing are the most important components of reading instruction, the teacher may want to plan other activities if students are challenged by aspects of specific narratives. For example, in making predictions, one group of fifth graders overlooked several details that turned out to be important to the story outcome. After reading, the teacher had them identify details they had missed but now realized were relevant to the story's outcome, and they decided that next time they needed to be more careful about noticing details. The teacher can use such occasions to help learners better understand their reading behavior and become more aware of how they might respond to texts in the future. The goal is not skill mastery or acquisition of strategies but the building of students' awareness through repeated experiences as thinking readers. When they fare well during the reading of a story, such instruction is not needed and may be counterproductive.

The Value of Authentic Reading Experiences

When we view a compelling serial drama on television with our families or friends, we engage in lively debates about what the characters will do next. We analyze their behavior and point out clues, sometimes basing inferences on a single word or gesture. We apply what we know about human nature and about other stories while keeping in mind that plots can be unpredictable. During the week, we share predictions about the next episode, heightening our interest in watching it. When we see an excellent film at the movies, we rehash our thinking afterward with companions, sharing the thoughts that occurred to us at different points in the drama and reliving our moments of greatest surprise or emotion. When we read a novel, we converse mentally with ourselves as we follow the action. In all our encounters with narratives, our active thinking brings us satisfaction and increases our desire to read and view other narratives. We want students to have these same kinds of experiences.

When we guide students' reading of narratives, our immediate goal is their comprehension and appreciation of the story. Our ultimate goal is developing in them the disposition to read alertly and thoughtfully and the expectation that reading narratives will be a rewarding experience. From the initial planning to the final moments of the postreading conversation, we are thinking actively about where to pause, what questions to ask, and how best to stimulate discussion and reflection. Our intellectual involvement is highly enjoyable to us as teachers, and our pleasure in what we're doing is readily apparent to our students.

Each comprehension experience we have with students is unique. The variation from one occasion to the next occurs because we don't follow scripts or use prepared questions. We ask certain questions repeatedly (e.g., *What do you think will happen next? Why do you think that?*), but most of our questions arise in response to what the students say, and we can never be sure what they will say. We don't think of what we do as "teaching the story" but rather as having lively conversations with students about the story. So although we are certainly teaching, our discussions are more authentic than the somewhat formulaic exchanges that are too often typical of guided reading. Students respond with heightened awareness of the text and of themselves as capable readers.

CHAPTER 3

The Power of Inquiry
Supporting Students' Reading of Informational Texts

When readers choose to read informational text, they do so because they have questions to answer. They may be interested in specific facts, a solution to a problem, a new perspective, or an understanding of a complex process. They have either generated the questions themselves or have become interested in questions raised by others. Even those who choose informational texts for leisure reading expect to learn something. Such real-world uses of informational texts are excellent models for classroom reading. Ideally, students become genuinely curious about something, are eager to discover the very information that is in the text, and have a satisfying experience of inquiry. Here is an example to illustrate.

Reading Informational Text: An Example

This lesson about bones was conducted in a third-grade class. Students sat in groups of three or four so that all could participate fully by discussing alternately in their groups and as a whole class. This was the first time the children had talked about the topic.

> *Teacher:* We're going continue our study of the human body and today will start learning about our bones. Let's think of what we already know or think we might know about the bones in our bodies. Take a few minutes to talk in your groups.

(The teacher circulated, showing interest in what the groups were saying but not indicating if they were correct. He asked occasional questions to encourage students to think more deeply or explore other possibilities, then reconvened the class to share ideas.)

Teacher: What do we know about the bones in our bodies?

Charlie: We talked about how bones break sometimes.

Teacher: And?

Charlie: Then you put it in a cast. You have to wear the cast a long time.

Teacher: Why do you think we need bones?

William: You have to have bones. Or you'd be like a jellyfish.

Dean: Yeah. You couldn't stand up. You would just flop over.

Teacher: Are there different kinds of bones?

Saira: Some are big. Some are little.

Charlie: Some are straight, and I think some are bent or curved.

Darren: Is your skull a bone?

Teacher: What do you think?

Darren: I don't know. It's hard, so maybe it is.

Teacher: What else did you talk about?

Zane: We have lots of bones. Everybody does.

Teacher: How many is a lot? *(Students shake their heads, puzzled.)*

Teacher: Well, do you think we have more than one hundred bones in our bodies or fewer than one hundred? What's your best thinking? Talk it over. *(Groups discuss briefly.)*

Teacher: What do you think?

Zane: Some of us think maybe twenty bones. But some of us think more.

LouAndra: We think maybe about one hundred bones.

Teacher: Talk about that.

LouAndra: Well, we have lots of bones in each hand and lots of little bones in our feet. And our arms and legs.

Marlo: We think maybe two hundred.

Avon: We think more than one hundred, but not two hundred. That's too many.

Teacher: Do we have all of our bones when we're born?

Several: Ooh. That's a good question.

Gaby: I don't think you could have all of your bones when you're a little baby. There isn't room to put them all. *(Several students laugh.)*

Saira:	Maybe they're all there. They're just very tiny.
Teacher:	What else?
Thomas:	We talked about whether your teeth are bones.
Teacher:	What do you think?
Thomas:	We think they are but we aren't sure.
Zane:	We think they are.
Teacher:	What's inside our bones?
Rhonda:	Is it bone all the way through?
Maria:	Are they hollow? Some birds have hollow bones, I think.
Eddie:	I think there's something inside. I'm not sure what it's called, but I think it's important.
Teacher:	How is it important?
Eddie:	I don't know, but I think the bones make you stay healthy. Something inside the bones.
Teacher:	What else?
Gaby:	You're supposed to drink lots of milk to make your bones strong.
Kylie:	I think you're supposed drink two glasses.
Gaby:	Every day.
Teacher:	OK, we have lots of interesting ideas. Let's read to ourselves and see if we can find answers to our questions. *(Students eagerly read the following text.)*

The Bones in Your Body

You were born with more than three hundred bones in your body. As you grow, some of the bones grow together, so when you are fully grown, you will have about 206 bones. Your bones make up your *skeleton*. Your skeleton protects and supports the organs and muscles inside your body. Tendons connect your bones to muscles so you can move.

Your bones were very soft when you were born. Your blood carries special cells into your bones, and they make your bones harder and stronger as you grow. Your bones have calcium and collagen, which is a kind of fiber. The calcium makes your bones strong, and the collagen makes them flexible.

Inside your bones is a soft and spongy material called *marrow*. Some is red, and some is yellow. The yellow marrow stores fat. The red marrow makes new red blood cells to replace old cells that die. It makes more than two million new red blood cells each second!

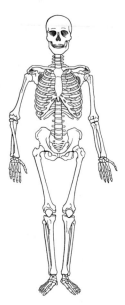

Your bones are connected by ligaments. Ligaments are made of collagen, so they're flexible. Because of that, you can bend and move easily.

You have different kinds of bones, for example: long bones, short bones, and flat bones. The big bones of your arms and legs are long bones. The main bones of your wrists and ankles are short bones that are as wide as they are long. Your rib bones are thin and flat, and you have twenty-four of them.

Your backbone is made up of thirty-three bones. You have twenty-eight different kinds of bones in your head. Eight are in the part of your skull that protects your brain. Others are in your cheeks, nose, and mouth. Each of your hands has twenty-seven bones. They are in your wrist, in the main part of your hand, and in your fingers.

Although your bones are strong, they can break. Where a bone breaks, it creates new cells and blood vessels. These cover over the broken parts and keep growing until the pieces grow back together. Then the bone is like new again.

Suppose you fall down hard and break a bone in your arm. First, a doctor will take an X-ray of your arm to see the broken bone inside. Then the doctor will move the broken pieces together and will put a hard cast on your arm to make sure they stay together. It will stay there for one or two months until the pieces grow together.

To keep your bones healthy, you need calcium and vitamin D. If you're between four and eight years old, you need about two eight-ounce glasses of milk a day, and you also need to eat foods that are high in calcium. If you are between nine and eighteen years old, you need at least three eight-ounce glasses of milk a day along with foods with calcium. Green vegetables like broccoli and kale have calcium. So do cheese, fish, and almonds. Milk usually has vitamin D, and you can get vitamin D from being in the sun for a short time every day.

Exercise is as important as calcium and vitamin D for healthy bones, but some exercise is better than others. The best exercise puts weight on your bones and makes your bones work hard. That's what makes them strong. Swimming and bicycling are good for you, but they don't put weight on your bones. Walking, running, dancing, and skateboarding all put weight on your bones, so they help your bones grow strong.

Students read silently and attentively but paused occasionally to express pleasure at finding answers. For closure, the teacher guided a lively postreading discussion:

Which of our questions did we answer? Students identified information that related to their questions and hypotheses. Zane and Saira talked about how you have more than three hundred bones when you are born and end up with 206 bones. Kylie remarked that bones have little sponges inside them. When Gaby said she didn't remember seeing that, Kylie read aloud the sentence referring to "soft and spongy material." Gaby said spongy material isn't the same as little sponges. The group discussed this and, with the teacher's help, better understood the nature of marrow.

What questions have we not answered and what new questions have we raised? Thomas and Zane wondered if teeth counted as part of the 206 bones. Saira wondered if milk is good for your bones, what might be bad for them? The group noted that the article said nothing about either point and decided to find the answers elsewhere.

What else did we learn that we didn't talk about or didn't have questions about? Students noted that they now realized the importance of exercise to bone health. The teacher brought up sports not mentioned in the article, inviting students to apply their understanding of the concept of weight-bearing exercise. Students also talked about bone marrow and discussed what they had learned about ligaments, calcium, and collagen.

What was the most surprising or interesting thing you learned from reading? Some students said they were most surprised to learn that people have more bones as infants than as adults, remembering that they had all thought just the opposite. Others said they were most surprised that bone is soft in the middle, that blood is made in the bones, and that the growth of red blood cells is so fast. They were also surprised by the number of bones in different parts of the body but realized they were confused by the numbers and body parts when they discussed them. To clarify, they reread selected passages aloud and discussed key statements.

What was the most important thing we learned today about our bones? Marlo pointed out that if you wanted to be a nurse or a doctor it would be important to know how many bones people have. Others noted information with practical benefits: how much milk to drink, the physical activities that are good for bones, and how broken bones are treated.

What do we know now about bones that we didn't know before? Students summarized the key points they had learned and also talked about bone flexibility. The teacher guided them to consider different degrees of flexibility so that they could understand how bones are hard and yet can bend.

This description can't fully convey the emotional tone of the lesson. Students leaned forward, listened attentively, eagerly contributed ideas, talked productively, read with enthusiasm, and reread thoughtfully. They became genuinely interested in bones. The teacher clearly enjoyed stimulating their thinking and seeing them find the information they sought. The positive climate strongly influenced the students' attention and comprehension.

Reflecting on the Power of Inquiry

This teacher used the power of inquiry to sustain students' interest and develop their comprehension. He invited students to share what they knew and accepted their ideas nonjudgmentally. As they talked, he probed further, leading them to think critically about their preconceptions. As questions arose, he invited them to form hypotheses and encouraged discussion of the different ideas that emerged. These four steps are vital to priming students effectively for reading informational text. Let's look more closely at how they work together.

- **Activate prior knowledge.** It is widely accepted that students benefit from recalling what they know about a topic before they read. However, although they may think they know some things and don't know others, they may be mistaken on both counts. They may also have knowledge that they don't realize is relevant and some that they think is relevant but isn't. In discussing, they will share misconceptions and say things that are incorrect, as the third graders did. Learners' "preconceptions" are a complex mix, as Bransford, Brown, and Cocking (2000) note.

- **Stimulate critical thinking.** Because students' prior knowledge is complex and imperfect, just asking them what they know is not enough. They must also be encouraged to think critically about their ideas. Thus, this teacher probed the nuances, depths, and accuracy of what students said. To sustain their uncertainty, he did not reveal any answers. Significantly, he knew that most of his questions were directly related to the information in the text. The students were not thinking of the text because it was not in front of them. They were focused only on the topic, and the more they thought, the more they questioned what they knew.

- **Invite hypotheses.** As uncertainties emerged, the teacher invited students to generate hypotheses, knowing these would make text details more salient during reading. He provided scaffolding as needed. For example, they were puzzled when asked how many bones humans have, so he gave them an anchor for their thinking: more than one hundred or fewer? This was not a clue to the correct answer. It was an encouragement to think further instead of saying they didn't know.

- **Encourage discussion and debate.** The teacher knew that interest would increase if the group considered different ideas. Discussing various hypotheses also intensified students' motivation. They didn't simply want to know the answers to some questions; they wanted to know if their tentative answers were the right ones. With their curiosity at its peak, they were well primed for reading.

This teacher knew exactly what he wanted the students to learn about the curriculum topic, and he was familiar with the text. His guiding of the conversation was thus an artful orchestration of the students' thinking. Notably, he asked the students to do far more than simply recall what they knew before reading. He asked them to *use* their prior knowledge to form hypotheses. This form of active thinking is highly beneficial to the learning of informational material, as Stauffer (1969) and Lindfors (1999), among others, point out.

A particularly important aspect of the lesson was how students' uncertainty aroused their curiosity, a mental state that is vital to learning, as Dewey (1910) noted and others have observed

Because students' prior knowledge is complex and imperfect, just asking them what they know is not enough. They must also be encouraged to think critically about their ideas.

since. Some students become curious as soon as they are aware they don't know something. Others, often those who have been frustrated by school, may become curious only later in a discussion like this. The third graders, used to hypothesizing, were developing the inclination to be curious and thus the ability to sustain interest in what they were learning.

Although such a prereading discussion does not need to be restricted to what is in the text, it can be counterproductive to focus too much on other information. For example, the teacher didn't encourage further discussion of birds' bones when Maria made her comment, knowing the text did not address that topic. However, even though the teacher deftly channeled the talk toward information that was in the text, these students felt they could talk about whatever they liked.

Properly nurtured, hypotheses change learners and learning. They are the students' questions and become the students' purposes for reading. The learners become intellectually and emotionally involved. No one has to force them to read; they genuinely want to find the relevant information. Scholars through the years have called attention to these aspects of the psychology of learning. For example, Kelley (1947) notes the vital role that learners' purposes play in motivating learning. Postman and Weingartner (1969) observe that if students are invited to engage in inquiry, they must develop an emotional connection to the subject; without that, the inquiry is superficial and hollow. Glasser (1992) asserts that students simply walk away, figuratively if not literally, if they are forced to learn information in which they have no interest. Markham (2005) points to the importance of making learning a matter of "sustained relevant discovery."

> *Properly nurtured, hypotheses change learners and learning.*

Reading Informational Text: A Second Example

This second example is from a high school class that had recently studied the American War for Independence and was now beginning a unit on the War of 1812. The teacher was especially interested in seeing how students would make use of what they had learned so far as they discussed the new topic.

Teacher: Today, we're going to learn about the writing of "The Star-Spangled Banner." Does anyone know who wrote the lyrics? (*Several students name Francis Scott Key, saying they remembered it from somewhere.*) OK. Let's take a minute to think about what we might

THE COMPREHENSION EXPERIENCE: Engaging Readers Through Effective Inquiry and Discussion already know about this. Talk in your groups about what you know or think you know about Key writing the lyrics.

(Students thought Key was looking at the American flag from a ship in the middle of a battle, recalling a painting of such a scene that they had seen some time ago. Most placed the event during the Revolutionary War; others suggested the War of 1812, noting that was the historical period they were about to study.)

Teacher: So if Key was on a ship, what was he doing there?

Wayne: He must have been fighting.

Ben: Maybe he was the captain.

Pat: Wasn't he a prisoner? I remember reading that somewhere.

Carrie: I think that's right.

Simon: So the British were holding him as a prisoner?

Pat: It must have been the British. Who else would it have been?

Larry: What about the French?

Pat: The French were on our side during the Revolution. Remember Lafayette and all that?

Teacher: Why would anyone be holding Key prisoner? What do you think he did?

Evan: Maybe he was a spy. They caught him and took him prisoner.

Jackie: He could have been an officer and they took him so his men would surrender.

Ronnie: But if he was a prisoner, how could he see the flag? Wouldn't he be below the deck in chains or something?

Pat: We don't know for sure that he was a prisoner.

Jeff: Where was the flag? On another ship or on the land?

Nathan: Maybe another ship. Maybe there was an American ship fighting the ship he was on.

Ben: Did the Americans have a navy at that time?

Teacher: If Key was on a ship, where do you think the ship was? Where did all this happen?

(Students conferred briefly in their groups. Some thought New York Harbor, saying that was a center for commerce; others thought Philadelphia or Washington D.C., noting that each was the capital at some point.)

Jeff: So where was the flag?

Teacher: Where do you think it might have been?

Kim: Maybe it was with the soldiers on land. They carried it into battle, and he saw it from the water.

Wayne: Maybe it was flying over a fort.

Simon: Yeah, a fort! The song goes, "O'er the ramparts we watched. . . ."

Teacher: What fort would that have been?

Students suggested several forts that they remembered from their earlier studies, debating which was most likely Key's location. After another few minutes of discussion, students read an account of Key's experience at Baltimore Harbor in September 1814, when he boarded a British ship to arrange the release of Americans who were being held as prisoners.

After reading, the teacher posed the six questions presented earlier. Students readily noted the details related to their hypotheses and discussed them with interest. They debated whether or not Key was actually a prisoner, pointing out that although he had not been captured, he was not free to leave. They said learning about this event would probably help them remember the War of 1812 and Fort McHenry because both of those details jumped out at them as they read. The lesson served as a springboard for later discussions of all four stanzas of the lyrics as the students continued their study of early American history.

This teacher engaged students regularly in forming hypotheses about upcoming topics. Sometimes they discussed and read in one class period, as in the example. Other times, they debated hypotheses for a longer stretch, then read and discussed multiple texts for several days. Sometimes they understood the material easily; sometimes they reread and discussed at length to clarify. Used to thinking ahead, they were becoming adept at applying what they had learned to new topics. Consequently, they experienced history as an interesting unfolding of related events. Such coherence is an especially useful characteristic of instruction, as noted by Applebee, Burroughs, and Stevens (1994, 2000), and enhances the pleasure of learning as well as depth of understanding.

Making the Case for Misconceptions

Many teachers are uncomfortable when students state incorrect information and are tempted to set them right quickly, but doing so is not particularly effective when the purpose is thinking. The value to learners of being wrong at the outset is actually high. Stauffer (1969) designed the

Directed Reading-Thinking Activity to make students aware of what they don't know about a topic as well as what they do know. Smith (1973) points out that for students to confirm what they already know is not as useful as being wrong initially and having to revise their thinking. McNeil (1984) advocates instruction that purposely creates cognitive dissonance. Bingham (2000) lauds the value of the "creative disequilibration" that results from purposely generating doubt in students' minds.

Dykstra (2005), reporting research on physics instruction, presents a strong argument for unearthing learners' misconceptions and speculations. As he explains, the typical physics teacher gives information, checks to see that students have received it, and assigns reinforcement activities. Students who receive such traditional instruction may be able to answer questions, especially if they are posed in the right way, but they can seldom apply information in actual problem-solving situations because so much of their knowledge is superficial. Even more significantly, Dykstra notes that studies dating from 1904 consistently show that this traditional approach fails to change students' initial misconceptions about physical phenomena. Furthermore, he expresses concern that the approach has negative impacts on learners' attitude toward science and toward themselves as students of science. However, he notes that when a teacher skillfully guides students to explore their misconceptions and build new understandings from their faulty knowledge, the students' understanding of concepts and phenomena improves dramatically.

In any subject, when students are about to learn something new, allowing them to voice incorrect information with impunity helps build a healthy psychological climate for learning. Students relax noticeably when told they are not expected to have all the answers. Thinking becomes enjoyable under these conditions. Students sometimes ask the teacher to hold off a little longer in handing out the text because they have "just one more idea" to share. They cheerfully admit they are probably wrong but want to say what they are thinking anyway.

As Holt (1964) notes in his classic work on the dynamics of failure, many students are painfully aware of not knowing the answers and fearful of looking foolish by saying something wrong. He gives a number of examples of students whose anxiety about what

> *When students are about to learn something new, allowing them to voice incorrect information with impunity helps build a healthy psychological climate for learning.*

It's not remarkable that the sensation of surprise—strongest when a hypothesis turns out to be wrong—helps to fix information in memory.

they don't know is so strong that it has debilitating effects on their ability to think clearly and use what they do know to figure things out. Tatum (2009) makes the same observation, pointing out that such feelings drive underachievers away from school altogether. Many others argue for the establishment of a climate for learning that encourages substantive student talk, accepts errors and misconceptions, reduces anxiety, and nurtures confidence. For example, Allington and Johnston (2002) note from their research that the most effective teachers engage students frequently in the exploration of ideas rather than merely the production of correct answers.

When competing ideas are explored, everyone benefits. Students listen to each other's reasoning and respond with their own best thinking. Even those who don't verbalize their thoughts become involved by following others' exchanges. A discussion of different ideas enables everyone to see more sides to the issue, reconsider initial ideas, and think more deeply about the topic. Debate sharpens thinking even when some of the ideas turn out to be wrong (Nemeth 1986). Such discussions provide what Hattie (2009) highlights as a sign of excellence: a focus on depth and complexity.

Whether or not a hypothesis turns out to be correct is essentially irrelevant, and students ordinarily are indifferent to the accuracy of their first thoughts, especially if the teacher does not call attention to it. More important is the pleasurable anticipation before reading and the heightened interest as answers are found during reading. As Jensen (2005) points out, excitement is one kind of emotional response that has a positive effect on cognition. Thus it's not remarkable that the sensation of surprise—strongest when a hypothesis turns out to be wrong—helps to fix information in memory.

Other Effective Approaches to Informational Text

Similar approaches can be used to prompt lively discussion and generate hypotheses before reading. Two that are especially effective are anticipation guides and the use of key words to stimulate thinking.

Anticipation Guides

An anticipation guide contains teacher-composed statements about a topic that students discuss before reading. After reading, they review their initial responses, revising as needed. To illustrate, here is a lesson about potatoes taught in a fourth-grade class.

Teacher: Here some statements to think about. Discuss each one in your groups and decide if you agree or disagree and why.

Potatoes

_____ 1. **If you put a potato in the ground, a plant will grow.**

_____ 2. **A potato plant has flowers.**

_____ 3. **Bees help potatoes grow fruit.**

_____ 4. **We eat the part of the potato plant that is called the root.**

_____ 5. **To grow a potato, you must plant potato seeds.**

Teacher: What have you discussed in your groups?

Group 1: We agreed with #1 at first, but then we read #5 and we weren't sure. So we agreed with both. We think you have to put a potato in the ground and a seed, too.

Group 2: We didn't agree with #1. We don't think it would work to put a potato in the ground. It would just get mushy and rot.

Group 3: We think you plant seeds because a potato is a vegetable and you plant seeds to get other vegetables, like squash and beans.

Group 2: Yes, that's what we think, too.

Student: My grandfather cuts potatoes up and puts them in the ground and they grow. So I think I agree with #1. But maybe it only works for the potatoes he grows. . . .

The groups shared their thinking about each statement. Some thought potato plants have flowers and attract bees like other plants; others thought not because potatoes grow underground. All agreed with #4, noting that because potatoes grow underground they must be roots. Each statement was addressed in the text they read: a short illustrated book about the life cycle of a potato plant. They discussed again after reading and concluded the lesson by revising or elaborating the original statements as needed to make them all true. For example, they revised the fourth statement to read: *We eat the part of the potato plant that is called the tuber. Tubers grow in the roots of the plant.* Finally, they wrote accounts in their own words about what they had learned.

Anticipation guides have considerable potential in grades K–12 when the statements are
simple but thought provoking and when
students discuss them. Simply writing
agree or *disagree* next to each does not
lead learners to think critically about the
statements, become curious, form hypotheses,
and read purposefully for answers. Thoughtful

> *Thoughtful discussion is essential if students are to become primed to learn more.*

discussion is essential if students are to become primed to learn more. Anticipation guides are
especially useful in information-heavy subjects such as social studies and science. For a more extensive discussion of this approach, devised by Herber (1978), see Nessel and Graham (2007).

Hypothesizing with Key Words

Another useful alternative is to present students before reading with the topic and several words
from the text. For example, here is an array given to a ninth-grade class:

Topic: Making Chocolate

nibs		ferment		winnow
		roast	molds	
beans	pods		rollers	blend

To start, the teacher said: *Today we are going to learn about how chocolate is processed into
chocolate bars and other forms. All these words have something to do with the processing. What do you
think the connections are? For example, what might rollers have to do with the process? What might be
blended with what? Talk in your groups first. Then we'll discuss as a class.*

The choice of words is critical. If students know too much about how the words relate to
the topic, they have little reason to wonder. That's why this teacher included *nibs*, *winnow*, and
ferment. He thought the words would probably be relatively unfamiliar in this context and thus
would arouse curiosity. At the other extreme, if too many of the words are specific and technical, students do not know what to do with them. That's why this teacher included *beans*, *rollers*,
blend, *pods*, and *roast*. He knew they would be familiar to students from other contexts and thus
would lead to meaningful, if not accurate, responses. After speculating about possible connections among the words, the students were eager to read. After reading, they discussed the words
again, pinpointing the role of each in chocolate manufacture.

This is an effective strategy to use when the students have relatively limited prior knowledge about the content to be learned. The words get the discussion going and prime students for reading. For a further discussion of this approach, created by Hammond (1984), see Nessel and Graham (2007).

The Value of Hypotheses in Reading Informational Texts

Students with clear hypotheses know what they are looking for and readily note relevant information when reading. Because they read with interest and attention, they learn other information, too, so their overall comprehension is high. Postreading discussion is purposeful, and because learners talk about the information in their own words, they are more likely to retain it. Word callers, in particular, benefit. Just as predicting outcomes helps them comprehend narratives, hypothesizing helps them comprehend informational texts.

Before reading, hypothesizing gives students excellent opportunities for critical thinking. They must judge the plausibility of their preconceptions and consider what they may have overlooked. After reading, they must decide if they should retain, revise, or discard their hypotheses in light of the text information. Learners may also consider the background of the author, the degree of bias evident, the publication date, and other features that might affect the validity of the information. This kind of thinking is useful at all grade levels but is increasingly valuable for older students, whose capacities for critical evaluation are usually more fully developed.

The six postreading questions (see Figure 3.1) prompt reflection and reconsideration of initial ideas. Each serves a useful purpose in stimulating discussion so that students' processing of information isn't too hasty or superficial.

Figure 3.1

Six Postreading Questions: Informational Text

1. Which of our questions did we answer?
2. What questions have we not answered and what new questions have we raised?
3. What else did we learn that we didn't talk about or didn't have questions about?
4. What was the most surprising or interesting thing you learned from reading?
5. What was the most important thing we learned today?
6. What do we know now that we didn't know before?

Asking students which questions they answered honors their hypotheses, invites them to state what they learned, and encourages them to bring up confusions or ambiguities. Further discussion may be needed if they have interpreted statements differently.

Noting unanswered questions and raising new questions invites students to consider what the text does not say. In some instances, distinguishing between what is addressed and not addressed is challenging and requires attentive rereading and further discussion.

Asking students what else they learned puts their recall under their control. They are not in the awkward position of being asked about details they may have overlooked. The regular use of this question leads students to expect that they will learn much from reading that goes beyond their initial purposes. Then, too, as students share ideas, some will mention details that others missed. All benefit from this review.

In the spirit of Rosenblatt (1978), asking about the most surprising or interesting details invites an aesthetic response to informational text. Most often, students find different bits interesting or surprising, so a lot of information is brought into the discussion. Hearing the responses, the teacher also gains useful information about the students' perspectives because they are deciding what they as individuals find noteworthy.

The term *important* in this context refers to what can be objectively considered significant or vital to remember. Students may judge certain nuggets of information both interesting and important, but they will be interested in some information even though it is not particularly important and will deem other information important but not all that interesting. The distinction between the two is thus useful for the shift in thinking that it entails.

Too many students think it's best to know the answers to all the questions at the beginning of the lesson, and teachers reinforce this belief when they place too much emphasis on what students know before reading. For this reason, it's especially useful to ask learners after reading what they know now that they didn't know before. The focus here is on relative gain: what new information they have acquired.

The enhanced comprehension that results from using hypotheses as purposes and having substantive discussions after reading also enables students to write with more confidence about what they have learned. In Chapter 5, we suggest a

Asking about the most surprising or interesting details invites an aesthetic response to informational text.

number of ways that writing can be used to refine and further extend comprehension of informational text.

Building Cognitive Capacities and Dispositions

Discussion provides opportunities to clarify or refine learners' comprehension and thinking. For example, fifth graders in Michigan have just read about the making of maple syrup. After discussing what they learned, the teacher stimulates further thinking:

Teacher: What do we know about where Michigan ranks in maple syrup production?

Hope: Michigan ranks third.

Teacher: How do you know?

Hope: In the second paragraph it says, "Only the syrup makers in New York and Vermont produced more." So that means Michigan must be third because this is an article about maple syrup in Michigan.

(Students look again at the paragraph from which Hope is reading orally.)

Many people think only of Vermont when they think of maple syrup, but Michigan is a major maple syrup state, too. Over 98,000 gallons of maple syrup were produced in our state last year. Only the syrup makers in New York and Vermont produced more . . .

Zoe: So New York is number one and Vermont is number two.

Rex: Wait. That may not be true. It doesn't really say which is number one. It just says that New York and Vermont produced more. Maybe Vermont is number one.

Zoe: That's true.

Teacher: Is there anything else we can conclude from this paragraph and other information in the text?

Kobe: Like what?

Teacher: Think about the sap.

Kobe: Oh yeah. It says it that it takes about fifty gallons of sap for one gallon of syrup. We could figure out how much sap came from Michigan trees.

Rex: You could multiply 50 times 98,00 gallons and get that answer. That would be a lot of sap!

Teacher: How much? Can we find out? *(Students compute and discuss.)*

The teacher raises the question about Michigan's ranking knowing that the text does not state the information explicitly. She is interested in seeing how students handle the implied information and is pleased when Rex questions Zoe because she has often talked with the group about reading closely, being alert to ambiguities, and not jumping to conclusions. In addition, the teacher is able to extend the students' thinking by using data about sap from another part of the text.

Such high-level thinking before and after reading develops useful dispositions over time. Students see learning as a form of discovery that generates a keen sense of intellectual satisfaction. The more they have these kinds of discussions, the more they learn to respond thoughtfully and reason with increasing sophistication. These are important aspects of the inquiry-based learning advocated by McCann et al. (2005). They also relate directly to the "intellectual character" that Ritchhart (2002) argues should be a priority of education. In addition, they reflect the idea that education should nurture the qualitative aspects of intelligence while helping students acquire information (Eisner 2002).

When students become adults, they will need to weigh pros and cons, consider implications, generate courses of action, form judgments, and make decisions under conditions of uncertainty. Consider, for example, how hypothesizing and associated critical thinking enters into the work of a scientist designing an experiment, a sales director creating a marketing campaign, a political advisor organizing an election campaign, a lawyer planning to defend a client, or a coach assembling a team of players. All operate from incomplete information in a context of uncertainty; all test their initial hypotheses against actual results and modify their thinking and actions accordingly. Examples exist across all occupations and professions. Students who have learned to keep their thinking within the bounds of what they know to be correct will not be as effective outside of school as those who realize, comfortably, that they may not always be right but can apply their best thinking. Such attitudes and actions lead to success in the world of work and human relations. See, for example, Covey (1989), Senge (1990), and Wallace (2010).

Students who frequently experience the kind of learning described here become comfortable about admitting ignorance. Given many opportunities to express their thoughts, they learn that no one is right all the time, and the need to be right diminishes. They must no longer feign forgetfulness or boredom to mask their lack of knowledge. Students' healthy skepticism about their own knowledge, coupled with their interest in learning more, creates a genuine climate of inquiry in the classroom that enhances these tendencies further. It is not surprising that "overall, inquiry-based instruction produce[s] transferable critical thinking skills as well as significant domain benefits, improved achievement, and improved attitude toward the subject" (Hattie 2009, 209–10).

Perhaps most important, students who experience this kind of teaching consistently learn that they are capable of thinking and take pleasure in it. They begin seeing school as a place that engages their interest and challenges them intellectually. Over time, their capacities for thinking, which have always been there, are brought to light, refined, and extended.

> *Students' healthy skepticism about their own knowledge, coupled with their interest in learning more, creates a genuine climate of inquiry in the classroom.*

Supporting the Spirit of Inquiry: The Essential Role of the Teacher

For students to feel comfortable revealing uncertainty and generating hypotheses, they must feel that their ideas have value. To discuss productively after reading, they must have developed genuine interest in the information and see it as relevant to their interests and purposes. Teachers who make students feel such comfort and engagement have these characteristics:

- **Their highest priority is thinking.** During prereading discussions, they focus on hypothesizing. After reading, they have students interpret, question, and evaluate the information as well as recall it. They consider accuracy more important after reading than before reading but also value the thinking associated with achieving accuracy.
- **They elicit and pose effective questions.** Before and after reading, they don't fish for right answers. They ask students to clarify, refine, extend, and articulate their thinking. Their questioning takes the discussion deeper and shows students the questions they might ask of themselves.
- **They guide students to evaluate their own thinking.** Before reading, they invite students to decide on the plausibility of their hypotheses, support their reasoning, and consider how sure they are of what they've stated. Teachers may introduce opposing viewpoints to sharpen students' thinking. After reading, they focus on what students learned, but they consider citing evidence to support an answer as important as the answer.
- **They do not give anything away.** Before reading, they lead the discussion without divulging the information the students will discover as they read. They remain neutral, not revealing by facial expression, body language, or vocal responses who, if anyone,

is on the right track. They avoid giving students the answers and may even give the impression that they do not know the answers. After reading, they have students turn to the text for information rather than merely telling them what is in it.

- **They set a tone of genuine inquiry.** They celebrate curiosity, listen attentively, foster collaborative thinking, and welcome a diversity of perspectives. They do not put students on the defensive nor allow a climate of one-upmanship to take hold.

Facilitating effective discussions before and after reading requires considerable skill; it cannot be scripted. The teacher must listen to what the students say and respond accordingly. Wells and Chang-Wells (1992) describe what is required: "moment-by-moment decisions about how to proceed, based on knowledge of the topic, understanding of the dynamics of classroom interaction, intentions with respect to the task, and a continuous monitoring of the ongoing talk" (46–47). This is challenging because one must think on one's feet.

For many, these needed teacher responses go against the grain. For example, when the history students suggested that Key penned his lyrics during the Revolutionary War, the teacher did not flinch. She also did not say *Good!* when others suggested the War of 1812. Her priority at this point was how the students used what they knew, or thought they knew, to respond to the challenges she posed. If they thought Key was on a ship, then where might the ship be and what might he be doing on it? If they thought he was a prisoner, why might he be held captive? Such thinking is more interesting and rewarding for students than trying to come up with correct answers before they have read anything about the situation. Such a discussion is also more satisfying to the teacher, who is not doling out praise to those who happen to know already what the class is about to learn. Praise for content accuracy is rightly reserved for the postreading discussion, when everyone has an equal chance to earn it.

Facilitating effective discussions before and after reading requires considerable skill; it cannot be scripted.

How Reading Informational Text Differs from Reading Narrative Text

The illustrative lessons in this chapter differ from those in the previous chapter because reading informational text is different from reading narrative text. Unfortunately, the profession has given scant attention to the differences. For example, the National Reading Panel (2000) did not investigate the differences or how instruction might need to vary accordingly, and the influential *Put Reading First* (National Institute for Literacy 2006) makes insufficient distinctions between the two. In the early grades, many teachers routinely refer to both texts as "stories." One day, students are told they will read a story about a boy who loses his mitten in the snow (with reference to a folktale); another day they are told they will read a story about snow (with reference to an informational text). At any grade level, instruction is most effective when it capitalizes on the differences.

Narrative texts contain artfully arranged sequences of events. Readers enter into the world the author has created or re-created and gain insight into the human condition. In contrast, readers don't expect things to "happen" in informational texts; they expect to acquire facts, learn opinions, obtain explanations, or find solutions to problems. Of course, information can be presented in narrative form (e.g., biography), and a story may include useful information, but readers ordinarily do not read narratives to obtain information, and they do not dip into informational texts to lose themselves in created worlds. Both kinds of texts can be equally fascinating and enjoyable, so the important distinction is not between "reading for pleasure" and "reading for information." The key is that readers approach the different texts with different purposes and expectations.

The different purposes lead to different kinds of reading experiences. When following a narrative, the priority is the unfolding story; with exposition, it is the information. Thus, the experience of reading a novel about a pioneer family is not the same as the experience of reading an article on the westward movement even though both are about the same topic. Conversely, the experience of reading exposition is much the same across subject areas although the content varies, and the experience of reading narration is similar across texts although settings, characters, and plots vary.

Another difference lies in the prior knowledge needed to engage successfully with the text. Most relevant to reading a story is an understanding of how humans think and act. Because all readers have acquired some of this knowledge from firsthand experience and from other stories or dramas, they can begin a new story without extensive preparation. In contrast, successful reading of informational text usually depends on readers connecting the new information to something they already know, including general or analogous knowledge if their topic-specific knowledge is sparse. Thus, more time and care are needed to activate prior knowledge in a way that primes readers to comprehend informational text.

Readers also approach these texts differently. They usually proceed straight through narratives, although they may look back occasionally to check a detail. Even when very curious, though, they seldom skip to the end, knowing that will spoil the suspense. In contrast, readers may check the summary of an informational text first to find the key points, or they may skim the text to get an overview. They may reread some parts several times and skip others entirely. Adept readers modify their pace and direction according to the nature of the text and their purposes for reading.

Yet another distinction lies in what is most important to remember after reading. The concepts and details in an informational text are the priority. Most, if not all, are worth discussing, understanding, and possibly remembering after reading. In contrast, details bring stories to life, but if they are not critical to the main story line, they are not usually important to remember. For example, it's more important to remember what happened to Cinderella at midnight than what her ball gown looked like. Thus, although students can be expected to note the details in informational texts, the point of reading a story is not to remember all the details.

An especially important difference lies in the kind of thinking ahead that is most useful when reading the two kinds of text. Predicting is appropriate for narrative texts because it involves forecasting events. Hypothesizing is suitable for informational texts because it involves generating tentative statements that can be confirmed or refuted by reading. The distinction is important, yet blurring occurs in classrooms. In particular, it is a common practice to ask students to make predictions when reading informational text, for example: *What do you think our text will tell us about bones?* or *What do you predict we will learn about Francis Scott Key when we read?* Questions like these put students in an awkward position. They don't know what information is in the text and so can only guess what details the author chose to include of all that were available. They may consider what they have seen in comparable texts to figure out what might be in this one, but they will still essentially be guessing and at some level may consider the question unfair. Asking students to think this way is like asking them to use a saw to hammer a nail. They can do it, but it's not the best cognitive tool for that mode of discourse.

Asking students to predict what they will find in an informational text, or what topics might be addressed in the text, deprives them of the kind of thinking that most enhances their comprehension. First, they have no need to use prior knowledge that is relevant to the topic. Also, the teacher cannot probe their thinking to generate uncertainty because their degree of uncertainty is as high as it can get. They don't know what's in the text, and they know they don't know. Moreover, they have no meaningful reason to think more deeply about their guesses or to discuss why they made them. Finally, because such predictions do not prime them well for reading, they may or may not notice the important information. Their reading is as superficial as their initial thinking.

Hypothesizing is a far better cognitive tool for informational texts because students think about specific questions related to the topic: *Do we have all of our bones when we are born? Where do we think Key's ship was located?* Finding answers to their questions is much different from finding out if they correctly guessed the kind of information contained in the text. The difference is significant.

*P*redicting is appropriate for narrative texts because it involves forecasting events. Hypothesizing is appropriate for informational texts because it involves generating tentative statements that can be confirmed or refuted by reading.

Making Better Choices for Teaching Informational Text

When planning lessons with informational text, teachers have choices. Some choices are effective, others less so. One choice is to assign the text for independent reading. Another is to provide an overview of the information and have students read to acquire the details. Still another is to have students read the text and write summaries. Yet another is to have students take turns reading the text aloud and responding to questions. These approaches are all common across curricula and through the grades, but they seldom lead to high levels of motivation, comprehension, or retention because they fail to engage students actively in thinking and constructing meaning. Other choices involve instructional strategies such as KWL (what we know, what we want to know, and what we learned; Ogle 1986) and Reciprocal Teaching (Palincsar and Brown 1984). These strategies can be effective, but teachers must guard against them becoming too routine. If teachers and students just go through the motions, the lack of intellectual and emotional engagement makes it less likely that learners will internalize and retain the new information.

If students are to gain the most from reading informational text, teachers must make thoughtful and astute decisions about how their students can most effectively interact with each new text to maximize understanding. Practices that encourage flexibility of thinking and responding are thus more effective than those that rely on fixed prompts or routines.

When we, as mature readers, peruse informational texts, we are driven by curiosity. We hear something that conflicts with what we thought we knew and want to clear up the discrepancy. We become aware of an intriguing issue or concept and want to know more. Our active pursuit of answers to our own questions makes reading pleasurable. Even if we don't find answers right away, we persevere until our curiosity is satisfied. Sometimes we find unexpected information that leads to more exploration and discovery. Our reading is both informative and enjoyable.

We aim to give students similar experiences. We arouse their curiosity, make them feel comfortable about not knowing everything, and increase their confidence about generating hypotheses. We probe their thinking and engage them in discussion to develop their naturally inquiring minds while helping them construct meaning. With each reading experience, we capitalize on the opportunities provided by the particular group of learners responding to a particular text. Thus, the dialogues we include earlier in the chapter are meant to be perspectives, not prescriptions; examples, not protocols.

This artful way of guiding students through informational texts is not only pleasurable to learners but also deeply satisfying to us as teachers. We are always fascinated to see how students think about a topic before they read and delighted to witness their pleasure when they find the answers they seek. We also like seeing how well they understand and retain the information from these reading experiences. In short, we find it the best way to nurture students' capacity to comprehend and respond to informational text.

CHAPTER 4

How Talking Supports Comprehension

Lectures, skill instruction, and question-answer exchanges take up a great deal of time in many classrooms, leaving students few opportunities to talk with each other about what they are learning. Although these teacher-dominant forms of discourse all have a place, student-to-student interaction is equally important for building comprehension. We gave some examples of effective discussions in the previous two chapters. Here we examine more closely how talking helps students understand and internalize what they are learning. First, we analyze two examples of classroom interactions.

Classroom Interactions: A View into Two Classrooms

These middle school interactions are based on the same text. Each teacher wanted students to review what they had read the day before without looking back at the text; each had comprehension and retention as objectives.

Interaction 1

Students faced the teacher. They raised their hands and waited to be called upon. When responding, they looked at and spoke to the teacher. The teacher aimed to call on each student at least once so as to give everyone a chance to respond. Students were familiar with the routine and the expectations and had no difficulty with either.

Teacher: Yesterday we read about Alexander the Great. Let's discuss it to make sure we all understand what we learned. Who can tell me where Alexander was born? Yes, Ronnie?

Ronnie: Macedonia.

Teacher: Macedonia. That's right. What was his father's name? Brenda?

Brenda: I think it was Philip.

Teacher: Philip. That's right. Who was Alexander's teacher? Brandon?

Brandon: I don't remember his name. It was a famous Greek guy, though, I remember that.

Teacher: Who remembers his name? Yes, Charlotte?

Charlotte: I think it was Aristotle.

Teacher: Right! It was Aristotle! Good for you, Charlotte. Now, how old was Alexander when his father died and he became king? David?

David: It said twenty, but is that really right?

Teacher: Yes, he was just twenty years old. He would scarcely have been old enough to vote if he had been alive today! Now, I know you remember that Alexander set out to conquer the Persians, who were led by King Darius, and that the battle is known as the Battle of Arbela. Did Alexander win the Battle of Arbela? Jason?

Jason: Yes. Even though the Persian king had a lot more men.

Teacher: Right! And why did he win it? Jeannette, do you remember?

Jeannette: (*using the exact words of the text*) He had a superior battle plan.

Teacher: You have a good memory, Jeannette! Now, class, what do you think was Alexander's greatest strength? (*Students look puzzled and do not raise their hands.*) We didn't talk about this yesterday. I'm just asking what you think. All right, Jennifer has an idea! Yes, Jennifer?

Jennifer: Well, he must have been smart because his father gave him a lot of responsibility.

Teacher: Yes, you could say that he was smart. What else? Yes, Michael?

Michael: He was a good soldier. When he went to war with his father, he was in charge of the cavalry, and he was successful.

Teacher: Yes, he was a good soldier. But what was really significant about Alexander was that he had a vision. He literally wanted to conquer the world, and he had every intention of doing that. He probably would have succeeded, too, if he had lived long enough. How old was he when he died? Clarence?

Clarence: I think it said he was thirty-three. That's younger than my father.

Teacher: Yes! Just imagine what would have happened if he had lived longer.

(The exchange continued.)

Interaction 2

Students sat in small groups, facing each other. Students looked at and spoke primarily to each other, talking alternately in their groups and as a whole class. They took turns without waiting to be called upon. Students were familiar with the routine and the expectations and had no difficulty with either.

Teacher: Yesterday we read about Alexander the Great. First, take a minute or two to decide in your groups what were the most interesting ideas you read. Be prepared to share your ideas. *(Students talk in their groups for two to three minutes.)* All right. What have you decided?

Jane: We all thought it was really interesting that he did all that stuff when he was so young. He was working in the government when he was sixteen.

Cindy: And he went to war when he was eighteen and led his father's cavalry. That's how old we'll be when we finish high school.

Rodney: We agree with that. But we also think it was interesting that he won that battle even though he didn't have as many soldiers. It said he did so well because he had a better plan.

Davis: We thought the horse stuff was really interesting.

Mary Jane: Yes, how he tamed the horse and rode it so far and then buried it in India. . . .

Carlo: And built a whole city around where he buried it.

Davis: That's right. It was a wild horse, and its name was . . . Butch something . . . *(looking at the teacher).*

Teacher: Can anyone pronounce it?

Cindy: I think it's Boo-CEFF-ah-lus.

Teacher: That's it. What do you remember about what he did after that? Talk in your groups first. *(Students talk for about a minute.)* All right. What did Alexander do next?

Dwayne: He traveled a lot.

Hal: And he wanted the people in the empire to cooperate.

Lucy: And he married a princess from Persia who was the daughter of the man that he fought against.

Rennie: And a lot of his soldiers married Persian women, too.

Teacher: What are your thoughts about any of that?

Lucy: Why did he marry the daughter of his enemy?

Teacher: What do you think might have been his reason?

Charlie: Well, when he married her that would change things between him and her father. They'd have to get along, wouldn't they?

Jane: So you mean it was like Alexander wanted to be sure they wouldn't be enemies any more?

Charlie: Yeah, I think so. It was like in that movie, where the two families had to get along when the man and woman married.

Teacher: Can you think of any other reasons?

(The exchange continued.)

Reflecting on the Examples

As is readily apparent, the first interaction is an example of a teacher-centered Initiation-Response-Evaluation/Feedback (IRE/IRF) sequence as described by Cazden (2001), among others. The teacher initiates the exchange; a student responds; the teacher evaluates the response or provides another kind of feedback. The teacher does most of the talking, and the pace is brisk. When a student doesn't respond, the teacher calls on someone else. Students know they aren't expected to express their own thoughts, ask questions, address each other directly, or respond to each other's ideas. They respond briefly, often with one or two words. The teacher's "wait time" before calling on the next student is brief, often as little as one second (Rowe 1987; Stahl 1994).

The second interaction is a student-centered discussion. The learners know they are to express their own thoughts, listen to each other, address each other directly, ask questions, and respond to each other's ideas. They focus on the topic, not on figuring out what the teacher wants them to say. They talk more than the teacher, use their own words rather than recall text or teacher language, and may talk at some length. The teacher's wait time is longer because the questions invite multiple responses and because students are often given time to discuss questions among themselves before responding to the class as a whole. Figure 4.1 highlights the contrasts between the two interactions.

Figure 4.1

Two Classroom Interactions

Interaction 1: A Teacher-Centered Discussion	Interaction 2: A Student-Centered Discussion
Purpose: have students state what they had read.	Purpose: have students state what they considered most interesting and in the process relate what they had read.
The teacher asked for facts directly and expected certain answers.	The teacher invited discussion of information and concepts and did not know what the students might say.
The questions required brief answers.	The questions required extended answers.
The teacher maintained a central verbal and visual position in the interaction.	The teacher stepped aside, literally and figuratively, from the central position.
The teacher repeated students' responses.	The teacher did not repeat students' responses.
The teacher verbalized a judgment about each response.	The teacher did not verbalize judgments about students' responses.
The teacher moved quickly from one question to the next.	The teacher lingered over the main questions, inviting multiple responses.
The teacher's questions were determined in advance.	The teacher based many of the questions on what students had just said.
Just one student answered each question.	All students answered the main questions in their groups; several responded to the group as a whole.
Students looked at and spoke only to the teacher.	Students spoke to each other in their groups or the whole class, except when one student asked the teacher for information.
The teacher made connections between the text information and current times.	The students made connections between the text information and their own lives.
Total words spoken: 361 Teacher words: 261 (72%) Student words: 102 (28%)	Total words spoken: 342 Teacher words: 89 (26%) Student words: 253 (74%) (The number 342 includes only the words shown here. Students also spoke in triads twice during the course of the activity.)

The comparative word counts in Figure 4.1 are telling. In the first interaction, the teacher speaks three words to every one spoken by students. Students say little although the teacher covers much ground. The reverse is true in the second interaction. Of course, word counts do not necessarily indicate the quality of thinking that is occurring. However, when the teacher does most of the talking, students ordinarily have few opportunities to become engaged with the topic and think in ways that deepen their comprehension.

Several reasons may explain the popularity of teacher-centered IRE/IRF sequences. Certainly, asking pointed questions is a quick way of getting students to state the correct information. Teachers with a sense of urgency about covering material may prefer this. Teachers may also elicit only certain bits of information, concerned about what students might say if allowed to talk more freely. Then, too, teachers may feel more in control when one student at a time is talking. Teachers may also feel more comfortable when they're doing most of the talking. As one teacher put it, "Silence panics me, so I start talking." Finally, teachers' own teachers very likely used this kind of interaction, shaping their perceptions about what teachers are supposed to do. The form may feel so right to many teachers that they don't think to question it.

Nevertheless, these exchanges are not ideal for promoting comprehension. Only one student responds at a time; what the others are thinking is left unsaid. The students who already know the answers usually produce them; those who don't know probably won't retain the information simply by hearing others respond. Some are too worried about being called upon to listen attentively. Furthermore, asking students to recall information they have previously been fed results in only superficial understanding, as noted by Applebee et al. (2003), Brady (2008), and others. Moreover, students in such exchanges generally aim to determine the meaning that the teacher has already found or inferred; they are essentially adopting someone else's understanding rather than developing their own. As Campbell and Green (2006) observe, this leads students to assume that the text has one meaning and discourages them from raising questions or thinking of other perspectives. Perhaps most important, when the teacher dominates the interaction, the teacher does the bulk of the thinking by determining what is important, what connections can be made, what can be ignored, and so on. Over time, this inevitably limits students' comprehension and affects their overall performance. For example, Taylor et al. (2002) report a negative correlation between teacher telling and student reading achievement. For all these reasons, it is preferable to allow students to interact more freely with each other when the goal is to develop comprehension.

When Students Do the Talking

Students may talk about a text, a teacher's explanation, a hands-on experience, a laboratory experiment, a video, or some other source of information or ideas. They may engage in dialogues between partners, small-group conversations, or whole-class discussions. In all these situations, they derive specific benefits from the peer interaction:

- **Talking is a primary vehicle for constructing meaning.** It helps students make sense of new information and reveals unsuspected areas of fuzziness that can be clarified. Adults almost always understand concepts and issues better when discussing them or explaining them to others. The same is true for young learners, as Britton (1967) noted some years ago and others have confirmed since. Giving students frequent opportunities during the day to talk about what they are learning is thus a critically important instructional strategy, often more important than the teacher's presentations or the instructional materials.

  Talking helps students make sense of new information.

- **Productive discussions enhance retention.** When students discuss what they are learning in their own words, clarifying as needed, they are more likely to retain the information and be able to retrieve it later. This is far better than repeating information on cue but quickly forgetting it. The use of talk to enhance retention has been recognized for many years. For example, it is a feature of the study strategy SQ3R (survey, question, read, recite, and review), introduced by Francis Robinson in 1946 (Robinson 1970), and it is an integral part of similar strategies advocated since then (Spache and Berg 1955; Robinson 1993).

- **Discussion shapes cognition.** Testing ideas in the public arena of a group leads learners to think more rigorously. In response to questions or challenges, they must clarify statements, give examples, or offer evidence. In a Piagetian sense, thinking in a group makes individuals less egocentric and thus more mature in their thinking. Paul (1987) describes it as "dialogic thinking," an active exploration of different ideas. Nystrand et al. (1997) assert that comprehension is enhanced by the "conflict, disagreement, and struggle of contrasting perspectives" (93). Even a typical discussion of a reading selection has a significant impact on participants' cognition. As Tharp and Gallimore (1988) note, this seemingly simple activity is a vitally important means of developing cognitive capacities. These viewpoints reflect the thinking of Vygotsky (1962) and Bakhtin (1986), for whom interactions with others are instrumental in developing cognition.

- **Collaborative efforts enhance the breadth and depth of comprehension.** The group is less likely than the individual to miss something. Conversation yields more robust understanding for all. Also, collaboration can be generative: Ideas ricochet around the group and emerge as new insights. At the same time, the selective comprehension of individuals is advantageous. One explains a point the others have misunderstood; another offers a fresh interpretation that shifts the group's thinking; another asks a question that leads the group to dig deeper. Hattie (2009) notes that performance improves when students work together with a sense of common purpose. Discussion is one example of such collaboration. Observations of classroom discussions show repeatedly how critical group effort is to comprehension. Wells and Chang-Wells (1992) give a number of instructive classroom examples to illustrate how group dynamics facilitate comprehension for the individual. Discussion is particularly important when learners are uncertain. As Duckworth (1996a) points out, it is not especially fruitful to discuss what everyone already knows but "it does serve a purpose to propose a tentative idea— because then people can help you think it through" (158).

- **When students note how others respond in discussion, their capacities for thinking improve.** The one who rereads to find evidence prompts others to do the same; the one who draws an analogy sparks analogical thinking in others. At the same time, those who present insufficient reasons to back up a statement, deviate needlessly from the topic, or refuse to consider other perspectives all serve as object lessons for the others. As students learn to weigh each other's contributions, they become more discerning and more adept at thinking, and as individuals improve, the group improves. Learners also become more capable of creative, critical, and productive thinking in other contexts. All this helps to build metacognitive awareness and the "intellectual character" that Ritchhart (2002) asserts is such an important goal of education.

- **When students have frequent chances to share different perspectives, they become psychologically comfortable with complexity.** This, too, has a positive effect on their thinking and learning. It is highly engaging to become aware of hidden depths in a subject or to find that looking at something from a different angle changes everything. Duckworth (1996c), in particular, argues for the value of increasing opportunities to grapple with complexity, pointing out that this leads to deeper thinking and more solid learning than responding to simplified materials and activities.

- **Effective student-to-student interactions shift the focal point away from the teacher.** The shift enables students to help each other learn. Moguel (2003) observes that students' understanding improves when they question each other instead of answering teacher questions, and Smagorinsky (2007) points out that student–student interactions allow for better learning precisely because students are not giving expected answers to teacher questions. The shift can sometimes be essential to effective learning, a point that Torbe and Medway (1981) make when they show how teachers can inadvertently derail collaborative thinking and learning with ill-timed interventions.

It is highly engaging to become aware of hidden depths in a subject or to find that looking at something from a different angle changes everything.

- **Discussions change the culture of the classroom.** When student talk is encouraged, learners feel their ideas are being heard and respected. Discussion is pleasing intellectually (because it stimulates thinking), emotionally (because it makes participants feel valued), and socially (because it generates a sense of camaraderie). These effects increase students' sense of being genuinely engaged in learning and being part of a vibrant learning community.

- **Productive discussions give students valuable practice with skillful communication.** Learning how to interact effectively with others may be the most important skill that students develop in school. The ability to exchange ideas and perspectives productively is important in the family and the wider community. Cox (2001) notes that when adults make positive use of the diverse opinions and perspectives in a group, their satisfaction increases while their performance in solving problems and completing other tasks is enhanced. Also, work environments are becoming less hierarchical, more egalitarian places where information sharing, peer review, collaboration, diverse perspectives, and intelligent contributions are valued and expected (Hamel 2009; Wallace 2010). Students simply cannot develop such strengths unless they have daily opportunities as learners to exchange ideas directly with their peers.

Many other scholars support the view that students need to talk to each other in order to learn. Wells (1986) shows how children use language to make sense of their worlds. Wink and Putney (2002) demonstrate how individuals negotiate meaning when interacting with others. Langer (2001) reports that collaboration among students is a key characteristic of instruction in the highest-performing schools. Allington and Johnston (2002) reveal that observed exemplary teachers consistently talked less than the students and actively promoted a climate conducive to exploratory talk. Keene and Zimmerman (2007) demonstrate how peer discussion in workshop settings deepens comprehension of literature. Allington (2007) stresses that discussion of texts, not quizzing about texts, is firmly supported by research as a highly effective strategy for developing understanding.

Learning how to interact effectively with others may be the most important skill that students develop in school.

To be clear, we are not advocating that the teacher step aside permanently or that students talk freely about whatever they want. We are simply pointing out that the skillful teacher balances teacher-dominant exchanges with well-planned student-to-student interactions, creates a climate conducive to collaborative thinking, and helps students learn to interact more effectively with each other.

How to Build Students' Capacity for Discussion

Many students have had little experience taking each other seriously in school as sources of information and insights. Then, too, individual and cultural differences among students may make it difficult to sustain discussion, as Wolf (1987) notes. For example, students' shyness or their belief that they should not speak out can work against a teacher's attempts to get students talking to each other. Also, social relationships strongly influence learners' ability to talk productively together, for good and for ill, as Cazden (2001) stresses. Students who know little about each other or feel uncomfortable with each other will probably not find discussions easy; friendly and cohesive groups will fare better. Of course, almost any class can improve its capacity for engaging in substantive talk.

The discussions described in Chapters 2 and 3 are examples of effective guided conversations about texts. Other classroom experiences build students' capacities further. Here are key actions the teacher can take to help students become better at using talk to improve their comprehension.

- **Pause for talk.** A simple yet powerful tactic is to pause periodically during instruction and ask students to talk for a few moments in twos or threes about what has just occurred. This gives them a chance to process what they have just done instead of merely listening to the teacher (McTighe and Lyman 1988). For example, a teacher may explain how a thunderstorm occurs, using a diagram of the process, then ask students to pair up and explain the phenomenon to each other while looking again at the diagram. Such pauses are particularly useful when the instruction is complex and lengthy, but stopping at any time for reflective conversation helps students learn more effectively (Jensen 2005).

- **Use conversational protocols.** One protocol that helps students with listening and turn taking is The Final Word (McDonald et al. 2007). Each group member identifies a sentence or two from the text to have the group consider; the others comment in turn; the first has the final word. Students who regularly use this protocol learn to function better in a group while making a deeper study of texts. The structure is needed only until students are able to participate actively in a text-oriented discussion, take turns, and respond meaningfully to each other's ideas. Once they have learned these basics, they no longer need to rely on the protocol.

- **Structure collaborations.** Collaboration can be easier within an effective structure. For example, each group can read one segment of text and decide how best to share the information with others. Together, they create notes or visual aids to capture key points. Then students form new groups to share what they learned, using their notes and visual aids. This activity, introduced as jigsaw learning by Aaronson et al. (1978), helps students comprehend more deeply. It is particularly useful when a text is lengthy or complex and bears repeated reading.

- **Encourage differences of opinion.** Students need to learn to express their differences effectively. Prereading discussions of predictions or hypotheses provide natural opportunities because competing ideas arise so readily. Then, too, students may interpret a text differently and can discuss their various perspectives after reading. At any time during any lesson, the teacher can ask *Is there another way of looking at this?* The key is to stress that differences are welcome, that competing ideas are worth considering thoughtfully, and that respect for all viewpoints is essential.

- **Promote question asking.** Students also need to ask questions about what they are learning instead of simply waiting to respond to the teacher's questions. Teachers can ask *What questions did you have as you read this passage?* or *As we talk, what questions are coming to your mind?* In time, students' questions become more thoughtful, and their tendency to raise questions strengthens. The propensity for learners to question has long been recognized as critical to academic success (e.g., Postman and Weingartner 1969; Robinson 1993), and the disposition is also useful for engaging in personal growth, making decisions, and setting directions for inquiry outside of school (e.g., Vogt, Brown, and Isaacs 2003). In fact, the greater students' capacity for asking astute questions, the better prepared they are for success in academic learning and in other life endeavors.

The propensity for learners to question has long been recognized as critical to academic success.

- **Vary group configurations.** Whole-class discussion is a challenge because spontaneity and engagement are reduced as students wait their turn, so other configurations are useful. With older students, a group of six or seven is optimal for discussing texts: small enough to be manageable yet large enough to yield multiple perspectives. In the early grades, a group size of four to five students seems optimal. Pairs or triads are useful for brief exchanges and collaborative tasks. The shift from pairs or small groups to whole class and back again is especially effective for keeping students alert and engaged. The key is to give all students opportunities to talk regularly so that all will feel part of the discussion.

As students become more comfortable talking with each other as learners, they can handle longer and more complex interactions. The Paideia Seminar, based on principles outlined by Adler (1982), provides a useful framework for more sophisticated interactions because it focuses both on the process of discussion and on the content discussed. Students prepare for a seminar by engaging with the topic. They receive coaching from the teacher on target behaviors, collaborate during the seminar to keep it going smoothly, reflect on the process afterward, and finish by writing a summary of what they discussed. For example, a high school teacher posed questions prompting comparisons between two events: historical and current. He organized students into small groups and assigned one question to each. Groups formulated responses. Individuals set personal goals for participating (e.g., making at least two contributions or building on others' responses). In the whole-class discussion, they used the ideas generated in their groups and raised new points as they listened to each other. After debriefing the discussion and assessing how well they had achieved their personal goals, they each wrote a final reflection on the historical event that was the original focus. Similarly, in a third-grade class, students used the same steps to discuss a garden project in which they had been involved. They prepared by thinking about questions the teacher posed, set goals for the discussion, debriefed afterward, and followed up by writing. For other examples, see Roberts and Billings (2008).

Students have different participation styles. Some are eager to talk right away; some talk only when pointedly encouraged; some are reluctant to participate at all. Students may veer off topic, interject amusing comments, or be preoccupied with details that others consider unimportant. In fact, students behave just as adults do in discussions, and the interplay of personalities and styles is part of what makes a discussion lively and interesting. At the same time, teachers can influence student behavior. Reminders to think carefully before responding help the talk-first-think-later students. Acknowledging thoughtful contributions helps everyone realize that quality matters. In shaping discussion behavior, the point is not simply to steer learners to be like one another but rather to encourage everyone to make use of their strengths, refine their rough edges, and collaborate with the others to have effective discussions.

Classroom interactions affect how students feel about themselves as learners, how well they work and learn together, how they comprehend, and how much they comprehend. Attending to the quality of classroom talk is vital to effective learning.

> *Attending to the quality of classroom talk is vital to effective learning.*

What Do We Want Students to Talk About?

Because talking is an important means by which learners come to understand, we want students to talk about whatever they are learning: literature, informational texts, mathematical problem solving, hands-on science and health activities, instructional videos, art and music lessons, and what they are learning about themselves as learners. We want students to talk about what they already know, what they are attempting to learn, how they are figuring things out, and what they are learning about their own thinking. As students talk, of course, we want them also to listen to the ideas and interpretations of their fellow learners, to their teachers, and to themselves.

An interesting example occurred in Ms. Kent's middle school class. Students had read an article about crocodiles that includes the weight of the baby crocodile and a statement about the adult-to-baby weight ratio. In discussion, when Ms. Kent asked how much an adult might weigh, the students responded that the text didn't say. Ms. Kent said that she had concluded that an adult must weigh about 1,000 pounds and invited the students to pair up and figure out how she arrived at that number. As pairs conferred, Ms. Kent listened in on one conversation:

Student 1: So we know the baby weighs 4 ounces. How do we get the adult weight?

Student 2: It says here that the ratio of the adult to the baby is 4,000 to 1.

Student 3: So?

Student 4: So that must mean that the adult weighs 4,000 times as much as the baby.

Student 3: Oh. So if we multiplied 4 x 4,000 we come up with . . . 16,000.

Student 4: 16,000 pounds? No wait. 16,000 ounces. We're multiplying ounces.

Student 3: OK. How do we get to pounds?

Student 4: How many ounces in a pound? 16?

Student 3: I think so. So 16 ounces would be 4 babies. So if we divide 4 into 4,000? That's easy. 1,000 pounds. And that's the answer!

Ms. Kent waited for all the pairs to finish before having groups discuss their answers. Another pair decided that 4 ounces was ¼ of a pound and multiplied ¼ times 4,000. Still another laughingly said they had figured out that an adult crocodile weighed 16,000 ounces and, knowing that 1,000 was the answer, concluded that there must 16 ounces in a pound.

The subtle shift from asking for the answer to giving the answer and asking for the thinking behind it made the task enjoyable, not extra work. What occurred is not measured on typical assessments, but such conversations have significant impacts on students' future learning and performance on assessments. The students were stimulated intellectually, seeing themselves as working on the teacher's level. They saw the value of collaboration and the payoff of perseverance. They were reminded that problems can be solved in different ways, and their success empowered them as learners.

For students to engage in substantive talk, they do not necessarily have to talk about ideas that are important to society at large, such as how to solve global warming or address world hunger. *Importance* is a relative term. The nature of marrow was important to the third graders learning about bones; the location of the flag was important to the adolescents learning about the national anthem; Ms. Kent's students became fully absorbed in crocodile weights. When teachers guide conversation effectively, students feel that they are engaged in talking about important ideas, and this helps them sustain attention to and interest in the topic.

Duckworth (1996b) makes this point when she relates the story of the child who had "a wonderful idea" that led him cleverly to deduce insights about an electrical circuit. She points out that his discovery was as admirable as an original discovery of an entirely new phenomenon and writes: "The more we help children to have their wonderful ideas and to feel good about themselves for having them, the more likely it is that they will some day happen upon wonderful ideas that no one has happened upon before" (14).

Classroom conversations are major contributors to developing a spirit of inquiry in students that leads to the discussion of important and wonderful ideas. Effective teaching promotes substantive dialogue that engages students and keeps them thinking.

> *Effective teaching promotes substantive dialogue that engages students and keeps them thinking.*

Building Teacher Capacity for Facilitating Discussion

Many teachers use *discussion* as a generic term, a habit that influences their perceptions of what the class is doing and may reduce their ability to lead discussions effectively. For example, a teacher presents information and asks questions to check students' understanding. He thinks the class is having a discussion; they think they are answering questions. Another teacher poses questions, receives no response, and answers them herself. She thinks of the activity as a discussion that isn't going very well; the students perceive it as a monologue.

Referring to lectures or question-answer sessions as *discussions* muddies expectations and can lead to what Freebody, Ludwig, and Gunn (1995) describe as "interactive trouble." A particularly worrisome "trouble" arises when teachers shift their expectations without making the shift clear to students. For example, a teacher might ask a series of factual recall questions, then suddenly invite opinions. The teacher in the earlier example introduced a different kind of trouble in asking for students' thinking about Alexander's greatest strength. When students offered opinions, the teacher said, *Yes . . . but what was really significant about Alexander was that he had a vision.* This belied the invitation to give opinions by suggesting she expected a particular response.

Of course, teachers may understand these differences and value genuine discussion yet still find that they talk more than the students and often more than they'd like. The following practices can help teachers encourage students to express themselves and value each other's ideas during discussions.

- **Have students talk directly to each other as much as possible.** Have them converse in pairs or small groups before sharing ideas with the whole class. To avoid saying something in response to each contribution, use nonverbal responses (nods, gestures). Unobtrusively break eye contact with students to encourage them to look at each other. Try moving slowly behind a speaker or acting in a way that signals thoughtful attention but gives the speaker unspoken permission to look at others.

- **Extend thinking and discussion.** Invite students to delve deeper and elaborate. Ask: *Would you talk about that a bit more? Can you tell us your reasoning? What else are you thinking?* Sometimes even a simple *And?* or *So?* invites elaboration.

- **Ask questions that have several possible answers, including some that cannot be anticipated.** Inviting predictions, opinions, interpretations, and judgments encourages students to voice their own ideas or perspectives. Even when the goal is to check students' understanding, questions can be worded to elicit a range of responses, for example: *In your opinion, what was the most important information we have learned? Which details did you find especially interesting?* Effective all-purpose queries are: *What do you think? Why do you think so?*

- **Avoid expressing surprise when hearing an unexpected response.** Surprise signals that the thinking has gone beyond what the teacher has already thought and thus may be questionable. Neutral acknowledgments (*Mm, All right*) are preferable. After all, outside the classroom discussants often think of ideas that have not occurred to the facilitator.

- **Allow time for thinking and responding.** Tell students to take time to think before they talk. Give them a chance to rehearse their ideas with one or more partners. Refrain from interrupting students, finishing their statements, or responding immediately to what they say. Allow them time to work through ideas on their own, and encourage classmates to do the same for each other. Also, realize that each discussion improves students' skill a bit more and that learning to discuss productively requires time.

- **Give students specific feedback about their thinking and talking.** Saying only *Good!* does not inform students of what they did well. Be specific about what was good (e.g., *That's an interesting connection with your own experience.*). Also be specific when suggesting the need for improvement (e.g., *You might make your point stronger if you could give us an example to illustrate.*).

- **Avoid parroting students' responses.** Repeating students' words discourages them from listening to each other and introduces an unnecessary extra "beat" into the rhythm of the interaction. If others have not heard something, ask the speaker to repeat it. Better, encourage students to ask respectfully for a classmate to speak up.

- **Be strategic in raising issues you think need to be addressed.** If a group does not bring up a point when you think of it, give them time. They may raise it eventually. Introduce the point only if it is vital to consider and it seems certain they will not think of it on their own.

As useful as these tactics are, however, a psychologically healthy classroom climate is equally important. The perceptions students have of themselves and their sense of comfort as class members strongly influence their behavior in discussions. Learners fare best when they feel honored as thinkers and contributors. Even casual interactions can shape students' thoughts and feelings about themselves as learners and affect their behavior. The more teachers become aware of the opportunities and pitfalls of their classroom language, the more likely they will improve their interactions with students and consequently their students' learning capacities. Johnston (2004), in his timely book *Choice Words*, makes particularly astute observations about teacher language that can help even the most experienced teachers develop greater self-awareness and effectiveness when interacting with students.

> *Learners fare best when they feel honored as thinkers and contributors.*

Examples of Effective Classroom Discussions

The exchanges around narrative and expository texts featured in Chapters 2 and 3 illustrate effective discussions. Here are other examples of productive talk that deepened students' comprehension while building their capacity for discussion. Although each was well defined and structured by the teacher, the discussion contents were not. Learners were expected to have original ideas and express them in their own ways.

Talking about books. A first-grade teacher regularly organized students into triads and gave each group a familiar classroom library book. She asked them to decide what they liked best about their book and be prepared to share their ideas with the whole class.

All of the children had something to say because they knew the books and had them in their hands. Consequently, they focused on interacting with each other. By standing to the side and not repeating what they said, the teacher directly influenced the students' behavior: Each speaker addressed the class; the class looked at the speaker; all listened carefully.

Sharing research findings. After reading an article about the writing of the Declaration of Independence, fourth-grade students generated questions they still had about the event. Groups divided up the questions and searched for information. When they gathered as a class to share their findings, they sat in their groups but formed a loose circle. The teacher asked students to respond to one another without waiting to be called upon and reminded them to take turns and to ask questions if they wished. Because the teacher kept his remarks to a minimum, the conversation flowed naturally from one student to the next once the first few spoke directly to each other.

Discussing opinions. A seventh-grade social studies class had been reading about a local issue in which the students were very interested: the building of a new recreation facility. The teacher wrote several statements of opinion about the plan, for example: *Putting a skate park at the center would create a dangerous situation. The center should have a playground for small children.* She organized the students into small groups, distributed the statements, and directed groups to consider the pros and cons of their statement. The whole class then convened to discuss the statements.

The small-group activities took just a few minutes but effectively primed the students to share their thoughts. Debriefing the activity, students said they liked working with different statements and having a chance to plan what they would say. They remarked that the preparation reduced their anxiety about speaking in front of the whole class. As one said, "You have a chance to see if others think your ideas are OK."

Digging into information. A tenth-grade science teacher wanted students to think deeply about an informational text on water pollution. The first day, he facilitated a discussion of hypotheses about the topic and had students read the text. The next day, he had students meet in pairs, then foursomes, to decide which points were the most important. After the discussions, students wrote individually about what they thought were the most important points. The activity is a variant of what Wood (1988) calls the Interactive Reading Guide. See also Wood, Lapp, Flood, and Taylor (2008). Using the different configurations for discussion contributed to the high comprehension that was evident in the closure writing.

Responding to literature. A twelfth-grade English teacher organized students into small groups and assigned each a character from a just-completed novel. The teacher then had students imagine that the characters board a bus for an extended trip. After several hours on the road, the bus has an accident, and the passengers must wait until help arrives. How will each fictional character react to the situation? What will they do and say? How will they interact? Groups made decisions about their characters, using evidence from the literary text to support their thinking, then shared their ideas in a whole-class discussion. Using what they knew about the characters was interesting and required higher levels of thinking than simply recalling character traits.

Fostering Self-Directed Student Talk

It is important for students at all grade levels to discuss on their own some of the time instead of always relying on the teacher to guide the conversation. In fact, the sooner students discuss regularly on their own, the sooner they will become capable of productive, self-directed talk. As they learn to handle their own discussions, a certain amount of socializing, along with false starts and digressions, will naturally occur. All are sometimes as useful as close attention to the topic.

Narratives are particularly effective vehicles for helping students learn to direct their own discussions. Here's a useful sequence for helping a reading group become more self-directed when discussing narratives:

1. Guide the group until students are used to making and discussing predictions and are talking confidently.
2. Note the increasing number of student-to-student responses between teacher responses.
3. Sit outside the circle a few times to gets students used to looking at and addressing each other.

4. Tell the group you think they are ready to go it alone. Give them stopping points and appoint a discussion leader.

5. When they finish, have them debrief the experience and set goals for improving their performance next time.

Ultimately, the whole class can be divided into groups and all can proceed independently while the teacher monitors unobtrusively. For example, a fifth-grade class is divided into four groups of five or six students for reading Betsy Byars' (1981) *The Midnight Fox*. Yesterday, they stopped at the point where Tom climbed out his bedroom window and let the baby fox out of the cage. Today, the teacher directs them to review where they are in the story and discuss what they think will happen next. One group begins this way:

Isaac: OK, he went down the tree and let the baby fox out. He broke the lock and the baby went off with the mother.

Melissa: Then he realized that he had to tell his aunt and uncle.

Rod: It was pretty dumb to go down that tree when it was storming and lightning, but I'm glad he did.

Amanda: I thought when he was breaking the lock the mother fox must have been close because he could hear her. That's sort of eerie.

Isaac: What do you mean?

Amanda: You know, it was like she was waiting for him to do it.

Will: So now he has another problem!

Christine: What do you mean?

Will: Well, he has to tell his aunt and uncle.

Rod: He could lie about it.

Christine: I don't think he'll lie. I think he'll tell them.

Will: Why do you think so?

Christine: That's how he is. Anyway, he thinks he did the right thing, so I think he'll tell for that reason.

Melissa: They'll know anyway, won't they? He's all wet and he's been outside and they have to let him back in.

Isaac: True. But he could just climb back up the tree.

Will: Maybe he'll wait until tomorrow.

Rod: Why do you think he'll wait?

Will: Sometimes it's good to wait. You can figure out the best way to say it.

Amanda: Maybe he'll tell Aunt Millie and she'll tell Uncle Fred.

Rod: Why tell Aunt Millie first?

Amanda: Well, Uncle Fred put the baby fox in the cage in the first place, so he would be really be angry that Tom let him out. But Aunt Millie might not be as mad.

Melissa: That's a good point. I didn't think about that.

The students continued for a brief time until they had firm predictions about what Tom would do next. They brought up important details, thought carefully, and handled themselves well. When the teacher elected to have them debrief, Rod mentioned an idea he didn't have a chance to explain, and Melissa said they didn't really discuss an important point. The students agreed, however, that they had made some very good predictions and were able to explain the reasoning behind their thinking. In addition, they noted that they had listened carefully to each other's ideas.

The feel of the discussion changes when the teacher isn't right there. Students rely on each other to think critically, raise questions, and call for evidence to support statements. They enjoy feeling that it is their discussion and that it's up to them to think, comprehend, and interact effectively. They are also somewhat freer to share their ideas. Alternating between teacher-led and self-directed discussions also makes students more aware of how the teacher facilitates discussions, and they can use this to improve their own efforts.

Other kinds of student-directed activities are equally valuable for building students' comprehension and thinking capacities. Chapter 7 addresses independent efforts in greater depth.

Creating a Culture of Dialogue

When we have discussions with colleagues and others about what we are reading, learning, or seeing in the media, we eagerly share our thinking and seek response. We listen to others' ideas, prepared to think anew about the topic. It doesn't matter if we agree with our companions or not; we benefit from the intellectual, social, and emotional stimulation that results from a lively discussion and from the new information and perspectives that we acquire. The more comfortable we are with such discussions, the more we profit from them.

Students deserve the same kinds of satisfying experiences. Simply asking them questions after reading is inadequate, as is telling them the information they need to learn and remember. A culture of dialogue is essential. Discussions refine students' thinking because they incorporate one another's ideas into their own frames of reference. The result is deeper understanding and the satisfaction that comes from successful collaboration.

Some students who are not used to discussing may not fare well at first, especially if they have experienced many years of teacher-dominant classroom discourse. Even the most reticent, though, will readily increase their capacities when they have opportunities for divergent thinking, active listening, intellectual risk taking, and reflection. Of course, the teacher is the key to establishing those foundations. Without question, the language, demeanor, and dispositions of the teacher determine the quality of classroom dialogue and thus the quality of the learners' thinking and understanding.

Whatever techniques the teacher might use to build students' capacity for discussion, successful discussions breed successful discussions. When students see that their contributions are honored and respected by the teacher and their peers, they join the conversation. In schools where students move from class to class, they usually become adept at adjusting to different teaching styles and classroom cultures. The more teachers work together to create a culture of dialogue in the school, with consistent expectations across all classrooms, the better students respond.

CHAPTER 5

How Writing Supports Comprehension

It is widely accepted that comprehension and composition are facets of the same underlying cognitive process of constructing meaning and are mutually reinforcing. Comprehending a text stimulates thinking and leads to expression, whether the reader jots a brief note in the margin or prepares an extensive written response. Similarly, various kinds of writing serve to develop, refine, and demonstrate comprehension. Because of the fruitful commonalities, many activities increase capacities in both areas. At all ages, students' writing improves when they learn to read like writers, noticing how others express their ideas. As students become authors themselves, their reading comprehension tends to improve as they become more attuned to the writing techniques and crafts used by the authors they are reading. Specific learnings such as vocabulary and encoding conventions also increase students' capacity as readers and writers, and as students are disposed to construct meaning through reading and writing, their knowledge of vocabulary and language conventions grows and matures. Even young children's spelling improves the more they see words in print and the more familiar they become with letters and letter combinations associated with different sounds.

Although reading and writing are equal and compatible partners in the world of literacy, each is worth pursuing in its own right without being coupled to the other.

Readers do not have to write in conjunction with reading to gain satisfaction from the reading, and writers often have their own ideas to express that do not relate to anything they have read. However, teachers often integrate the two because they are so mutually reinforcing and enhancing, and that is our focus here. In particular, we concentrate on writing that supports and extends comprehension while developing writing capacity.

The Characteristics of Skilled Writers

In Chapter 1, we enumerate the characteristics of skills readers as noted by Anderson et al. (1985). We see close parallels between these and the characteristics of skilled writers:

- **Skilled writers are constructive.** They use what they know and what they have learned to express meanings from their own perspectives in their own words.
- **Skilled writers are fluent and efficient.** They have learned to organize and articulate their ideas in an efficient manner so that they write with ease.
- **Skilled writers are strategic.** They know when their writing does not make sense or is in need of further revision, and they know how to improve it.
- **Skilled writers are motivated.** They are eager to write, and they write for long stretches even when the task is challenging.
- **Skilled writers see writing as a lifelong process.** They continue to develop their capacities through their school career and beyond to share what they know, have learned, or are imagining about the world.

These principles are reflected throughout this chapter as we discuss how writing is best used to support comprehension of informational and narrative texts and how youngsters can best develop a disposition to write.

Writing in Response to Informational Texts

Students can use writing to develop their thinking as they are learning, to demonstrate their comprehension after they have learned, or to share what they have learned with an audience. All three purposes enhance comprehension while refining expressive capacity. All involve students in "writing about text," which has a positive influence on reading achievement (Graham and Perin 2007; Graham and Hebert 2010).

Writing to Comprehend Information

Writing, like talking, develops understanding when it takes the form that Britton (1970) calls "expressive language." Unpolished writing in the expressive mode is comparable to talking to oneself or discussing informally with others. It is a primary vehicle for constructing meaning when learners use it to mull things over, state information in their own words, make connections, raise questions, and clarify points. Britton contrasts it on the one hand with "transactional" writing, which is used to inform, persuade, or in other ways communicate formally, and on the other hand with "poetic" writing, which is an artful shaping of language to represent experience or the fruits of the imagination. Although transactional and poetic writing are certainly suitable for the classroom, writing in the expressive mode is particularly supportive of comprehension.

Writing informally in one's own words fortifies comprehension and retention in ways that copying or completing exercises cannot do. As Cramer (2004) observes, "Writing makes effective use of prior knowledge, creates new knowledge, and stabilizes concepts currently under study" (268). When students begin writing to learn in kindergarten and first grade and do so frequently from then on, writing becomes an ever more powerful vehicle for constructing meaning. Here are some effective ways to stimulate expressive writing.

Learning logs. Students keep logs of what they are learning, writing in their own words. They can write before learning to focus thinking, during learning to respond, and after learning to reflect, summarize, and apply. Primary-grade students might write a few words or sentences; older students might write lengthier pieces. Learners may also draw pictures or diagrams to accompany their writing. The discussion prompts suggested in Chapter 3 can be used: *What was the most surprising or interesting thing you learned? What was the most important thing we learned today? What do you know now that you didn't know before?*

McCrindle and Christensen (1995) report that such writing has a positive influence on students' metacognition. Graham and Perin (2007) note that writing summaries is a particularly effective way to

When students begin writing to learn in kindergarten and first grade and do so frequently from then on, writing becomes an ever more powerful vehicle for constructing meaning.

reinforce comprehension for students in grades 4–12. Learning log writing also tends to improve overall writing, probably because students are more deeply engaged in thinking about and representing information than they would be if they were simply answering questions or completing a worksheet (Hillocks 1986). The key is allowing students to approach the topic in their own way, representing what they are learning in their own words and images. More information about learning logs and examples can be found at www.learninglogs.co.uk.

Writing and mapping. Visual representations are particularly effective learning aids for enhancing comprehension (Marzano, Pickering, and Pollock 2001). The Frayer Model is one example of how learning can be reinforced graphically. Students discuss four dimensions of a target concept, capturing their ideas in a chart (see Figure 5.1 for an example). Students then use the chart as a basis for writing. For more information, see Frayer et al. (1969) or Nessel and Graham (2007).

The set of eight Thinking Maps devised by David Hyerle (1993) is another example. Each map is used to represent a specific kind of thinking. For example, the Double Bubble Map is used for comparing and contrasting and the Tree Map for categorizing. With these

Figure 5.1

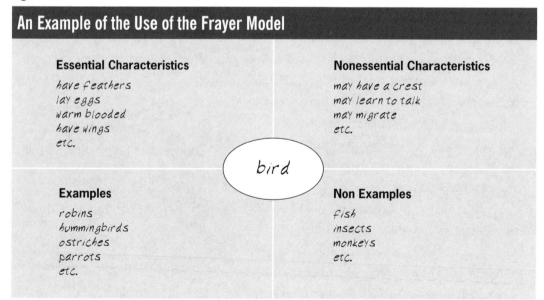

An Example of the Use of the Frayer Model

Essential Characteristics

have feathers
lay eggs
warm blooded
have wings
etc.

Nonessential Characteristics

may have a crest
may learn to talk
may migrate
etc.

bird

Examples

robins
hummingbirds
ostriches
parrots
etc.

Non Examples

fish
insects
monkeys
etc.

THE COMPREHENSION EXPERIENCE: Engaging Readers Through Effective Inquiry and Discussion graphic tools, students can structure information in ways that help them understand and remember it. For more information, see: http://en.wikipedia.org/wiki/Thinking_Maps or www.thinkingfoundation.org. Yet another form of visual representation is the Mind Map, a unique web that the student constructs to represent relationships among concepts and details (Buzan and Buzan 1993). For more information, see: http://en.wikipedia.org/wiki/Mind_maps.

These various forms of representation can be thought of as visual enhancements of expressive language. Collaborative construction of such charts and maps during learning is especially fruitful in developing comprehension because learners talk things through as they represent their thinking visually. In the early grades, the teacher may construct a chart or map for students, incorporating their ideas as they discuss the topic.

It is important to recognize that representing information in maps and charts is a legitimate form of writing. For many students, a graphic is a useful and welcome first step to writing about information, and in some instances, the visual representation can be the end product.

Visual representations are particularly effective learning aids for enhancing comprehension.

Talking and writing. Students can also combine writing with talking to strengthen their comprehension as they read. One activity is especially useful: Key Word Notes (Nessel and Graham 2007). For example, in studying mail delivery in the nineteenth century, middle school students read the first segment of text and chose three to five words related to key points, following the teacher's direction: *Choose words that you think will help you remember the most important information.* Then they paired up and explained their choices to each other, referring to the text as needed. They did the same with the next three text segments. Then they put the texts aside and wrote individually about the information, using their key words as memory aids. Figure 5.2 shows one student's key words and the beginning of the summary she wrote.

Working together helps students stay on task. Being selective in choosing words encourages careful thought. Conversation fortifies comprehension, and the closure writing, in the student's own words, aids retention. This activity can be used with oral or visual texts. For example, a teacher may pause during a video or a demonstration and have students

Figure 5.2

An Example of Key Word Notes

GOMC 1 Year 165 stations 1,200 horses (station) 750 men	1858 most finished San Francisco–St. Louis 35–40 days (24)
in SF big crowds cannon, bands Overland stuff	600 Comanches 5 hours Go swift

A man set up the Great Overland Mail Company to take mail across the West. He had a year to build 165 stations and get everything ready for stagecoaches to take the mail. Some stations had 1,200 horses there at one time. And they had to have food and water for the horses and places to fix the wagons and take care of the horses. He had to hire 750 men....

select key words to write down and discuss with each other. Students may also draw pictures or symbols instead of writing words.

Enhanced note taking. Students do not necessarily know how to take notes on their reading but are often expected to do so, especially in the upper grades. Many only copy the words in the book. To make note taking more effective, students can go through their notes periodically to condense them. Each time, they create a new, one-page representation of important concepts and relationships, integrating new information with what they have already learned. The process helps them comprehend, internalize, and retain the information. It is most appropriate for high school students but can be adapted for younger learners. For details and examples, see Robinson (1993).

Other age-appropriate writing-to-learn activities can be devised that are specific to subject matter. For further discussion and additional suggestions, see Atwell (1989), Elbow (1994, 2004), Fulwiler and Young (2000), Langer and Applebee (1987), and Zinsser (1988).

Writing to Demonstrate Comprehension of Information

Students can also use writing to demonstrate what they have learned once they have understood and internalized the information. Reports, research papers, and examinations are commonly used for this purpose, but these assignments too often lead students simply to reproduce information. For example, they print out downloaded text from the Internet, regurgitate teachers' explanations, copy source text, or paraphrase material poorly. To show understanding effectively, learners need to organize and explain learned information in their own ways, using their own organization and their own language. Here are some examples.

I-Search reports. An effective approach to reporting involves the student telling about the search process as well as the information unearthed. Learners begin with substantive questions that emerge from topics of personal interest or concepts they have been studying and want to know more about. They think about where they might find information and devise a plan to guide their search. They may interview people or consult books, websites, and other sources. As they search for information, they keep track of where they are looking as well as what they are finding. Their final report details their search process and relates the information they found in their own words. The reports usually involve the students' own connections between what they learned and what is important to them as individuals. Young children may express their findings in drawings as well as words; older students may write extensive compositions. For example, a fifth-grade group found information about the Vietnam War in books and on Internet sites but also interviewed veterans in their neighborhood. They used some of the veterans' information in their reports but were so interested in the stories that they compiled the interviews into a separate booklet, included photos of the interviewees, and offered copies to the school and town libraries. I-Search reports are more personal and motivating than reports on assigned topics in which students may have little interest. Also, I-Search writing is less likely to include copied material. For more information, see Macrorie (1988).

Digital demonstrations. Today's technological tools provide students with many opportunities to demonstrate comprehension as they build composing capacity. Video documentaries,

> *An effective approach to reporting involves the student telling about the search process as well as the information unearthed.*

digital animations, slide shows, and other media can be used in conjunction with writing in ways that challenge learners to think more deeply about their topics. For example, instead of simply writing reports about animals, a fourth-grade class took photos of local wildlife and created digital presentations with informational voice-overs accompanying the photos. Instead of writing five-paragraph essays about recycling, ninth graders created brief videos to show local efforts and provide detailed information about basic principles. Such projects can be a part of I-Search writing or of other assignments. They are likely to appeal to students who prefer hands-on activities, and the process of putting them together enables students to write as well as use other media. The satisfaction students derive from using technological tools can also lead them to write and speak more easily and enthusiastically about what they have learned.

Performances of understanding. Performances of understanding challenge learners to think in new ways about what they have learned to accomplish a specific purpose. For example, an eighth-grade science class had been studying the effects of earthquakes. As a performance of understanding, one group staged a current affairs program in which they posed as experts to discuss lessons learned from past earthquakes. A group of tenth graders dramatized an event from the Civil Rights era in three ways to represent three perspectives. Fourth graders who had studied local water pollution conducted a panel discussion to highlight issues they had learned about. For these performances, students needed to select, order, and express information in new ways. Their comprehension improved as they made their decisions because they were doing much more than simply restating the information. Although writing was not the end product, the activities all involved extensive writing. For more information, see Perkins and Blythe (1994) and http://learnweb.harvard.edu/alps/tfu/info3e.cfm.

These forms of expression position writing not simply as a summative assessment but as a process that improves students' expressive abilities and yields important and appealing products. Because the process is as important as the product, students cannot wait until the last minute to throw something together. Genuine interest propels the activities, so learners ordinarily become more engaged than they do when they are simply completing an assigned report or taking a test.

Writing to Share Information in Print and Online

A third purpose for writing about information is for students to share their knowledge and their perspectives as communities of readers and writers. This, too, fortifies comprehension while developing writing capacity. Students may collaborate to create documents and other products or work individually. The activities can be optional rather than expectations for everyone, but they are likely to appeal to quite a number of students and can become the basis of special units of study that extend to audiences beyond the classroom.

Letters. Students of all ages can learn about letters to editors by reading and discussing them in class, either as part of a newspaper unit or in conjunction with studies of current events. Writing their own is a natural next step. For example, in a suburban high school, a schoolyard incident led to considerable publicity in the local paper, including letters from concerned citizens. Students in one class discussed the incident, critically evaluated the paper's coverage, and drafted letters to express their views. Three of the letters were published and led to further exchanges on the editorial page among students and other readers.

Blogs. The ready availability of tools for creating online blogs enables students to share information and perspectives with audiences outside the classroom. Although many blogs are personal diaries, content- or issue-oriented blogs can be set up by individuals or groups as an extension of their classroom learning. For example, when a third-grade class was studying pond life, they began a class blog to record observations, research, and commentary, including photos they took at a local pond. Their appreciative audience included students in other classes, parents, and other community members, all of whom contributed comments regularly. A high school civics class was following a local election and began a class blog to share their thoughts about key issues, the candidates, and the media coverage of the campaigns. The experience brought to life their studies of the first amendment to the U.S. Constitution. A number of Internet sites provide blogging tools. Two are www.blogspot.com and http://blog.com.

Online collaborations. Wikipedia (www.wikipedia.org) is one example of a website that can be modified by those with access permission. It is a useful model for collaborative, network-based classroom writing. The class, or groups within a class, establishes one or more wikis to present information about topics they choose, adding more as they learn more. Because wiki readers can modify the content, those who are involved must read it regularly to see if they agree with what is being added or if they want to revise the additions. Creating and tending a wiki can be especially motivating to students who are drawn to digital creations (Leuf and Cunningham 2001). Other online tools can also be used for collaborative writing. PBWorks, with its controls and security measures, is especially appropriate for classroom use: http://pbworks.com/content/edu+overview.

These ways of sharing information give students control over their writing, foster a sense of community, and lead to high levels of involvement. For these reasons, they are noteworthy examples of information-based writing that goes beyond simply relating information that others have already presented in writing.

Writing in Response to Narrative Texts

Students can write before, during, and after reading a narrative to fortify comprehension and stimulate reflection. Some of the activities described in the previous section are also suitable to use with narratives. For example, students can use reading logs to record their thoughts during and after reading or graphical tools to represent aspects of narratives. They might also use digital tools to show their interpretations or engage in performances of understanding to illuminate the narratives.

The capacity to respond thoughtfully to narratives develops over time and is influenced by the number and quality of discussions students have about literature. Young students can write about the character they like best and why. Older students can write more sophisticated responses that improve the depth and quality of their thinking. When reading long narratives, students can read and write predictions and reflections as homework, allowing more time in class for discussion. For more information about this use of writing, see Dixon and Nessel (1992) and Elbow (2004).

Chapter 2 suggests several dimensions of response to use in discussions. These are equally useful for writing about narratives or about poems, films, and other works of art. For example, *Sarah, Plain and Tall* (MacLachlan 1985) is about a pioneer man who has lost his wife and advertises for a new one. Sarah responds. She comes from Maine to become his second wife and the mother to his children, Caleb and Anna. The prompts in Figure 5.3, individually or in combination, can be used to stimulate writing in response to the story.

When students have a range of prompts to choose from, they are more likely to write in depth with enthusiasm. Of course, it's best if they respond to only one or perhaps two prompts for any given literary selection. With each new selection, they can choose a different prompt or two so as to gain experience and comfort with each and learn to respond from different perspectives.

Young writers also benefit from opportunities to talk in pairs or small groups before they write. Talking with peers confirms that students' ideas are worth writing about, helps them formulate their thoughts, and may give them new ideas. Just a few minutes of conversation can

Figure 5.3

Writing Prompts for Responding to Narrative Texts	
Interpretive	Why do you think Caleb worried when Sarah drove to town by herself?
Thematic	What is this story really all about?
Visual/Imaginative	Which scene did you find especially vivid? Describe what you imagined.
Writer's Craft	What are some interesting words or techniques used by the author to describe the characters and settings?
Metacognitive	Did your thoughts and feelings about Sarah change from the beginning to the end of the story? How? Why?
Moral/Ethical	Was it all right for Sarah not to tell the family why she wanted to go to town on her own? Why or why not?
Intertextual	Does this story remind you of any other story? In what ways are they similar? Different?
Analogical	Tell of a similar situation in which someone moved from one home to another.
Elaborative	Sarah described herself as "plain and tall." How else would you describe her?

make an enormous difference in the quality and quantity of writing in comparison with simply choosing a topic and beginning to write. For example, near the end of a group's discussion of *The Relatives Came* (Rylant 1985), the teacher asked: *Did you like the language in this story?*

Students: Yes!

Teacher: Talk about that.

Alexa: I like the part about all the hugging. Then it was hugging time. All those hugs.

Gary: It said they had an old station wagon that smelled like a real car.

Teacher: And?

Gary: Well it looks pretty junky and they had been eating all that food and they had been riding all day. It probably just smelled. (*laughter*)

Teacher: Nice thoughts. Here's what I would like you to do. Find a phrase or sentence in the story that you would like to talk about and share it with the person next to you. (*Students discussed their choices in pairs, then as a group.*)

Pattie: Kerry and I liked where it said: "Then we crawled back into our beds that were too big and too quiet."

Teacher: Why did you pick that one?

Kerry: Well, that's the way it is when you have lots of company and then everybody leaves. It's so quiet.

Pattie: It is.

Alan: I picked this: "It was different with all that new breathing in the house. . . ."

Teacher: (*after several other students have shared*) Nice thinking. Now use your favorite lines and write about why you like how Cynthia Rylant used the language she did. We'll share your writing later today or tomorrow.

The conversation took only a few minutes but gave students a chance to hear different ideas and formulate first thoughts. This helped them begin writing with confidence and purpose.

In another classroom, the teacher steered a discussion of the same book toward an analogical response after the reading and near the end of the conversation about the story.

> *J*ust a few minutes of conversation can make an enormous difference in the quality and quantity of writing in comparison with simply choosing a topic and beginning to write.

Teacher: Does this story remind you of an experience you have had?

Students: Yes!

Chris: Every summer we visit my relatives in Tennessee. It takes us all day to get there from Michigan. We leave early in the morning. My Dad drives, and so does my Mom. We always stop at the same place for lunch.

Teacher: What else can you tell us?

Chris: Well, we try to get there before dinner but our relatives call it supper. I have three cousins and we play outside every night until dark. We swim in the lake and sometimes we go to a big amusement park that is close by in the mountains.

Teacher: Who else has a relatives story? (*All students raise their hands.*)

Teacher: Turn to the person next to you and tell your story—either visiting relatives or having relatives visit you.

(After four or five minutes, nearly all were eager to share a story. The teacher selected two students to share and invited the group to ask questions, which led the speakers to describe their experiences in greater detail.)

Teacher: These are wonderful stories. They are so good that I would like each of you to write your own. You have reminded me of a relatives story of my own from when I was your age, so I'm going to write one, too. Let's share our stories tomorrow or the next day.

These discussions allowed everyone to relate an experience, consider the level of detail they might include, and begin writing confidently. Because students talked in pairs, everyone had a chance to tell a story before writing. Then they were primed to express their thoughts. For further discussion of how extended writing can become such a natural process, see Cramer (2001).

Exploring Forms of Discourse

Reading and writing capacities are also extended when students purposely explore the structural elements of different kinds of texts. They can transform one form of discourse into another, combine forms of discourse, and use common text structures or features as writing models. Such explorations involve close reading and careful thinking. They enhance students' reading and writing capacities while providing interesting cognitive challenges. Here are some examples.

Transforming Forms of Discourse

The original Readers' Theatre is a particularly effective transformational activity. Students work together to dramatize a narrative text by creating a written script that they rehearse and perform. They must determine which roles to include, which scenes and props they need, what the actors will say and do, and if a narrator is needed. The need to be selective and accurate challenges their thinking while inviting them to respond creatively. The activity also enhances students' visualization of the narrative as they figure out how to stage the scenes. Different groups can easily generate different but equally effective scripts from the same text. For example, one group might enact the whole of "The Wager," while others might dramatize only the ending kitchen scene. For more information on the value of this activity with literature and informational texts, see Flynn (2007), Latrobe (1996), and Moffett (1968a). Students may also read from scripts that have been prepared for them, but this alternate form of Readers' Theatre, though enjoyable and useful for developing fluency and camaraderie, does not build comprehension or reading–writing connections as effectively as students' creation of original scripts from stories they have read and discussed.

Here are other examples of how students can transform one form of discourse into another:

- Create a story based on the details of an informational account, such as a sporting contest or a brave deed.
- Write the plot of a story as a newspaper article. For example: *Corduroy, the Bear, went in search of a lost button last night and had a real adventure. . . .*
- Choose a memorable scene from a novel and capture its essence in haiku or another poetic format, such as cinquain or diamante. (For examples, see www.cinquain.net and http://en.wikipedia.org/wiki/Diamond_poem.)

Creative transformations are appealing, especially when the end products are shared with appreciative classmates. First attempts may be awkward, but the quality of the end product is not as important as the cognitive effort.

Combining Forms of Discourse

Yet another interesting exploration involves combining forms of discourse. One example begins with Sensory Writing, also known as Saturation Reporting. Students make firsthand observations of a place or an event, incorporating actions, bits of overheard dialogue, and interesting sensory details. This is not an objective report from an impartial observer. It is a subjective account of how the writer experienced the place, including the sights, sounds, smells, tastes, and textures that contributed to that writer's unique impression of the place at that moment in time. This kind of writing, recommended by Moffett (1968a), can be used at all grade levels. Primary-grade students can visit and write about the media center or the playground at the school. Older students may do their observing outside of school, perhaps at a sporting event, a museum, or another place in the community. Different people can be in the same place at the same time and yet have different impressions of the experience, so the finished reports are always interesting to share.

When students are comfortable with this firsthand reporting, they can combine it with issue-oriented composition, creating their own versions of the feature articles that appear in newspapers and magazines. For example, fifth-grade students integrated their observations during a trip to the zoo with their study of endangered species. Here is the beginning of one student's composition:

You can hear the birdcalls before you get to the tropical aviary. When you enter, you see lots of color—white, bright blue and green, yellow and red. Cockatoos with yellow crests screech and bright green parrots squawk. It's fun to see the beautiful birds, and the zoo takes good care of them.

But it is sad to see them, too, because it makes you think about how tropical birds are taken from their native habitats around the world and sold to pet stores and individuals. This is having a terrible effect on the birds....

The firsthand narrative establishes a context for the information and brings it to life. Many possibilities exist for such writing. For example:

Visit . . .	When Writing About . . .
a fire station	firefighting efforts and tactics
a supermarket	food distribution
a train station	public transportation
an animal shelter	abandoned animals
a war veteran	America's role in a specific war

Other combining activities are also fruitful. For example, students can include letters as part of a fictional account based on a historical period. Creating digital presentations combining text, graphics, and audio can also be engaging. For example, students can summarize the plot of a story with digital images or animations and text, or they can combine video images with a persuasive speech to intensify the persuasion.

Using Texts as Models

A long-standing tradition in reading/language arts classes is for students to focus on specific text structures to understand their features and use them as models for their own writing. Learners can work individually or collaboratively, imitating models explicitly or simply using them to inspire their own writing. Following a model helps students become more attentive to language patterns and encourages them to read like writers. Some models, ordinarily referred to as *frames*, provide a specific structure with blanks into which students put their own words. Genres, such as the argumentative essay or the memoir, can be used as another type of model. Students immerse themselves in examples of the genre, then write compositions that share the same characteristics.

Imitating Models

Imitation builds deftness with language while encouraging close reading. The model can be a sentence, a paragraph, or a longer piece of text; the charge is straightforward: Write one like this. The imitation can adhere strictly or loosely to the model.

In a commonly-used approach, students copy the original mindfully, attending to the specifics of the pattern and the meaning. Next, they substitute synonyms for key words. This step encourages thoughtfulness about word choice, strengthens vocabulary, and deepens comprehension. Finally, students create their own by adhering to the structure of the original but changing the topic. This brings the writer's attention more firmly to the structural elements of the model and further enhances comprehension of the original. See Figure 5.4 for an example of imitation writing at the sentence level. The writer has adhered strictly to the pattern in that the two imitations match the original exactly in terms of sentence structure, numbers of words, and punctuation.

The models chosen or created by the teacher can be similar to the students' own language patterns, reinforcing what is familiar, or can challenge the students to use language in ways that they might not generate on their own. Both are useful tactics. With this effective blend of comprehending and composing, students learn to read more closely while they develop versatility with written expression. For more information about this kind of writing, see Butler (2002) and Hillebrand (2004).

Figure 5.4

Imitation Writing of Sentences	
Original sentence	The timid, quiet boy sat at the back of the auditorium and read a magazine.
Copy of original	The timid, quiet boy sat at the back of the auditorium and read a magazine.
Same sentence with synonyms for key words	The shy, silent male remained at the rear of the hall and perused a periodical.
Imitation sentence (new topic)	The regal, watchful hawk perched at the top of the tree and surveyed the beach.
Imitation sentence (new topic)	The daring, eager swimmer balanced on the edge of the pool and awaited the signal.

Using Writing Frames

Various writing frames can be constructed for students to use. Figure 5.5 shows an example that is consistent with the process of reflecting on informational text discussed in Chapter 3. For more examples, see Lewis and Wray (1995). While providing structures for student composing, frames also illuminate commonly used elements of text organization, such as transitions. As students become familiar with these elements by seeing them repeatedly in frames, they begin to notice the elements in the texts they read, and the awareness benefits their comprehension.

Using Texts as Inspiration

Students can also use specific texts as inspirations for their own writing. Lunsford (1997) describes how to help students improve their introductions by studying lead sentences in published books. Freeman (1991) shows how students can use engaging informational texts as models for sharing their learning. For example, an animal alphabet book can inspire students to create an alphabet book of a country's features or a historical event.

Almost any text can become a source of inspiration. *The Important Book* (Brown 1949) is popular for this purpose. The same language/conceptual pattern is repeated from page to page:

The important thing about _____ is that _____.

It is true that _____, and _____, and _____ .

But the important thing about _____ is that _____.

Figure 5.5

An Example of a Completed Writing Frame

Before we learned about *bones*, I thought that *you probably had about 25 bones in your body.* I also thought that *babies had less bones than grown-ups.* I had never thought about the idea that *bones help make cells that keep us healthy.* I was really surprised to learn that *we have more bones when we are born and we have over 200 bones in our body.* I also learned that *there are different groups of bones.* I still have these questions: *Are teeth bones? What causes bones to grow?*

Deciding on an important point for a lead and a conclusion requires careful thought. Eventually, students can prioritize important points and decide on the *most* important thing. They can compose their own Important Books individually, or each can write a page for a collaborative class book. For example, after studying the U.S. presidents, fourth-grader Emory wrote:

The most important thing about George Washington is that he was the first president of the United States.

It is true that he was a surveyor and a farmer.

He was the General of the Continental Army.

He crossed the Delaware River at Christmas to surprise the British.

He lived at Mt. Vernon in Virginia.

But the most important thing about George Washington is that he was the first president of the United States.

Other such pattern books can be used as models for writing in the early grades, for example, *The Very Hungry Caterpillar* (Carle 1969), *I Unpacked My Grandmother's Trunk* (Hoguet 1983), and *Too Much Noise* (McGovern 1967).

Middle and high school students can use other texts for inspiration. One eleventh-grade English class read and discussed a feature article in *Smithsonian* about a New England town known for its fishing industry. They liked certain turns of phrase the author had used and remarked on them when they discussed the text. A few days later, they drafted descriptive compositions about a place they had visited as a class, and, with teacher encouragement, used elements of the *Smithsonian* article as inspiration to make their writing more colorful and interesting. In the weeks that followed, they began to read with writers' eyes, jotting down examples of phrases or sentences that appealed to them and that they wanted to use as models for their own writing.

Genre studies can inspire original writing across grade levels. For example, a class of fifth graders read a number of European folktales and spent several days discussing their common characteristics. They noted that important events often happen in threes, that main characters usually undergo trials, and that elves and other such creatures often provide help. They also noticed certain language structures and vocabulary, such as: "The king refused the girl's request for he was sorely displeased with her." In addition, they discussed recurrent themes of abandonment, courage, and battles between good and evil. Small groups then collaborated to compose their own original folktales that included the features they discussed. Bomer (1995) presents other examples of the way genre studies positively influence the ways students think and write.

The Promises and Limitations of Discourse Explorations

Text structure explorations and manipulations develop students' command of language in intellectually challenging ways while increasing their flexibility as readers and writers. In addition, most students find it more interesting to engage in creative activities such as Readers' Theatre than to respond briefly to questions or fill out worksheets. Working with text structures also gives students a sense of control over their reading and writing, building their confidence.

Models and frames do have advantages. Models show students what an effective end product looks like, and frames make some types of composing easier at first. These aids help students internalize structures that they can later use spontaneously and are especially helpful to students who are reluctant to write. Many youngsters take pleasure in following a model or filling in a frame successfully. They may be using someone else's structure, but the ideas are their own and the end product can be praiseworthy.

On the other hand, if activities are too contrived, they can fall flat. Readers' Theatre, for example, has little value if done mechanically. It is most effective when the students have been deeply involved in reading and discussing the narrative and are enthused by the prospect of writing their own script to dramatize it. Also, some exercises with models and frames are best described as "writing without composing" (Applebee 2000) because they result in writing that reflects the originator more than the student writer. Such supports are best compared to training wheels on a bicycle. They can get students off to a good start and give them a welcome feeling of accomplishment, but if they are used too extensively, they can foster dependence and limit students' vision of what they can accomplish in writing. Learners benefit from some use of models and frames, but they will be hampered as writers if they never get beyond such aids.

> *Learners benefit from some use of models and frames, but they will be hampered as writers if they never get beyond such aids.*

Genre study engages students in working with forms at a more abstract level. Rather than following a specific model or filling in a frame, learners develop and apply a broad understanding of the features and purposes of different genres. Such writing can be interesting and intellectually challenging, and because the model is a category of discourse rather than a specific text, students have considerably more leeway when they "write one like this." At the same time, a good reason should exist for studying a genre other than its existence as a requirement in the curriculum. Ideally, students have become interested in the genre because they see the form as useful to their own purposes.

Applebee (2000) stresses that novice writers vary in the way they learn to write, in the specific composing strategies they use, and in the kinds of writing that appeal to them, noting that a single approach will not work for all students in all contexts. He calls instead for redefining the act of writing as part of ongoing "important conversations" in the classroom. For example, instead of learning historical facts and restating them in writing, students can discuss and write about the issues that are relevant to the era as well as factual information about the era. Applebee's perspective suggests that student writing will improve only to the extent that learners are more deeply engaged in what they are reading and learning and have many opportunities to think critically and creatively about the subject matter. That is, attention to the context within which writing is done is at least as important as attempts to improve students' writing by means of contrived assignments and exercises. For excellent discussions of how to nurture such authentic writing, see Cramer (2001).

The kinds of text explorations described in this section are likely to strike learners as personally meaningful, intellectually challenging, and emotionally satisfying. As such, they are examples of how writing experiences, like reading experiences, can be designed for maximum engagement and effectiveness.

> *Attention to the context within which writing is done is at least as important as attempts to improve students' writing by means of contrived assignments and exercises.*

Revision and Comprehension

Effective writers evaluate their writing from the point of view of prospective readers and revise accordingly, but this may not be uppermost in young writers' minds. When they read their drafts, they can easily overlook ambiguous sentences, confusing statements, or omitted ideas or words. However, with practice, they can learn to reduce their egocentricity and consider their audience by asking themselves, *Does this make sense? Have I stated my ideas well and in an organized fashion? Do I need to say more?*

Revision involves attending closely to constructed meanings, so the process increases students' capacity to comprehend. Young writers are most likely to approach revision willingly and thoughtfully when they realize that a first draft is merely an early step in a process and that the need for revision does not mean they are inadequate writers. They do not need to be intimidated by the thought of revising. They need only understand that it involves four interrelated processes: (1) adding ideas; (2) taking out ideas, or "pulling weeds" as William Zinsser (2006) calls it; (3) restating ideas; and (4) moving ideas around. They also need to understand that revising is distinct from editing, which addresses grammar, usage, and mechanics such as spelling and punctuation.

> *The process of revision increases the students' capacity to comprehend.*

Teachers can take a number of actions to promote the kinds of revising that strengthen students' comprehension and improve their writing. Here are some suggestions:

- Talk to students about their writing, individually and in small groups, always beginning with strengths (e.g., *This part of your writing is especially effective*). Be specific.
- Encourage students to reflect on their own writing. Refrain from always telling them how you think they can improve it.
- Have students respond to each other's writing in ways that encourage them to revise. For example, when peers ask questions to clarify statements or elicit more details, writers see a need to revise.
- Help students see that revision is central to the communication of ideas, whereas editing makes the piece presentable and attractive to an audience. They need to understand the distinction.
- Demonstrate the revision process so that students can see you revise as you do it. As you revise, articulate what you are thinking.
- Display early drafts and later drafts side by side and celebrate the growing strength in students' writing as it goes through several revisions.
- Talk to students about revision in the same way you talk to them about monitoring their comprehension. Engage them in conversation about the skills of good writers.

- Elicit from accomplished writers statements about and examples of their own revision practices and samples of their initial and final drafts.
- Have students write to authors to inquire about their revision practices.
- Make sure that students have the opportunity to share their revised pieces with an appreciative audience so that they experience satisfaction following their efforts.

Revising is essential to producing writing of high quality and has a positive effect on reading comprehension and thinking. However, students do not need to revise everything they write. Ideally, they will always have several works in progress in their writing folders and can periodically choose a favorite to revise.

Developing a Disposition to Write

When writing is integrated with reading at all grade levels in the ways suggested here, students become comfortable expressing themselves in writing, finding it almost as easy and natural as speaking. The greater their comfort, the greater the chance they will develop the disposition to write—that is, to use writing regularly as an aid to learning as well as a means of reflection and self-expression. This increases their capacity for writing still further and has an increasingly positive influence on their reading.

At all grade levels, teachers can develop the disposition to write with the assignments they give, the attitude they convey about writing and about the students as writers, and the way they handle the evaluation of students' writing. The following practices are especially useful.

Present writing as a meaning-making process. When children first begin to write, usually before they enter school, they concentrate entirely on expressing themselves. Meaning comes first; form follows. When these priorities are sustained in school from kindergarten onward, students continue to see writing as the expression of meaning. In the primary grades, invented spelling nurtures meaning-oriented writing as does substantive talk before writing to help students generate and formulate ideas. Although the temptation may be to focus on mechanics and usage in the early years, doing so almost always leads to less writing and less interesting writing because students concentrate on not making mistakes. Instruction in spelling, language usage, and other conventions is useful and worthwhile, but at any grade level, form should not be the priority until students have acquired considerable confidence and fluency in communicating their ideas.

Keep the writer in the writing. Have students write in their own words rather than copy, finish incomplete sentences, or perform other tasks that divorce the writer from the writing and require only minimal thought. Students are more inclined to write when they are communicating their thoughts instead of completing an exercise. This is particularly important in the early grades, when students are first developing their perceptions of writing. When first and second graders write about what they find most interesting about a topic they studied, they see that writing involves formulating and expressing their own thoughts even when they are relating facts. Upper-grade students also need opportunities to express what they think about what they are learning even when they summarize and synthesize others' ideas.

Provide response to the content. Students need substantive response to what they write, both from teachers and peers. The more others show interest in their ideas, the more inclined they are to write. Opportunities for young writers to share their compositions with each other formally and informally are essential to a focus on content. Students can meet in small groups to respond to each other's writing. They can share compositions by reading them aloud to the class. They can publish their writing by posting it on the classroom wall, compiling classroom collections, and uploading it to a class website.

Give students control. Students are more likely to develop the disposition to write when they have control over the process, and choice is an important way of giving them control. They can be given choices of topics. They can write several drafts and choose the ones they like the best to revise and submit for evaluation. They can be allowed to choose between writing individually or writing with a partner, illustrating their writing or not, sharing a draft with a writing group or keeping it to themselves. The more choices students have, the more enthused they will be about writing.

Create a community of writers. Students are more inclined to write when they see those around them writing and valuing writing. A workshop atmosphere in the classroom is helpful, one in which some students are writing drafts, others are sharing their writing in small groups, and still others are engaged in revising and proofreading. The buzz of productive energy in such classrooms is agreeable; students see others engaged in a variety of writing activities and want to join in.

In one Virginia elementary school, sixth graders gather voluntarily in a writers' café to share and talk about their writing with minimal adult supervision. The atmosphere, often with juice and cookies, is festive. Any K–6 student is encouraged to join the group to share drafts and talk about their writing. Four times a year, the group sponsors a schoolwide writers' conference. Both activities help young writers celebrate their accomplishments and inspire others.

These practices are parallel to those that develop the disposition to comprehend when reading. In both writing and reading, it's vital to focus primarily on constructing meaning rather than on the mechanical aspects of the process. It's also important to give students control by engaging them in topics and ideas rather than simply asking them comprehension questions or assigning writing tasks. The key is to create a lively community of thinking readers and writers by leading the kinds of discussions that engage students deeply.

Fostering Meaningful and Satisfying Writing

When we write, we do so most willingly and eagerly when we are writing about something that is important to us. We experience great satisfaction when we write to share what we know and what we think with others who might be interested. We also frequently enjoy the craft of writing. We take pleasure in composing an especially effective memo, proposal, report, or letter. Ordinarily, writing that we have chosen to do for our own purposes and in our own ways is more satisfying than writing to meet someone else's expectations or requirements. When our writing stems from a genuine desire to have our say or to craft a piece in our own way, we take extra time to make sure we choose our words carefully, structure our sentences well, attend to the flow of ideas, and clean up the mechanics. We also find that highly meaningful writing improves our thinking about the topic and our comprehension of it. As we write, we read or reread other texts and discuss our thoughts with others, continually refining, extending, and clarifying our thoughts. In the end, having immersed ourselves in the topic, we often know more than when we started, or at least we are thinking more clearly than when we began.

Knowing that the same is true for students, we aim to help learners find good reasons to write and have satisfying writing experiences. We invite them, when appropriate, to write before they read to activate their thinking. We guide them to write while they are reading to keep track of ideas, clarify points, and raise questions. We lead them to write after they read to summarize, reflect, and respond. We sometimes have them play with text structures in ways that deepen their comprehension while refining their capacity to write, and we help them venture beyond predetermined structures to find their own voices, styles, and messages. We are most gratified when we see students developing the disposition to write and the interest in continuing to grow as writers, increasing the depth and sophistication of their written expression. We know that those students are on their way to having success with academics and being able to function well in society beyond the classroom and school community.

CHAPTER 6

The Importance of Comprehension Instruction in the Primary Grades

Comprehension instruction is seldom a top priority in kindergarten, first-, and second-grade classrooms because it is widely believed that young children must focus primarily on decoding (i.e., deciphering the words on the page). After all, the argument goes, comprehension cannot be addressed until students can read the words. Several influential models of reading embrace this principle of phonics and decoding first and comprehension later. For example, in Chall's model of the stages of reading, comprehension is not addressed in any substantial way until second or even third grade, well after students have learned to decode written text (Chall 1983). Complementing this stage model is the automatic processing model: the idea that word recognition must be rapid and accurate—virtually automatic—before the reader can attend to comprehension (LaBerge and Samuels 1974). These models have prevailed in recent years. For example, the Reading First programs, established under the auspices of the No Child Left Behind Act of 2001, embrace Chall's model. Moreover, the draft *Common Core State Standards*, proposed in March 2010 for nationwide adoption, lists only fluency, phonics, and word recognition as "foundational skills" for grades K–5 with the addition of print concepts and phonological awareness for K–1.

Aspects of reading related to comprehension are discussed elsewhere (www.corestandards.org). A third model, known as the Simple View of Reading (Gough and Tunmer 1986) holds that reading comprehension is a product of listening comprehension and decoding skills. The theory is that if decoding skills are sufficiently developed and students are skilled at understanding oral language, reading comprehension will naturally follow, thus implying that reading comprehension, per se, does not require instructional attention.

When instruction is based on any of these models, the result is minimal attention to reading comprehension in the early grades. We consider this most unfortunate and present the view here that comprehension instruction must be a major component of any early literacy program.

Building the Case for Early Comprehension Instruction

A strong case exists for making comprehension a priority in early literacy programs. Four supportive arguments relate directly to what will most help students learn to read well.

1. Focusing on comprehension from the earliest days of school develops the disposition to make sense of text. How young children are taught initially shapes their perceptions of reading over the long term. When they are engaged in constructing meaning from their earliest days in school, they learn to perceive reading as a way to discover, interpret, and reflect on ideas that others have written. In contrast, an almost exclusive attention to phonemic awareness, letter–sound correspondence, and oral reading fluency develops the perception that reading is about sounds, letters, rapid word recognition, and oral reading performance. When students are focused consistently on these aspects of reading, many do not expect texts to make sense and often are not aware when what they read doesn't make sense.

It is not surprising that decoding-first advocates lament the phenomenon they call the "fourth-grade slump" (Chall, Jacobs, and Baldwin 1990; Chall and Jacobs 2003). Fourth graders are expected to respond to longer narratives and informational texts of all kinds. If they have not previously been expected to attend to meaning to any significant degree and have not developed the habit of constructing meaning as they read, it should not be surprising that they experience difficulty when comprehension suddenly becomes the priority. The "slump" is very likely a consequence of delaying substantive comprehension instruction in the early grades.

When teachers and students view reading as a meaning-making process from the earliest days of kindergarten, youngsters have a greater chance of being successful with comprehension through the grades and across the curriculum. In fact, the widely accepted mantra "first learn to read, then read to learn" should be reversed: Read to learn; learn to read. Comprehension must be a priority in the early grades, not merely a goal to be reached only after other aspects of reading have been mastered.

2. An emphasis on comprehension builds on the existing strengths and dispositions of young children. Young people are skilled at constructing meaning before they come to school. Children are notorious question askers as early as three or four years of age. They ponder, make connections between concepts and events, and persevere in their quest to make sense of their world. They are exemplary meaning makers as Wells (1986) and others have noted. Placing comprehension at the center of the primary-grade curriculum builds on this strength and makes students' success with reading more likely.

When teachers and students view reading as a meaning-making process from the earliest days of kindergarten, youngsters have a greater chance of being successful with comprehension through the grades and across the curriculum.

3. The process of comprehending facilitates and strengthens all aspects of reading. When learners think about and understand what they are reading, they read more fluently. They also become more familiar with letter–sound correspondences, morphology, and other aspects of word knowledge. In addition, they increase their vocabularies and their knowledge base. Of particular importance is the reader's use of context: the language and meaning cues that are available in the text. As good readers move through a text, they continually consider the meaning they are constructing. Thus, context and a complex array of information available to the reader are significant aids to word processing and word recognition (Schwartz and Gallant 2009). However, if students are focused heavily on sounding out words and identifying "sight words" they have memorized, they tend not to focus on comprehension and thus make minimal use of the language and meaning cues that facilitate the reading process.

4. Making sense of text is satisfying. Young readers like to find out what happens next in their story and learn from informational texts. Just as importantly, they like to do this on their own, without relying on someone to read to them. Comprehension-centered instruction develops genuine satisfaction with reading. Because the students enjoy reading so much and have growing confidence with the process, they read even more, increasing their competence further.

We argue for comprehension as a priority because beginning reading instruction has been heavily skewed in recent years toward "code cracking." However, phonics knowledge is useful to readers only if they are, first and foremost, attending to meaning when they look at the words in phrases and sentences. If learners are not attending to meaning, they are not reading, no matter how accurately and rapidly they pronounce the words. In the most effective early literacy programs, phonics does not precede comprehension. Decoding and comprehension are consistently taught in tandem so that each supports the other.

If learners are not attending to meaning, they are not reading, no matter how accurately and rapidly they pronounce the words.

What Comprehension Instruction Looks Like in the Primary Grades

Most important is the manner in which teachers guide students' reading of age-appropriate texts, including wordless picture books, illustrated narratives, and informational texts. When young children read a text under the direction of the teacher, they are attentive to what the teacher expects and do their best to provide it. The way the teacher proceeds thus shapes children's perceptions of reading and their reading behavior. Following are three examples of primary-grade teachers effectively guiding their students' reading and thinking. We use the term *guided reading* in the most general sense here to mean a teacher facilitating students' reading of a text, not any specific program or procedure that other educators may call "guided reading."

A Visit to a First-Grade Classroom

It is mid-January in Ms. O's room. The thirteen girls and eight boys come from the surrounding blue-collar, middle-class neighborhood. Desks and tables are arranged in clusters so that children can work collaboratively. Books of all kinds are on display: predictable books, leveled books, chapter books, and big books. Each child has a writing folder. Some are stacked in piles; others are with the writers. Most children also have self-made books that contain stories and accounts they have composed orally and dictated to the teacher. The children's writing, featuring invented spelling, is on display throughout the room. A word wall, required by the district, is in use. Interspersed with the compulsory high-frequency words are: *Ferndale*, *pizza*, *state fair*, *Thanksgiving*, *hockey*, *turkey*, *pumpkin*, and *birthday*. Also visible are art displays, posters, and a few strategic student-constructed charts with reminders about what it means to be a good writer, reader, mathematician, and scientist.

Several children are writing or illustrating their writing; some are reading independently. A few are reading with a partner, and still others are making collages of interesting words they know, having cut them from periodicals. Two are sorting words. The children are absorbed in their independent work but eagerly read aloud to visitors what they have written or an excerpt from a book they are reading. The overall tenor of the classroom is of a community of literate individuals, busily and comfortably engaged in reading or writing.

Ms. O is about to guide six students in their reading of *Lost*, written and illustrated by David McPhail (1990). The story is about a bear that climbs into a delivery truck while the driver changes a tire near the woods. When the bear awakes, he finds himself lost in the city. A friendly boy offers to help. Eventually, after they make numerous attempts to find the bear's home, they board a bus that takes them into the forest, where the bear recognizes his home and runs off. When the boy realizes that he is lost, the bear returns to help him.

Ms. O begins the story by having the children examine the cover, title page, and the first two illustrations (Figure 6.1) and talk about what might happen in the story. The children discuss who might be lost, the boy or the bear. One child notes the bear climbing into the truck and suggests that he's after snacks, pointing to the picture with the word *snacks*. The children then read the first three pages of the story. Four read silently; two read quietly to themselves.

When Ms. O invites the children to discuss what they have learned so far, they confirm that the bear is the one who is lost and is crying and afraid.

Ms. O: What else do you think?

Alex: I think they're in the city. There are tall buildings.

Eric: And there are lots of people.

Ms. O: What do you think is going to happen?

Samira: I think the boy is going to help him.

Figure 6.1

Tatiana: I think so, too.

Ms. O: Let's find out. Read the next page to yourself.

The children read the next page silently, discovering that the boy asks the bear where he lives and offers to help.

Samira: We were right. The boy says, "I will help you."

Ms. O: How is the boy going to help?

Rafi: Maybe the bear will just tell him where he lives.

Carla: But he's lost. He doesn't know where he is.

Ms. O: What can he do?

Alex: He could ask a policeman.

Tatiana: Or take him home to his mother to help.

Eric: Maybe he will take him to the zoo.

Ms. O: What do you think of these ideas?

Carla: Yes, but maybe the zoo will keep him.

Ms. O: And?

Carla: And then he couldn't go home to the woods.

Ms. O: Well, let's find out. Read the next four pages.

The children continue reading silently. When one encounters a word she doesn't know, Ms. O. responds, "Think about what you are reading. What word would make sense?" The child thinks briefly, looks at the picture, and reads on.

At the end of this segment, the boy voices the idea of taking the bear to a tall building.

Ms. O: Why do you think they may go to a tall building? (*Students ponder this.*)

Carla: The bear hasn't seen one, so the boy wants to show him.

Rafi: That's a good idea.

Ms. O: That is a possibility. What could they do if they went to the very top of the building?

Alex: Well, they could look out and see everything.

Tatiana: (*referring to the illustration*) The building has lots of windows.

Samira: They could see where the bear lives!

Ms. O: How are they going to get to the top of the building?

Eric: Take an elevator.

Rafi: That's what I think, too.

Ms. O: Let's read and find out.

As the children read silently, they learn that the two take an elevator to the top of the building and look out over the city.

Ms. O skillfully guides the children's thinking. She knows the plot but does not give it away. When Rafi agrees with Carla's idea, Ms. O recognizes that the idea makes sense from their perspective and acknowledges their thinking, then prods them to think more. Her question about how the characters might get to the top of the building is strategic because she knows the students will probably think of an elevator. Once they mention it, she is confident they will use the idea and the upcoming picture clue to identify the word in print. Identifying the word for themselves gives them a greater sense of accomplishment than they would have had if she had taught it beforehand.

The reading and discussion continue. The students are actively involved in thinking about the story, using the text, the pictures, and their own knowledge of the world to make sense of the developing plot. The teacher guides the readers deftly so that they see the story as a kind of interesting puzzle to solve. Rather than simply recalling what they read at each stopping point, they use what they have read to think ahead. Near the end, when the boy and bear have returned to the bear's woods, Samira smiles and says, "Now the boy is going to be lost!" Others agree, seeing the sense in this prediction.

> *The teacher guides the readers deftly so that they see the story as a kind of interesting puzzle to solve.*

Ms. O continues to develop the children's thinking after they have finished the story, moving them to a higher cognitive level as they consider how the story illustrates a concept or theme.

Ms. O: What is our story about?

Alex: It's about a boy finding a bear and helping him.

Ms. O: And?

Rafi: And he took the bear home and then he got lost.

Ms. O: Who got lost?

Rafi: The boy got lost because of the tall trees.

Carla: The bear said he would help him.

Ms. O:	So what else do you think this story is about?
Samira:	It's about helping people?
Eric:	If you help somebody then they will help you.
Ms. O:	Yes, it is about that, isn't it?
Tatiana:	The boy helped the bear, and the bear helped the boy.
Ms. O:	What did the bear say when the boy said he was lost?
Alex:	*(reading)* "Don't worry," he said, "I will help you."
Samira:	They helped each other.

Not all stories have a clear thematic element, but this one does, and Ms. O uses it to stimulate thinking. Next, she leads the children to reflect on their thinking when they were reading the story: what they thought might happen, the clues they used to predict, when they first began to realize that the boy was going to get lost, and so on. They return to selected illustrations and discuss how the illustrator used these to make the story more interesting. They also select favorite passages to read orally. Throughout, these first graders are deeply engaged in constructing meaning.

A Visit to a Kindergarten Classroom

Near Ms. O's room is Ms. K's kindergarten classroom. Along with manipulatives, art supplies, and games, books are displayed throughout the room, primarily wordless picture books and picture books with predictable texts. On the wall and on chart holders are accounts the children have dictated about various class activities. Ms. K has also established a word wall, and, like Ms. O, adds words that the students find especially interesting: *Tyrannosaurus rex* appears just below *to*, and *popcorn* appears just above *put*. The eighteen children are engaged in various activities. Some are drawing; some are looking at books, some are writing, and some are making collages from familiar logos and words they have cut from old magazines.

Ms. K gathers the children onto a rug and displays *Frog, Where Are You?* (Mayer 1969), a wordless picture book. She tells the children that they will be reading the book together and holds up the front cover (Figure 6.2).

Ms. K:	Girls and boys, what do you think our story is going to be about?
Tanya:	There's a boy and a dog.
Jay:	And they're on a tree.
Ms. K:	Anything else?
Jawan:	The boy is yelling.

Figure 6.2

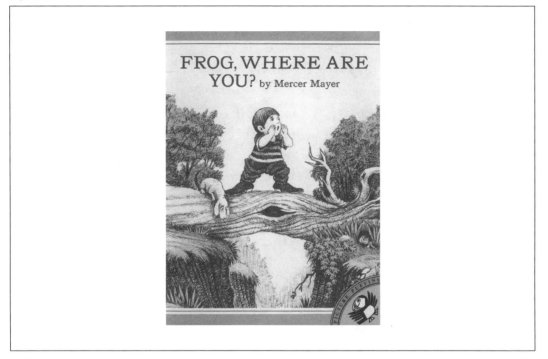

Anthony: And the dog looks like he's going to fall off.

Donna: He's looking for something, I think.

Ms. K: What do you think the dog is looking for?

Marcella: I don't know.

Ms. K: What do you think?

Marcella: Maybe he's looking for a frog.

Ms. K: What makes you think that?

Donna: *(pointing to the words on the cover)* Because it says "Frog where are you?"

Jawan: Oh! The boy is yelling for the frog!

Ms. K: What do you think he may be yelling or shouting?

Students: *(several in unison)* Frog . . . where are you?

Jay: It's a funny picture.

Ms. K: Yes, it is, isn't it? Would you like to find out what is going to happen in the story?

Students: *(in unison)* Yes!

Ms. K opens the book to reveal the next picture (Figure 6.3).

Students: *(in unison)* There's the frog!

Sierra: He's in a big jar.

Jerry: And the dog is looking in the jar.

Davon: The boy is looking, too.

Ms. K: Anything else?

Anthony: I think they caught him and put him in the jar.

Jay: The boy looks happy.

Donna: The dog is wagging his tail. He's happy too.

Ms. K: What about the frog?

Tanya: He looks happy too.

Ms. K: So what do you think is going to happen?

Tanya: I don't know.

Marcella: Maybe they're going to keep him.

Sierra: Maybe he's going to stay all night.

Davon: Maybe he's going to escape.

Ms. K: That's an interesting idea. Why do you think that?

Davon: It says, "Frog where are you?"

Ms. K: What do we know about frogs?

Jawan: Frogs jump. So maybe he's going to jump out.

Ms. K: *(turning the page)* Well, let's find out.

Ms. K turns the page, allowing the students to examine the next picture (see Figure 6.4).

Anthony: The frog is getting out.

Donna: They're sleeping and the frog is getting out.

Davon: They don't know that he's escaping.

Ms. K: What is going to happen when the boy and his dog wake up?

Marcella: They are going to be surprised.

Sierra: Maybe the frog will come back.

Ms. K: What do you think the boy and dog might do?

Tanya: They'll go looking for him.

Ms. K: Well, let's find out.

Figure 6.3

Figure 6.4

Ms. K turns the next page in which the picture shows the boy and dog waking up, noticing that the jar is empty, and looking everywhere for Frog.

Jawan: The frog is gone.

Donna: They can't find him.

Ms. K: Do you think he is in the room?

Tanya: He could be under the bed.

Ms. K: Could be.

Jay: No frog.

Jawan: Oh. The window is open. The frog jumped out the window.

Ms. K: So what are they going to do?

Tanya: They're going to go look for him?

Marcella: They're going to try and find him.

Ms. K: Where do you think they will look?

Donna: All over.

Jay: Everywhere.

Ms. K. Any special places?

Davon: In a pond?

Marcella: Under a tree?

Ms. K: *(turning the page)* Let's find out.

The students continue to follow the adventures of the boy and his dog as they search for the frog. At one level, these five-year-olds are looking at pictures and enjoying a story. At a deeper level, they are constructing meaning with the pictorial information. They are making interpretations, using their existing knowledge and schema. They are using picture details to draw conclusions and make inferences. They are exploring possibilities and predicting what is going to happen next. Perhaps most importantly, they are establishing the habit of thinking about the information provided in books. They are deeply engaged in comprehension.

A Visit to a Second-Grade Classroom

In the adjoining wing of this elementary school is Ms. W's second-grade class. This room, too, has many books and other print materials on display, and children's writing is posted on almost all the available wall space. Here, too, the twenty-four students are fully engaged. Everyone is reading, writing, or engaged in related activities individually, in pairs, or in small groups.

Ms. W calls five students to the back table. While the rest of the students proceed independently, she will guide these five in reading an informational text, *Elephant Families* by Arthur Dorros (1994). She knows these students need more experience in reading extended text silently, so that is one of her aims. Her other purpose is her usual one: engaging students in thinking and learning. She gives each student a copy of the book but asks them not to begin reading until they have talked as a group. She asks them first to look at the cover (Figure 6.5).

Ms. W: Who would like to read the title?

Aaron: *Elephant Families.*

Ms. W: What do we know about elephants and their families?

David: They are big.

Sam: Elephants or their families?

David: Elephants. I don't know how big their family is.

Ms. W: Who might be in an elephant family?

Tricia: The mother, the dad, the kids.

Martin: Sometimes you see big herds of elephants, so probably more than that.

Sam: Maybe cousins and relatives and stuff.

Ms. W: What kind of stuff?

Sam: Oh, you know, maybe grandparents and uncles and aunts.

Ms. W: What do we call a mother and dad elephant?

Tricia: Parents.

Sam: Wait . . . I think the dad elephant is called a *bull*.

Ms. W: And the mother elephant?

Sam: Cow?

Ms. W: And the baby elephant?

Tricia: Cubs?

David: Calf?

Ms. W: Who do you think the leader of the family might be?

Martin: Probably the bull.

Tricia: Or the oldest elephant.

Ms. W: Any other possibilities?

David: Could be the biggest or the strongest.

Figure 6.5

Tricia: Probably the strongest.

Ms. W: What do elephants eat?

Martin: *(in unison with Tricia and Aaron)* Peanuts!

Ms. W: What besides peanuts? *(after a long pause of four to five seconds)* Well, are they meat eaters or plant eaters?

Sam: Plant.

Tricia: Plant.

Ms. W: What kind of plants?

Aaron: Maybe grass or hay.

David: You know. Plants and leaves and stuff.

Ms. W: Would they eat fruit?

Sam: Hmmm. Probably.

Martin: Maybe oranges and bananas, fruit like that.

David: Monkeys eat bananas. I don't know about elephants.

Tricia: I bet they do.

Ms. W: If elephants eat an orange or banana, would they peel it first?

Sam:	No way. They'd just eat the whole thing.
Tricia:	(laughing) They couldn't peel it.
Ms. W:	What else do we know about elephants?
David:	I think they travel from place to place.
Ms. W:	Why?
Aaron:	To stay away from enemies and to find food to eat, maybe.
Tricia:	They are probably looking for food.
David:	Or a water hole to drink.
Ms. W:	If an elephant was moving, could you hear it?
David:	What do you mean?
Ms. W:	Well, could an elephant sneak up on you?
Martin:	No way.
Tricia:	Not me.
Sam:	Me neither.
Ms. W:	Let's see if we can find answers to our questions. Read to the bottom of page 15.

(Students read silently and examine the illustrations on each page.)

Out in the grasslands of Africa, a baby elephant is born. Mother helps the baby stand up. Sisters, brothers, cousins, aunts and grandmother watch. They are all part of a family. Elephants live in families.

The baby takes its first wobbly steps. Big sister helps the baby along with her trunk. She helps take care of the baby. She is a baby-sitter.

Sometimes the baby-sitter is a cousin or aunt. Almost all baby elephants have baby-sitters.

The baby drinks milk from its mother. The older elephants eat grass, seeds, fruit, leaves, even branches and tree bark.

Elephants eat almost all day. An elephant can eat more than 300 pounds of food each day. You would need to eat a lot, too, if you weighed three or four tons like a grown elephant. That's as much as a large truck!

Elephants often wander far to find enough to eat. An elephant family may walk forty miles a day, looking for food.

Grandmother elephant leads the way. She knows where to find the best food. The other elephants follow her. Each elephant family is led by the oldest female elephant.

Elephants can walk very quietly. The bottoms of their feet are soft, and elephants walk carefully on their toes! A family of elephants could walk right by you and you wouldn't hear them.

Elephants are surefooted. They can walk on logs or narrow trails.

Mother and big sister help the baby up a steep bank. They show the baby where the trail is.

Grandmother leads the family to trees full of fruit. She remembers how to get here for ripe fruit every year.

The elephants shake the trees with their trunks and tusks. A trunk is like a nose and hand combined. Elephants can pick leaves or peel fruit with their trunks faster than we could with our hands. The tips of the trunk are used like fingers. Tusks are useful too. Elephants use them to dig, to push over branches or trees and to strip off bark to eat. (Dorros 1994, 1–15)

The students read silently with no interruptions, finishing in about four minutes. As the first student finishes, Ms. W. whispers to her quietly: *Be thinking about what you want to talk about with the others.* This student reviews pages selectively. As other students complete their reading, they do the same, rereading quietly or pointing out something to one of the others. When all have finished, the discussion continues:

Ms. W: What did we learn? Did we find answers to some of our questions?

Aaron: Lots.

Tricia: They do eat fruit and they peel it with their trunk.

Martin: The grandmother is the leader.

Ms. W: Did that surprise you?

Martin: Yeah, I thought it would be the bull elephant. And the baby is called a *calf*.

Ms. W: What else?

Sam: There are cousins and aunts and brothers and sisters.

Tricia: They travel to find food. It says they can travel forty miles a day.

Ms. W: Anything else?

David: And they can walk quietly. They can sneak up on you sometimes.

Sam:	I don't think an elephant could sneak up on me.
David:	That's what it says.
Sam:	I hope not. *(Several children laugh.)*
Ms. W:	What else did we learn?
Tricia:	Elephants have baby-sitters.
Ms. W:	Talk about that a bit.
Tricia:	*(referring to the text and reading aloud)* "Sometimes the baby-sitter is a cousin or an aunt. Almost all baby elephants have baby-sitters."
Ms. W:	What else did we learn about their eating and how they find food? *(The discussion continues.)*
Ms. W:	What was the most surprising or unusual thing we learned?
Martin:	That they peel fruit.
Aaron:	Me too.
Sam:	That the oldest female is the leader. That surprised me. I thought it would be the biggest or maybe the bull elephant.
Tricia:	I was surprised that they could sneak up on you.
David:	That's what surprised me the most.

Ms. W. now shifts the discussion before the students go on to the next part of the text.

Ms. W:	What haven't we learned or what questions would we like to find answers to?
David:	I would like to know who their enemies are.
Aaron:	And how long they live.
Aaron:	I would like to know how fast they can run.
Ms. W:	How fast do you think?
Aaron:	Hmmm. As fast as a person?
Tricia:	Or a horse?
David:	They couldn't run as fast as a horse. I bet they're really slow.

The conversation continues briefly, generating individual and collective purposes for reading the next part. For example, the children wonder about the elephant's sense of hearing because of their big ears. Students are obviously interested and engaged. They read the last segment silently and are well prepared to discuss what they learned. Ms. W. uses the questions provided in Chapter 3 to guide the children in restating and reflecting on what they have learned.

Before reading, Ms. W skillfully elicits prior knowledge, probes to stimulate critical thinking and wonderment, invites hypotheses, and encourages discussion and debate. She accepts all ideas and encourages additional speculation, focusing strategically on information that she knows is in the text. Her questions also relate to information that is located at different places in the text so that the students will be motivated to read right to the end. To elicit elaborated responses, she uses effective prompts: *Talk about that. What else? Why?* She also scaffolds her questioning. For example, when students mention only peanuts as elephant food, she continues questioning to encourage further thinking: *Are they meat eaters or plant eaters?* When they say *plants*, she counters with *What kind of plants?* The teacher does not summarize for the students what they will be reading. She accesses their preconceptions and leads them to become curious. After reading, she leads them to compare what they read with what they thought initially, knowing this will generate in them a sense of satisfaction about what they have learned.

> *The teacher does not summarize for the students what they will be reading. She accesses their preconceptions and leads them to become curious.*

Additional Reflections on the Classroom Visits

In all three primary classrooms, visitors can identify practices that focus students firmly and purposefully on comprehension. Reading, talking, writing, and listening are all aimed at meaning making. Two features of the instruction are especially notable: quality and quantity of language and authentic and cumulative instruction.

Quality and quantity of language. Although the quality of the groups' discussions is noteworthy, the ratio of student language to teacher language is also revealing. For example, in the *Elephant Families* lesson, the initial dialogue contains just over three hundred words. The teacher speaks approximately 44 percent of these, the children 56 percent. Of the fifty-five initiated utterances, nineteen come from the teacher, thirty-six from the children. The children are doing most of the talking, and each utterance is relevant to the text.

The balance between teacher talk and student talk varies from lesson to lesson in primary-grade classrooms, but our own classroom observations have shown that, unfortunately, teachers ordinarily do 60 percent to 70 percent or more of the talking in guided

reading lessons. Examples of guided reading in the
professional literature show a similar pattern.
When teacher talk is extensive, it's usually because the teacher is telling more
than asking: giving directions, trans-
mitting information, explaining, and
restating what students say. In contrast,
primary-grade teachers who are oriented
to comprehension focus on eliciting students'
thoughts and preconceptions and listening to what
they have to say. They ordinarily keep their talk to less than 50 percent of the total.

Primary-grade teachers who are oriented to comprehension focus on eliciting children's thoughts and preconceptions and listening to what they have to say.

Authentic and cumulative instruction. In reflecting on the way these teachers guided
their students' reading, we note that they did not teach the children *about* comprehension nor give them practice exercises in comprehension. Rather, they engaged the children
directly with an interesting and meaningful text and guided them to think about it as they
read. Moreover, they will continue doing this week after week and month after month, with
multiple texts. It is such cumulative experiences that help students develop the capacity
and the disposition to comprehend deeply and think critically as they read.

Additional Instructional Components of a Meaning-Centered Curriculum

The three classroom visits showcase real teachers and students talking about texts. Discussion
about predictions or hypotheses is a critical component, but the teachers also use other practices
to orient the children to reading as a meaning-making process. These are enumerated below.

Student-Dictated Stories and Accounts

All three teachers make effective use of student-dictated stories or accounts,* using basic principles of the Language-Experience Approach (Stauffer 1970; Nessel and Jones 1981). Children
relate their ideas about a topic or experience to the teacher. The teacher prints or keyboards the
children's language to create the text. The children then read the texts with teacher support as

---

*These compositions are sometimes called "experience stories" although they are not necessarily narratives. We aim to call
them *stories* when they have a narrative structure and *accounts* when they relate information.

necessary. Individuals may dictate, or small groups may dictate collaboratively. These creations are highly meaningful to students because they reflect the children's own experiences written in their own words. Using them as an integral part of the literacy program allows children to feel like readers from the beginning and develops an ongoing sense of confidence.

Ms. K involves her kindergartners about once a week in dictating a new story or account as a group. For example, when they visited a nearby pond, she engaged them in talking about the experience, wrote down several of their statements on chart paper, and read them back to the group (Figure 6.6). The children then read the account several times, chorally and individually, with teacher support as necessary.

The teacher schedules a few minutes several times a week to work with these stories and accounts, using them to teach the children to track print from left to right, develop their concept of what a word is, and help them realize that printed text conveys meaning. The kindergartners regularly identify words they know on the charts, building a core vocabulary of words they recognize immediately or "at sight." Ms. K uses these words in selected word study activities and places the most popular ones on the classroom word wall.

Ms. O engaged her first graders in creating dictations the first week of school and uses dictation extensively throughout the year. Each student has an opportunity to create a dictated story or account at least once a week. As the children learn words from these creations, they store their known words on cards and use the cards for word study activities. Most of the children are soon able to read their dictations independently and learn a number of words from their new stories and accounts each week. Like Ms. K, Ms. O realizes that limiting her focus to high-frequency words would limit her students' learning.

Figure 6.6

A Group-Dictated Account

Visiting the Pond

We heard frogs at the pond, and we saw minnows. There were cattails by the water. Some were fluffy. We blew on them and made the seeds fly. Birds use the fluff in their nests. We brought back leaves and flowers.

Ms. W. uses student dictation in second grade as well but on a more limited basis. Sometimes she records a group chart, with contributions from various students, to commemorate a special event or project, but her primary use of the stories and accounts is with two students who need extra support. One is an English language learner for whom the Language-Experience Approach is particularly effective (Nessel and Dixon 2008).

To summarize, the use of student dictations is most effective when:

- The students compose stories and accounts orally that the teacher records in print for them.
- Students use their dictations to develop reading fluency and to build their reading vocabularies.
- Student dictations are used for instructional purposes and also for independent reading.
- The student-created texts are used flexibly and are gradually phased out when students are comfortably reading texts from other authors.

Word Study and the Study of Language Patterns

Ms. K focuses on rhyming words and initial sounds with her kindergartners. Ms. O does the same for her first graders, adding ending sounds along with vowels, diphthongs, and digraphs. Ms. W does the same as needed and also engages her second graders in more sophisticated within-word sound and meaning patterns. Students in all three classes often sort words to explore auditory and visual patterns, as described by Bear et al. (2007), and they have daily opportunities to learn new words by going from the known to the unknown. The teachers consider selected phonemic awareness activities, phonics, and other kinds of word study to be important components of their programs, but they think of these as corollary and parallel learnings rather than prerequisites to comprehension. The teachers sometimes work with the whole class and sometimes with students in small groups. All three know that word recognition cannot be learned effectively from worksheets and other paper-and-pencil activities.

To summarize, word study is most effective when:

- Students spend about twenty to twenty-five minutes daily on phonics and other word study activities with an emphasis on common visual and auditory patterns in words.
- The exemplar words for word study come primarily from the words the children see every day in their dictated accounts and other texts.

- The learning of phonics and other elements of word recognition involves the full participation and interaction of the teacher and students, with paper-and-pencil activities kept to a minimum.

Independent Reading

In all three classrooms, the children read books of their own choosing silently or occasionally in whispers, focused entirely on comprehension. The kindergarteners read wordless picture books, familiar books with predictable language patterns, and their dictated accounts. The first graders read books their teacher had previously read aloud, new books with predictable language, and their dictated accounts. In second grade, some students read books with predictable language and other easy-reading fare, but most are comfortably handling lengthier picture books, chapter books, and a variety of informational texts. Spending time with a good book is an integral part of their daily routine. The significant time the children spend reading independently every day is invaluable, not only for increasing their competence with the process of meaning construction but also for developing in them the disposition to read. During any given week, the students conference with the teacher individually at least once, twice if possible, about their independent reading. The students also regularly talk about their reading in pairs or small groups and use book talks to share what they are reading more formally with their classmates.

The time the children spend reading independently every day is invaluable, not only for increasing their competence with the process of meaning making but also for developing in them the disposition to read.

To summarize, independent reading is most effective when:

- Children read books of their own choosing independently each day.
- The amount of time children spend reading daily increases from the beginning of the year to the end.
- The teacher confers with selected children daily about what they are reading, speaking to them in small groups or individually.

Read-Alouds for Promoting Comprehension and Thinking

All three teachers read to the children each day, and the children are intellectually engaged at these times, not merely listening passively. The teachers pause periodically in narratives to ask students what they think will happen next, and they invite students to form hypotheses as they listen to informational texts.

Reading to children brings them great pleasure and creates a special bond between teacher and students. It also exposes students to literature that they are not yet able to read on their own. It strengthens their listening comprehension, generating strong foundations upon which they build their capacity for reading comprehension. Reading narratives to children also helps develop their sense of story and written language patterns, knowledge components that are critical to their success with reading (Purcell-Gates 1988). Reading informational texts aloud reveals the fascinating information available in books.

To summarize, students benefit most from teacher reading when:

- Teachers read aloud daily, twice a day if possible.
- Teachers read from a variety of texts: fictional narratives, biographies, informational texts, and poetry.
- Some materials are read aloud just for fun; others to stretch students' thinking; still others to stimulate discussion and writing.
- Students are actively involved with the text before, during, and after a read-aloud.

Shared and Collaborative Reading

The three teachers also use Shared Reading or Shared Book Experiences (Holdaway 1979) to varying degrees. Ms. K. uses Shared Reading to develop students' concept of word and ability to track print while engaging them in reading extended discourse. She understands that her kindergartners are going to learn to read by actually reading. Starting the first week of school, Ms. O has daily Shared Book Experiences with big books such as *Brown Bear, Brown Bear* (Martin 1996), *The Very Hungry Caterpillar* (Carle 1969), *Mrs. Wishy Washy* (Cowley 1999), and others with strong picture support and predictable sentence patterns. She uses the books to help her first graders develop fluency and build their reading confidence. Ms. W. uses Shared Reading selectively with the students in her class who need extra support to develop fluency and confidence. At all three grade levels, extensive classroom libraries of predictable books are available.

All three teachers use one or more collaborative reading activities daily. Buddy Reading is a favorite in all three classes. The children look at books with a partner, talk about what they are reading with each other, and read to and with each other. Sometimes, the teachers allow the children to choose their own partners, and sometimes they engineer pairs to give the children different experiences. The regular shifting about builds a strong sense of community in the room. Everyone is regularly a buddy to everyone else.

Collaborative oral reading activities are also common in all three rooms. The teachers sometimes use Choral Reading (all students reading at once) and sometimes Echo Reading (teacher reads; students repeat). The activities build students' fluency while giving them additional practice processing print. They also develop students' sensitivity to language patterns and rhythms, for example, the cadence of language in predictable books, the structural patterns in folktales, and the rhymes and rhythms in poetry.

To summarize, shared or collaborative reading is most effective when:

- The materials are chosen for their age-appropriateness and their appeal to the students.
- The texts have predictable language patterns and strong picture support so that students will experience fun and success in reading them together.
- The activities vary from day to day so that none becomes too routine or mechanical for either teacher or students.

Writing

The children in all three of the primary-grade classrooms write every day, generating their own stories and accounts. Topics come from their firsthand experiences, what they are learning, and what they are reading. In all three rooms, the children are allowed and encouraged to spell at their own level, so the writing in each class represents all the stages students go through in learning to encode the language as described by Bear et al. (2007), Henderson and Beers (1980), and Gentry (1981). The teachers realize that invented spelling does not inhibit spelling development but encourages it (Cramer 1968; Stauffer and Hammond 1965; Henderson and Beers 1980). The students write freely and with confidence. Most produce a combination of drawing and writing. Some draw and then write captions for their pictures; others write, then illustrate their compositions. Because students feel considerable ownership of their writing, they enjoy reading their narratives and accounts to each other and posting them on the wall for others to read.

The teachers monitor how the children's word study increases their understanding of letter–sound associations and influences their spelling. As they become more attentive to letter–sound patterns in words, they gradually replace their invented spellings with standard spellings. Their daily reading also has a positive impact on their spelling. Seeing conventional spellings in print leads to growth in spelling capacity. Ms. W is equally mindful of this predictable growth but also engages most of her second graders in formal spelling instruction. In addition, the teachers find opportunities to have students notice and discuss such language conventions as punctuation, capitalization, and sentence structures. The children's growing awareness of these patterns is readily evident in their writing. See Figure 6.7 for an example of writing from a first grader in late February of the school year. Alex's use of invented spelling since kindergarten contributes to the ease with which he writes. His book about money shows considerable command of his written expression as well as a clear indication of what he currently understands about the concept of money. This writing was not assigned; writing the book was his idea. Like many children in an environment that celebrates ideas and wonderment, Alex happily shares what he is learning, in the classroom and at home.

Daily writing is critically important to the development of young readers' comprehension ability. In fact, comfort with writing and the disposition to express ideas in writing must be established in the earliest days of school. Writing is a pure form of meaning construction. It provides powerful opportunities for youngsters to think creatively and critically. Writing also provides meaningful texts for reading—for the writers and their classmates

To summarize, primary-grade writing activities are most effective when:

- Learners write every day in their own words about topics and experiences of genuine interest to them.
- Writers use invented spelling so as to focus primarily on meaning.
- Writers share their compositions frequently by reading them aloud to classmates and by posting them for others to read.
- The teachers monitor students' writing, noting growth in their command of encoding, sentence structure, and organization of ideas and using the observations to plan instruction.

Creative Drama

The three teachers use creative drama on a regular basis with their classes, following the "acting out" principles presented by Moffett (1968a). Most often, the teachers encourage the children to do impromptu enactments of their favorite stories with simple props as

Figure 6.7

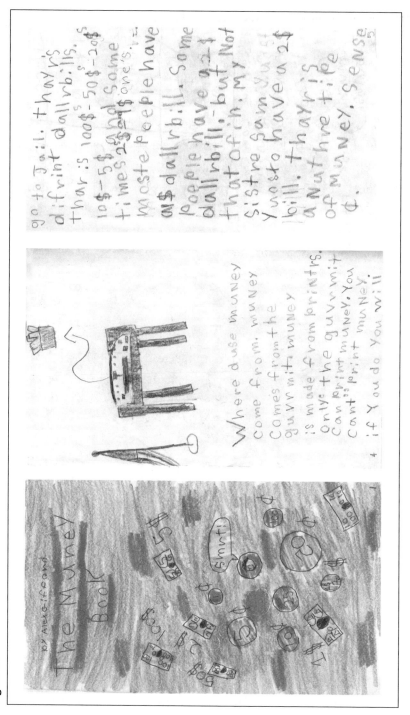

needed. The dramatizing gives children excellent opportunities to visualize and recreate the stories, thereby deepening their comprehension. For example, Ms. O's students love hearing her read *One Fine Day* (Hogrogrian 1971), the story of a fox that loses its tail and goes through a series of ordeals to get it back. The children ask to hear the story repeatedly, and it has become a favorite for creative drama. A favorite in Ms. K's class is *The Mitten* (Tresselt 1964), the story of how a lost mitten becomes the improbable winter shelter for one animal after another. The children engage in repeated enactments of the story. The second graders are most interested in enacting scenes from the chapter books and folktales they are reading. A few of the children have begun to write simple scripts, based on favorite stories, and to put on their plays.

To summarize, the use of creative drama is most effective when:

- Learners have regular opportunities for informal or impromptu enactments of familiar stories.
- Students are allowed to act out the same story repeatedly as long as they are still interested in it.
- With each enactment, students are encouraged to think about how they want to represent the story they have heard or read.

Metacognition

A strong metacognitive thread is evident in all three early literacy classrooms. The teachers model for students and discuss what good readers do, remind students to use these strategic behaviors, and celebrate the students' use of them. For example, the teachers demonstrate how skillful readers use the context as well as letter–sound clues to figure out unfamiliar words. When students encounter an unknown word, the teachers remind them: *Think about what you are reading. What word might make sense here? Does that word sound right? Does it look right?* Children come to understand that good readers use multiple cues and strategies when figuring out unknown words in texts. By beginning with the meaning cue in most instances, children are repeatedly reminded that reading should make sense. In addition, these teachers illustrate how skillful readers reread and rethink when something doesn't make sense. The students understand that good readers often reread text for clarification and better understanding. In all aspects of their literacy development, the children's learning is based on the metacognitive principle of being aware of how they are thinking and consciously using the known to learn the unknown.

To summarize, students learn to be metacognitive most effectively when:

- Teachers discuss with students how good readers think and what they do as they read.
- Teachers model metacognitive behaviors for students and remind them to engage in these behaviors as they read.
- Teachers encourage students to articulate what they are thinking before, during, and after reading.

Early Comprehension Instruction: What Effective Teachers Don't Do

We have focused on the exemplary practices of three teachers, but to some extent their teaching is also defined by what they *don't* do. For example, they spend little time teaching sounds in isolation, having students blend sounds to generate words, or assigning phonics worksheets. Nevertheless, their dedicated attention to patterns within and across words develops in their students a firm knowledge of letter–sound associations and the capacity to use that knowledge, along with context, to figure out unfamiliar words when they read.

Similarly, these effective teachers do not spend time drilling their students on high-frequency words. The children readily learn these words in the course of the meaningful reading and writing they do because they see and use them so often in different contexts. In addition, because Ms. O focuses on decoding by analogy and going from a known word to an unknown word, children begin to see patterns within high-frequency words such as *make* and *take*; *no, go, so*; and *would, could, should*. Consequently, the learning of the high-frequency words becomes far more manageable for both the teacher and the students.

These teachers also do not aim for students to reach a certain level of fluency (as measured in words per minute) as a prerequisite to comprehension instruction. They also do not have their children take turns reading texts aloud, a popular practice often called "round-robin" reading. Nevertheless, the students are developing their fluency from their many experiences with meaningful texts and the significant amount of oral reading they do in their daily activities. Choral Reading, Echo Reading, Buddy Reading, and the reading of dictated accounts and books with predictable language patterns all directly build fluency.

The teachers rarely use picture walks, an activity that involves students looking at all or most of the pictures in a book to discern the plot before they read the words. Although this is a common practice in many of today's primary-grade classrooms, we feel strongly that it tends to divulge too much information and detract from the pleasure of reading the story. If students already know the plot, reading the words is anticlimactic—more like an assignment than a means of discovery. Although the three teachers avoid picture walks as a standard practice, they do have students make use of pictures as they read to make initial predictions, revise predictions, and gain a better understanding of story events. The illustrations contribute to their comprehension, but their primary understanding comes from the meaning they construct with the print. When the text is a word-less picture book, the teachers also do not have the children "walk" through the whole book before they begin to read it together. Because the pictures tell the story, the teachers treat these books as regular texts, having students pause periodically to make predictions about the outcome based on the details in the pictures seen so far.

> *These effective teachers do not spend time drilling students on high-frequency words. The children readily learn these words in the course of the meaningful reading and writing they do.*

These teachers also rarely teach words before reading. For example, when Ms. O engaged her students in reading *Lost*, she did not prepare them by teaching them *elevator* or any of the other words in the story. She knew they knew most of the words and was confident that they would be able to figure out most of the unfamiliar words by combining the print context of language and meaning clues, picture clues, and their growing knowledge of letter–sound associations. Ms. O and the other teachers make note of any words the children have difficulty with and use those words, and words with similar features, in future word study activities. At all times, the teachers are less concerned with the children's ability to identify specific words than they are with their ability to use intelligent strategies for processing text and constructing meaning.

In addition, the teachers do not ordinarily refer to the children's activities as "work" in the sense of assignments to complete, nor do they suggest that unfamiliar words or texts are hard and that the going will be difficult. The perceptions shared by students and teachers are that substantive and enjoyable reading and writing are going on every day and that the children are developing solid capacities as readers and writers.

Program Continuity Across the Primary Grades

The teachers showcased in this chapter are admirably knowledgeable about language learning and teaching methodology. Seeing their programs in action demonstrates that meaning-oriented instruction is highly doable at these early grade levels. However, what these teachers accomplish as a team is their real strength. Students who are in these classrooms in their first three years of school do not have to adjust each year to new activities or new expectations because the programs are closely synchronized. The students develop their capacities each year in meaning-oriented contexts with ever more challenging texts, activities, and expectations.

Each teacher's program includes critical threads: student-dictated accounts; the study of words, phonics, and language patterns; independent reading; read-alouds; shared and collaborative reading; writing; creative drama; and, perhaps most important, guided reading with a focus on predicting or hypothesizing. These threads in the early literacy "rope" are complementary and interdependent. None is strong enough individually to develop literacy maturity, yet each has a significant contribution to make, and each enhances or strengthens the other threads (Hammond 1999). To remove even one weakens the whole.

The three teachers featured here base their instruction on what is known about how children learn. They give the children meaningful and engaging texts, from the students' dictated accounts and their own writing to a variety of books that are attractive, age-appropriate, and written to delight children. There are no contrived texts in these classrooms. The instructional materials, used in conjunction with the highly effective learning activities, develop in students a love of reading and the perception that reading is an enjoyable and stimulating meaning-making process.

Rethinking Early Literacy Instruction

We could say more about these teachers' instructional programs, but it is not our purpose here to provide detailed guidelines for teaching beginning reading. Rather, we simply make the point that delaying attention to comprehension until after so-called "basic skills" are in place fragments the reading process and leads students to lose sight of the purpose of reading.

The foundational principles for comprehension instruction in the early grades are compelling. Young children are natural meaning makers. They easily learn language and come to understand their world. When they begin reading and writing, they can readily use their natural inclination to make meaning if encouraged to do so. By allowing them to read engaging texts that make sense to them and by supporting them in doing so, we make the process of reading and learning to read easier and more satisfying for them. We ensure that making meaning is not only the goal of their reading but also is a major means by which they learn to read.

Unfortunately, prevailing trends periodically divorce early reading instruction from meaning. Reductionist and linear views of reading focus heavily on decoding skills as prerequisites and delay substantive attention to comprehension. To the everlasting credit of young children, they often tolerate this meaningless approach to learning to read. Perhaps they are simply used to doing what adults ask. Perhaps they have been informed that if they do the decoding exercises long enough, they will eventually be able to read real stories and books. However, we owe emergent readers more than skills instruction and delayed gratification.

A related issue is that early literacy instruction is too often polarized, forcing teachers to make either/or decisions: either phonics *or* comprehension, either invented spelling *or* spelling instruction. Such contrasts are unnecessary and unfortunate. Learning to read is about making sense, but it is also about using language, visual, and phonetic cues to process text. Writing is about constructing ideas but also about gaining command of writing conventions. All of the important components of literacy need to be addressed concurrently from the beginning, not introduced step by step in a linear fashion. Most importantly, the commitment to meaning making by both teachers and students must be real, transparent, and continual.

In the hundreds of primary classrooms that we have visited or worked in, we can say without reservation that meaning-oriented, comprehension-first instruction produces the highest rates of success and the most joy for both students and teachers. The children in these classrooms come to school eager to read and write and share what they are learning about the world. They return home each day confident that they are becoming skilled readers and writers and ever more capable learners.

CHAPTER 7

Reading and Thinking Without the Teacher

Much of what occurs in classrooms is under the teacher's direct supervision or guidance, but ultimately learners must learn to read and think independently because that is what they will be expected to do in successive grades and in their lives outside school. Thus, to a significant extent, teachers' efforts are best measured in terms of what students can do on their own both in the classroom, when the teacher is not right with them, and outside of school. Students can learn very early to function independently. Kindergarteners can learn to browse and read on their own. First graders can read independently and share in partners or triads. Primary-grade students can also write independently, either after conversing with the teacher or on their own without teacher prompting. As children mature, their independent performance can become more sophisticated, more extensive, and more effective.

At all grade levels, students need a balance of teacher-directed reading and self-directed reading. The two are natural companions and should not be placed in either/or opposition, but their relationship is critical. Ideally, teacher-directed activities prepare students for and complement their independent efforts. We address this important concept in this chapter. We also discuss two aspects of instruction that are critical to promoting self-directed reading: developing metacognition and building the capacity to handle vocabulary independently.

Independent Reading: The History and Rationale

Notable pioneers of independent reading were Jeanette Veatch (1959), Russell Stauffer (1969), Lyman Hunt (1970), and Walter Barbe (1961; Barbe and Abbott 1975). To a great extent these proponents were reacting to the dominance of controlled-vocabulary commercial reading programs of the 1950s and 1960s that took students in lockstep through basal readers and workbooks. These pioneers wanted to increase the variety, quality, and quantity of children's reading with a range of literature and informational texts from which students could choose. They also believed that children tend to read best and read more when they are genuinely interested in what they are reading, and they believed trade books to be more appealing than anthologies. Terms such as *personalized reading* or *individualized reading* were used to describe these programs. They either supplanted the basal or counterbalanced it. Stauffer (1969), for example, recommended a fifty-fifty balance between teacher-directed group reading of teacher-selected materials and individualized reading of self-selected materials. Central to these programs were classroom libraries of books so that students could choose from a wide variety of topics and genres across a range of reading levels. Classroom time for independent reading and teacher–student conferences about the reading were also central to these programs.

Sustained Silent Reading (SSR) emerged at about the same time, popularized by Fader and Shaevitz (1966). The intent was to increase the amount of time students spent reading, regardless of what they were reading. Paperbacks, magazines, and newspapers appeared in classroom libraries to provide even more appealing choices to students. Ordinarily, the teacher also read silently during SSR to demonstrate the importance of reading in the adult world. Conferences were not usually a part of SSR programs. Students simply read independently for a set amount of time every day and perhaps maintained a simple log to keep track of titles and daily page counts.

A belief in the importance of individualized, independent reading endures today, and some programs, such as Readers' Workshop, include significant time for independent reading. At all grade levels, teachers want students to enjoy reading, to function well when given time to read on their own, and to read widely outside of school. Some students do so, but many do not. All can benefit from an instructional program that develops and refines their capacities to become independent, self-directed readers and thinkers.

Fostering Independence in Readers

The key to fostering independence is to make the bridge between teacher-directed reading and independent reading as easy to traverse as possible. That can be done by guiding student reading in ways that develop independence and provide an effective variety of independent reading experiences to engage students and build their interest in reading.

Shaping the Guided Reading Experience with Independence in Mind

What students experience during guided reading strongly influences their independent reading behavior. Ideally, their experiences with guided reading lead to effective independent functioning. With that idea in mind, consider what students must do when they read independently in comparison with what they do in two different models of guided reading. Figure 7.1 highlights the comparisons.

Reflecting on the contrasting models leads us to conclude that the instructional practices of Guided Reading A encourage a form of dependency on the teacher when they are used routinely through the grades. For example, when the teacher habitually provides an overview of the text, students learn to count on such help and do not proceed well on their own in the absence of a teacher's overview. If teachers ordinarily set students' purposes for them, the students are not likely to set their own purposes when reading independently. When the teacher identifies and teaches most of the "new" or challenging vocabulary before reading, learners are deprived of the opportunity to learn how to handle such words on their own and may skip them or confront them ineffectively. When comprehension is defined as answering the teacher's questions, students are less likely to think about meanings on their own as they read.

What students experience during guided reading strongly influences their independent reading behavior.

We are not arguing against instruction or teacher direction; quite the contrary. We are arguing for the kind of teacher-guided instruction that develops effective habits of thinking and leads students toward resourceful independence. If teachers do the thinking for the

Figure 7.1

Two Guided Reading Models Compared with Independent Reading

Guided Reading A	Guided Reading B	Independent Reading
Before reading, the teacher provides background information.	The teacher aids students in accessing their prior knowledge.	Students must access prior knowledge on their own.
The teacher provides an overview or summary of the text.	The teacher invites predictions or hypotheses. Thinking ahead primes students for reading and shows them what they can do when reading on their own.	Readers must orient themselves to the text on their own.
The teacher addresses selected words before students read the text.	Students are encouraged to figure out words on their own as they read and to discuss words of their choosing after reading. Vocabulary instruction usually occurs after reading.	Readers deal with vocabulary on their own as they read.
The teacher typically conducts a "picture walk" to preview story events or informational topics.	The teacher guides students to use individual illustrations as they read when they become relevant to the students' reading purposes and understanding of the text.	Readers use illustrations on their own during reading as the illustrations become relevant to the readers' purposes and understanding of the text.
The teacher sets the purposes for reading.	The teacher guides students to set their own reading purposes by formulating predictions or hypotheses.	Students set their own purposes for reading.
Students often read the text orally.	Students read silently except when they read aloud segments to make specific points in discussion.	Students read silently.
After reading, the teacher poses questions to check students' comprehension.	The teacher facilitates discussion about what students discovered through reading, using questions they can use for reflection when they are reading independently.	Students reflect on their own about what they have read.

> *If teachers do the thinking for the students, they will not learn to think on their own, no matter how much teachers may model the process.*

students, they will not learn to think on their own, no matter how much teachers may model the process. For this reason, we think a major goal of guided reading must be to develop independence and self-direction while providing support for comprehension and thinking.

The dialogues in previous chapters show rich conversations among students, stimulated by but not dominated by the teacher. The instruction that promotes these conversations keeps students from becoming dependent on the teacher as they read and makes it more likely that they will perform effectively when the teacher is not present. Functioning well independently is important not only when students are reading for their own purposes but also when they are studying and when they are taking district or state assessments.

Engaging Students in Independent Reading Activities

In addition to teacher-guided activities that foster independence, an effective literacy program provides specific opportunities for students to engage in self-directed reading, individually and collaboratively. Of the various possibilities, we focus on three here that we consider especially valuable: independent literature discussions, the Interest Area Curriculum or Inquiry Circles, and individualized reading of self-selected materials.

Independent Literature Discussions

In an independent literature discussion, students meet to discuss books thoughtfully and responsibly without a teacher. The teacher's role is to develop the setting for student-led discussions, establish the procedures, debrief with students when appropriate, and be available when needed to support students in developing independence. When students meet in self-directed groups, they do so almost always as part of a balanced literacy program that includes instruction, selected guided reading, and an emphasis on writing. Some teachers allow children to choose their own reading selections; others arrange for the selection of literature related to a particular theme. Students may read an entire book and then gather to discuss it, or they may meet periodically during the reading to discuss their reactions and expectations. Some teachers use the Book Club program for these kinds of discussions, and some use Literature Circles. We discuss each briefly here. Because the two share some characteristics but have different features, we recommend further reading to understand the similarities and differences in the philosophies and practices associated with each.

Book Club emerged in the early 1990s as a literature-based response or alternative to the commercial basal reader programs commonly used at the time. The program is based on a strong foundation of social constructivism, with the belief that students need to read and discuss high quality literature. A substantive writing component is a critical feature as well. Central to the Book Club program is the Teachers Learning Collaborative, a strong network of teachers who share ideas and work together to refine their curricula and classroom practice. Book Club and Book Club Plus have been carefully monitored and studied by both practitioners and researchers. Children's work that emanates from the Book Club experience exhibits high levels of performance in thoughtful discussion, inquiry, and writing. For further information, see McMahon, Raphael, Goatley, and Pardo (1997), Raphael, Florio-Ruane, and George (2001), and Raphael, Pardo and Highfield (2002).

A related practice is known as Literature Circles. This activity involves students selecting their own reading material, with teacher guidance, and forming discussion groups based on their choices. Students prepare for their discussions and may meet several times in the course of reading the book they have chosen. Once students finish their books, the groups usually dissolve, and new ones form when the students decide what to read next. For further information on this and related practices, see Daniels (1994) and Harvey and Daniels (2009).

Students need preparation for such self-directed conversations to be fruitful and productive; they cannot simply be turned loose to talk. They need to have participated in teacher-guided reading experiences in which they have done the vast majority of the talking, listened carefully to classmates' ideas, raised and answered their own questions, and interpreted texts for themselves. They also need to have developed a strong age-appropriate sense of metacognitive awareness: knowing what it means to be a skilled reader and having practiced effective reading behaviors. Finally, they need to have developed facility with language in conveying their own ideas and a strong appreciation for the language used by authors.

Questions suggested in earlier chapters are highly useful in student-directed discussions. For example, when students meet periodically to talk about a narrative they are reading, they can use the questions similar to those presented in Figure 2.1, for example: *What is happening in our story? What were we thinking as we were reading? What interpretations are we making? What do we think might happen next? Why do we think so? How might the story end?* If the students have read the entire story, they can reflect on what they thought about these various questions as they were reading and can also use the postreading response options suggested in Chapter 2: discuss themes, compare the story with other narratives, respond metacognitively, and so on, as discussed on pages 40–41.

Keeping students on task in a discussion is sometimes challenging, even for a teacher. For a student leader, it can be a daunting task at first. Selecting an effective leader, helping a leader prepare, ensuring cooperation among the other members of the group, and debriefing with the students all help ensure a smooth process. Here are a few suggestions for each.

- **Selecting discussion leaders.** Most students have the capacity to be good leaders, but to get a group off to a good start, it is usually helpful to select a student who has what Gardner (1993) calls strong interpersonal intelligence. Natural leaders may or may not make the best facilitators; it depends on how readily they can take turns and encourage others to talk. Daniels (1994) and others have advised that all group members assume specific roles, such as a *vocabulary enricher, literary illuminator, illustrator, summarizer,* and so on. However, more recently Daniels has suggested that role assignments may actually restrict students' thinking and affect their ability to engage after the novelty of the roles wears off (Harvey and Daniels 2009). We agree with this assessment.

- **Preparing.** It is helpful for the teacher to meet with the discussion leader to talk about what the group might address and suggest an opening question, such as *What would you like to talk about?* or *Who would like to share their thinking about the story we are reading?* Usually this is enough to get the discussion started. The leader might also write down questions or issues to raise or might enlist a trusted peer to raise points or questions if other students are reticent. The teacher might also remind the leader to keep the discussion focused and to facilitate rather than dominate.

- **Ensuring cooperation.** Participants need to be schooled in their responsibilities as discussants: listen carefully, share time and ideas, avoid getting off task, and show the discussion leader the same respect and courtesy that they show the teacher. They must also come to the circle with ideas and issues they would like to talk about and may bring sticky notes or journal entries to share.

- **Debriefing.** A group debriefing can be very helpful. If things went well, the group can identify what they did that was effective. If things did not go as well as hoped, the group can focus on how they can be more effective in the future. Blame and negative comments should be avoided.

Independent literature discussions are powerful additions to any literacy program. They are used most often in second grade and beyond although some first-grade teachers use them effectively. However, no matter how successful and enjoyable they are, student-led discussions are complements to teacher-guided reading, not replacements for it.

The Interest Area Curriculum or Inquiry Circles

Besides discussing literature, students can also have self-directed conversations about informational text. The opportunity to study one concept or subject area in depth has considerable value. As Eudora Welty has remarked, "One place comprehended can make us understand other places better" (Ritchhart 2002, 11). Student choice of topic and reading material are critical elements in such investigations.

In our work some years ago with Russell Stauffer, we helped initiate a self-directed learning program that came to be known as the Interest Area Curriculum. We were influenced at the time by David Elkind's *World of Inquiry Schools* (Elkind, Dick, and Brown 1974). In such schools, students spent approximately half of the school day investigating and researching their own areas of interest. The same premise and procedures underlie the Inquiry Circles more recently advocated by Harvey and Daniels (2009). Although we like the term *Inquiry Circles*, we will use the term *Interest Area Curriculum* because it is the more familiar to us.

To begin an Interest Area Curriculum, teachers put aside commercially produced materials, including reading anthologies and skill exercises, and use their reading/language arts time for the self-directed inquiry. In the primary grades, the Interest Area Curriculum might last a week; in the upper grades, it might last a month or more. The procedures are extensions of the guided reading of informational text discussed in Chapter 3.

A third-grade class in a mid-Atlantic state provides a good example. The teacher began by asking students what they would most like to learn about if they had a choice and could devote several weeks to an investigation. Several expressed interest in birds and other animals; several wanted to learn about space travel; others wanted to learn more about Benjamin Franklin or other historical figures. Students could elect to work in small groups, in pairs, or individually.

The class devoted the first two days to deciding on topics, forming partnerships, and generating initial questions. One student, David, said he would like to learn more about bridges. Below is part of the conversation he had with the teacher on the first day:

Teacher: What is it about bridges that interests you?

David: Well, there are different kinds of bridges. Like drawbridges and just little bridges, but I think I want to learn more about really big bridges.

Teacher: Talk about that a bit.

David: There are a lot of bridges around here.

Teacher: Such as?

David: I've been over the Delaware Memorial Bridge and the Summit Bridge and the Chesapeake Bridge. I think they're called suspension bridges. We went over the Bay Bridge tunnel, which is really something. First you go over a bridge and then you go into a tunnel and then you go on another bridge and then another tunnel and then another bridge!

Teacher: Is that a suspension bridge?

David: I don't know. Maybe not. I think it has to have those high wires to be a suspension bridge.

Teacher: What do you wonder about these bridges?

David: One thing I wonder is how do they actually build them?

Teacher: Good question. Think about other questions like that. When you are ready later today or tomorrow, we'll meet again. You should probably write out some of your more important questions. Let's see if someone else is interested in bridges and might like to work with you. Your topic sounds very interesting, David!

The teacher had similar conversations with small groups and individuals for two days. The thoughtful discussions of topics and questions served to heighten interest and motivation even more.

When the teacher met with David the next day, he had worked out a number of questions that he wanted to investigate. He had talked to his parents about the topic, and they helped him shape his thinking, but the questions were clearly his:

How do bridge builders get started?

How do they get those columns at the bottom of the bay underwater?

Do the columns just sit there on the bottom?

Do they make the columns first and then put them in the water?

How long did it take to build the Chesapeake Bay Bridge?

How dangerous was it?

Which bridge was built first, the Delaware Memorial or the Chesapeake?

Who owns the bridges?

Why did they use tunnels for the Bay Bridge Tunnel, near Norfolk?

Were those islands already there?

What is a suspension bridge?

What is the longest bridge in the world?

When they build a bridge, how can they meet in the middle?

To deepen David's thinking, the teacher encouraged him to speculate on possible answers, and he enjoyed this. For example, he thought it would probably take four or five years to build a large suspension bridge and that the islands were already there for the building of the Bay Bridge tunnel. He thought perhaps the columns for suspension bridges were built and then put in the water, but he wasn't sure. His speculations and hypotheses framed his upcoming research and enhanced his sense of excitement.

For the next three weeks, David researched bridges, working almost entirely on his own, consulting the school and town libraries. He also wrote to three state authorities to request information. At the time, his school did not have access to the Internet, which would have been a welcome resource. He made notes and drawings of his findings. The large block of time each morning when he could research bridges became his favorite part of the school day. His interaction with his teacher was minimal but strategic; they discussed briefly what he was learning, where he would go next, and what additional resources he might use. He was mindful that he would have a chance to share with his classmates what he had learned, and he planned accordingly. David was not merely learning about bridges; he was learning how to learn and developing the confidence that comes from learning in depth.

David's efforts were similar to those of his fellow students, most of whom were working in pairs or small groups. One of his best friends was learning about automobile engines, and they often shared how they were getting their information and what they were learning. Their teacher circulated daily, able to give her full attention to supporting and guiding the students because she had been released from working through a prescribed curriculum.

The children did not work diligently all of the time. They socialized occasionally and spent time just looking through books without finding relevant information. However, they remained enthused and focused. Impromptu visits to the classroom convinced other teachers, the principal, and parents that something special was occurring. The children were intellectually engaged. They persevered. They worked collaboratively and individually. They made many of their own decisions about where to turn next in their inquiries, sometimes going to considerable effort to help each other find resources. They read widely and deeply and wrote purposely. Although the teacher's guiding hand was much in evidence, students did not need her close supervision on a continuous basis.

At the end of the four weeks, the students shared what they had learned in substantive and interesting presentations to the class. They explained things in their own words, showed illustrations they had made, talked with authority, and skillfully answered questions from classmates. Their engaging talks were reflective of the performances of understanding mentioned in Chapter 5. Following their foray into the Interest Area Curriculum, students returned to regular teacher-guided reading activities with commercial materials or trade books and also engaged in occasional independent literature discussions. They knew that in the coming weeks or months they would have more opportunities to immerse themselves in interest areas of their own choosing.

The Interest Area Curriculum was not an add-on at this school; it was the curriculum for a month at a time periodically during the school year. Able to concentrate entirely on the self-directed study during these times, the teachers embraced the opportunities with gusto. They supported students as they searched for answers, held frequent conferences with them, and monitored what they were learning about their topics, about reading, and about self-direction.

Our assessment of this program is subjective and mostly anecdotal. Standardized test scores tended to increase in reading, mathematics, and social studies. This should not be surprising because during the Interest Area Curriculum periods, students were reading and writing a great deal more than they usually did and were discovering quite a lot about their world that they shared

Students were learning, even in their early years of schooling, how to research and investigate ideas and concepts in an in-depth and sustained fashion, and doing so mostly in an independent and self-regulated manner.

with each other. Vocabulary development and concept learning were at high levels. Perhaps most significant was the impact on motivation and engagement that both teachers and parents noted and the resulting influence on students' attention and work habits. Students stayed focused for longer stretches, expressed considerable interest in what they were learning, and clearly enjoyed the workshop environment. Students were learning, even in their early years of schooling, how to research and investigate ideas and concepts in an in-depth and sustained fashion, and doing so mostly in an independent and self-regulated manner.

Individualized Reading of Self-Selected Materials

In a curriculum oriented to independence, a core component is the reading students do individually in self-selected books and other materials. There are at least three types of individualized reading, and each type has variations. All contribute to a comprehension-centered curriculum; all help students get better at reading by reading.

The first is the reading that students elect to do on their own with no responsibilities to report on what they are reading. Students may read fiction or may pursue an interest such as sports or horses. Much of this reading is done outside of school, but students may also keep a book nearby in class and choose to read it whenever they have extra time.

A second type of individualized reading is done when school time is set aside expressly for this purpose. The teacher ordinarily reads as well and does not monitor the students' reading except to ensure that each has access to texts and appears to be engaged in reading self-selected texts during the allotted time. This has become an integral part of many classroom programs, whether labeled Drop Everything And Read (DEAR), Sustained Silent Reading (SSR), or Uninterrupted Sustained Silent Reading (USSR). One caveat is important: All of the children must actually be reading. Good readers tend to value this time, but more reluctant readers may view it as downtime and only pretend to read. It is critical that even the most reluctant readers are engaged in reading. For a detailed discussion of this kind of reading, see Routman (2002).

A third type of individualized reading involves learners reading self-selected materials and conferring with the teacher periodically about what they are reading. At the elementary level, these conferences are typically one-on-one interactions in which the teacher invites students to talk about what is happening in their story, what they think of the characters, what might happen next, how the book compares with others by the same author, and so on. In sharing informational texts, students can talk about what questions they had when they began, what they are learning, and what they are currently reading to find out. Readers might also share favorite passages with the teacher. The key is to make the conference a conversation, not an inquisition. Teachers do not have time to confer with each student on each book read, nor is this necessary. Some have conferences with several students at once who are reading different books. Ordinarily these conversations center on a common theme or event that is relevant to each book. Students may also keep logs of what they are reading, and these can serve as the basis for conferences as well.

Allowing students to choose from a wide range of materials is critical to building their interest in reading. Classrooms at all grade levels must have books, magazines, newspapers, and other reading materials displayed enticingly. Ideally, the teacher talks briefly every few days about what is available, noting the contents of a book or perhaps reading a few lines to arouse interest. Most teachers at the elementary level do this as a matter of course, but it is just as important for secondary subject area teachers to have reading materials in their classrooms and to talk to the students about them. Science teachers can provide newspaper articles on scientific discoveries along with science-oriented books and magazines. Math teachers can showcase articles about the way mathematics is used in daily life along with books of logic puzzles or other popular math-oriented publications. And so on for the other subject areas.

In elementary classrooms, it is important to allow time every day for students to read self-selected materials and to increase the time from the beginning of the year to the end. The goal at all grade levels is to give students the experience of becoming engrossed in reading so that they derive genuine pleasure from reading. The sensation of enjoyment is most likely to lead them to acquire the habit of reading and to read even more outside of school than they do in the classroom.

When students are able to engage productively in self-selected classroom reading, an added benefit arises for the teacher: more flexible use of time, either to conference with children, aid in book selection, or perhaps conduct a guided reading group. For students, independent reading is almost always more beneficial to their

When students are able to engage productively in self-selected classroom reading, an added benefit arises for the teacher: more flexible use of time, either to conference with children, aid in book selection, or perhaps conduct a guided reading group.

growth as readers than spending the same amount of time working on skill exercises. Also, when students read more, they begin spontaneously talking about books and recommending books to each other. Individualized reading of all types can thus provide the foundation for group activities such as literature circles.

Some form of individualized, self-selected reading, with some combination of independent literature discussions and the Interest Area Curriculum (Inquiry Circles), will promote the development of students' literacy maturity. The balance among these activities may vary from class to class, grade to grade, and school to school, but all provide students with valuable opportunities for developing their language, cognition, and comprehension abilities.

Providing Opportunities for Metacognitive Thinking

Although we have alluded to metacognition in previous chapters, it merits special attention here because thinking about one's own thinking is so critical to independent functioning. We suggest five core metacognitive behaviors that are especially useful for readers to acquire. It is best for students to begin learning these in kindergarten and continue refining and internalizing them through the grades and across the curriculum. They are characteristic of skillful, self-directed readers.

- **I begin with what I already know and what I wonder.** For example, if I am going to read about the heart, I ask myself: *What do I already know about the heart?* Well, I know I have a heart. Everybody has a heart. Sometimes my heart beats really fast when I run or when I get nervous or excited. I wonder why? I know it is a pump and that it pumps blood. I wonder what makes it go? Your heart is in your chest and. . . .

- **I read with a purpose.** I know why I am reading and what I am reading to find out. I have questions I want to answer to satisfy my curiosity. I know that having clear purposes makes it easier for me to stay on task and keep my mind from wandering or daydreaming.

- **I always try to make sense of what I am reading.** I know that good readers really think to make sense of the text. We stop to think about whether we understand the text or if something is unclear. Sometimes we reread to clarify. Sometimes we read more to see if information further on will help us make sense of what we don't understand. We are always thinking as we are reading.

- **I ask myself questions before, during, and after reading.** Although I start reading with a few questions in mind, I ask more as I read. I keep wondering. If I am reading a story,

I'm always thinking ahead about what might happen next. If I am reading about a topic, I raise new questions as I read. After reading, I think about what I learned, what was most important, what was most interesting, and so on. I also think about which of my questions are still unanswered.

- **I know that rereading is often necessary to improve my understanding.** Even when I think I understand a text, I know that when I reread some portions of the text I will get more out of it than I did the first time. I may see things I missed or come up with new interpretations, or I may just remember it better because I took the time to reread it.

These behaviors turn into dispositions when students are aware of their relevance and begin to use them spontaneously. Some teachers place these statements on a wall chart or on bookmarks as a reminder and discuss the behaviors with students frequently. As several elementary school principals have said on numerous occasions: "No student should leave our school without knowing and practicing these metacognitive behaviors." These five dispositions are not a complete list. Individual teachers may add to them or modify them and, of course, express them in language that is age-appropriate. The key is to help students build their metacognitive awareness whenever they read. This serves students well from the primary grades through secondary school and beyond.

Similar behaviors are hallmarks of skillful, self-aware, and independent writers:

- **I write about what I think and what I know.** I share my ideas and my knowledge—in writing.
- **I write with a purpose.** I know why I am writing, what I want to say, and who my audience is.
- **I always think about what will make sense to a reader.** I reread what I have written to see if something is unclear or could be stated better or if I need to say more.
- **I know that revising almost always improves my writing.** Even when I think I have written well, I know that when I reread my draft critically I will see ways of improving it.
- **I edit my revised writing carefully.** I do my best to present my writing in the best possible way.

As mentioned in Chapter 4, group discussions provide excellent opportunities for metacognitive growth as students share their different viewpoints. We are reminded of an able graduate student and middle school language arts teacher who reflected in a university class one day: "You know, when I drove to campus this morning thinking about this literature selection we would be discussing, it never occurred to me that anyone would seriously interpret it differently than I did. Yet now I have an entirely different way of looking at it!" Such a response is not unusual. Most adults have similar experiences when discovering that others have different interpretations of a literary work. Group dialogues also open students' minds. Discussions of informational texts yield similar insights. Students see how their classmates focus on different aspects of the information, have different understandings, and find different concepts to be the most important or interesting. They also discover that however carefully they read, they may miss something that others note or, in turn, notice something that others overlook.

When learners regularly share different views in discussions, they are more likely to ask themselves when they are working independently: Is there another way of thinking about this? Is there another interpretation? Is there something I may have missed?

When learners regularly share different views in discussions, they are more likely to ask themselves when they are working independently: *Is there another way of thinking about this? Is there another interpretation? Is there something I may have missed?* This metacognitive questioning of their own thinking makes readers smarter and wiser. It is a "habit of mind" that is acquired as a result of accumulated experience (Costa and Kallick 2000) or a disposition that forms part of the learner's intellectual character (Ritchhart 2002). Students need regular opportunities and encouragement to think critically about their own perspectives and assumptions.

Students may shift into thinking about their own thinking at any point in a discussion. For example, a group of fifth-grade students were discussing Chapter 8 of *Hatchet* by Gary Paulsen (1987), in which Brian realizes that to survive the winter he must make a fire for warmth and safety. That night, he senses something (a porcupine) entering his shelter. Frightened, he throws his hatchet. It misses the intruder but hits a rock and creates a shower of sparks.

> ***Darian:*** I knew the hatchet was going to be important in this story but I didn't think about using it to make a fire.
> ***Gary:*** Brian didn't either until he had a dream about it.
> ***Judith:*** I didn't either. I didn't think about the sparks when I was reading it.

Teacher: Why do you think that was so?

Judith: I think I was so worried about what animal might be sneaking in the shelter that I didn't pay any attention to the part about the sparks.

Camille: Maybe it was a good thing the porcupine tried to get in the shelter and Brian had to throw the hatchet.

Ian: Oh. I hadn't thought about that.

In this snippet of thoughtful conversation, metacognitive responses arise naturally, without teacher prompting, because the students were so focused on the story. The teacher's question leads Judith to reflect further on her own thinking and results in a thoughtful insight about the selective nature of a reader's thinking.

Similar prompts spark metacognitive responses at any age or grade level when students are talking about informational text. In fact, the types of questions recommended in Chapter 3 put metacognition fully in play. Before reading informational text, questions like these require students to evaluate their own thinking: *Which idea do you think is the most likely? Which of these ideas are you relatively sure about? Which are you unsure about?* After reading, questions like these require students to express awareness of what they had learned and how their thinking had changed: *What do we now know that we didn't know before we began reading? Which things are still unclear or what questions are still unanswered?*

Metacognition can be a natural and integral part of discussions about texts if teachers ask the right kinds of questions. The more they make use of opportunities, the more likely the students will regularly reflect on their own thinking. This disposition can be strengthened throughout the school day when students are solving problems in mathematics, working in the science lab, learning to use different media in art, and so on. A metacognitive disposition helps learners act strategically and intelligently to attain higher levels of intellectual performance. As they reflect on their own behaviors, students become more self-reliant and thus able to perform well without close teacher support.

Growing Vocabulary and Language

Also relevant to our discussion of fostering independence is how best to teach vocabulary. This has been of concern to teachers for a long time. In recent decades, important research has contributed to our knowledge of how very young children learn language (Hart and Risley 1995; Wells 1986) and how children learn words in school (Nagy, Anderson, and Herman 1987; Nagy, Herman, and

Anderson 1985). More recently, others have framed the profession's thinking about the nature of vocabulary growth and have suggested instructional approaches (e.g., Beck, McKeown, and Kucan 2002). From this research, we can extrapolate a few fundamental principles:

- **It is possible to read a text, not know all of the words, and still understand the text quite well.**
- **It is possible to know the meanings of all of the words in a text yet not understand the text well enough to retain and make good use of the information.**
- **Most word learning is incidental, that is, not taught directly.** School-aged children learn on average about three thousand new words per year (Beck and McKeown 1991). Yet when researchers attempted to increase students' vocabulary through intentional instruction, they were able to teach the equivalent of about four hundred new words during the year (Beck, Perfetti, and McKeown 1982). Thus, intentional instruction can account for only a small percentage of the typical child's rapidly growing vocabulary.
- **Language, including vocabulary, is developed through interactions with others.** Talk, both in terms of quality and quantity, begets language and vocabulary development from birth through adulthood (Brown 1973; Wells 1986; Hart and Risley 1995; Nystrand et al. 1997). Similarly, the more widely and deeply students read, the greater their growth in vocabulary and their facility with language.
- **Vocabulary growth is always a work in progress.** It is not so much that a word is either known or unknown. Learners may have a notion of what a word means but are not comfortable using it, or they may understand a word in one context but not in another. They may also achieve deeper understandings of a word's meaning over time as they see it in different contexts and come to appreciate its many connotations.

With these principles as a foundation, we can construct a framework for vocabulary development that serves students well in school when working with the teacher or independently, individually or in a group, in or out of school.

Because talk facilitates vocabulary growth, rich conversations that enhance comprehension inevitably enhance vocabulary. The teacher's consistent use of a variety of words is also critical, including words and expressions that students may not have heard before. The profound effect that language interactions have on students' vocabulary cannot be overestimated.

It is generally accepted that vocabulary learning enhances comprehension. However, the opposite is also true: Comprehending texts enhances vocabulary learning. When students are

It is generally accepted that vocabulary learning enhances comprehension. However, the opposite is also true: Comprehending texts enhances vocabulary learning.

reading with a purposeful focus on understanding, they are highly attuned to the words and phrases they are encountering. They attend to word meaning because they are constructing meaning as they read and are less likely to skip over or ignore unfamiliar words.

Children who read often and read widely, purposely focused on meaning, encounter many more words and expressions than they hear orally. The context often provides adequate support for acquiring an understanding of many new words, and readers learn many new words almost effortlessly in this way. Each new text contains new words and concepts that engage learners' thinking and extend their understanding of word meanings. This happens most readily when the readability level of the material is appropriate to the student's own reading level. As a general rule, it is best to ensure that students spend most of their time reading materials that contain welcome but not overwhelming vocabulary challenges. When students are allowed to choose their own reading materials, they choose books that provide the right level of challenge most of the time or can readily learn to do so.

Retrospective discussion that focuses on students' attention to words while they were reading is also useful, especially when it reminds them of how much they can learn simply by thinking about word meanings as they read. For example, consider the word learning opportunities in the passage below.

Life During the Middle Ages

In the Middle Ages, people in Europe lived a way of life called *feudalism*. All the land was owned by the king or other important nobles, such as dukes or counts. A noble would allow less important people to use parts of his land by granting them certain rights. In return for the land, these people became the noble's vassals. Each vassal had to promise loyalty to the noble man, usually called the lord. The vassal would promise to fight for his lord and to give his lord weapons and men when the lord needed them. . . .

The nobles lived in castles with high walls made of stone. A castle was usually surrounded by deep ditch, filled with water, called a *moat*. . . .

The poorest people lived outside the castle on the estate of the noble. They were called *serfs*. The serfs worked as farmers and lived in small, crude homes near the fields. They could not protect themselves, so the noble watched over them. In return for noble's protection, the serfs gave the noble part of the food they grew. . . .

Several key words are defined or partially defined by the context: *feudalism*, *moat*, and *serfs*. Note how this teacher discusses words and word learning with students after the group has read the material, focusing on how the context can help.

Teacher: Let's talk about some of the words in this selection. Did you wonder about any of the words when you first read them?

Barney: The word *feudalism*.

Teacher: How did you handle that?

Barney: Well, I knew it was a new word for me, and then I read the rest of the paragraph.

Teacher: And?

Yvonne: It told us what *feudalism* was. It said there were kings and nobles who lived in castles. And they gave their land to vassals who agreed to fight for them.

Raymond: I didn't know what a serf was at first but then I read on and found out.

Teacher: OK. Any other words?

(The discussion continues.)

Not all contexts define words as well as this, but many do. Most importantly, the dialogue illustrates an effective conversation about words. The teacher is not simply telling the students meanings but is conducting a conversation about how language works and how to think about words. The specific words discussed were less important than the students' awareness of how new words might be learned and their developing disposition to think about word meanings as they read. It is this learning that will most help them when they are reading independently.

Deeper study of selected words also promotes vocabulary growth. The Frayer Model (Figure 5.1) may be used to build conceptual understanding. The word mapping procedure advocated by Schwartz and Raphael (1985) is another effective approach. These scholars contended that students often have difficulty developing a definition of a word or term because they lack a well-developed concept of what a definition is. They noted that most concepts are subsumed in at least one higher-order category, that each has properties or defining elements, and that each can be illustrated with examples. Once students understand how to use this structure for discussing words, they can use it independently. The following dialogue shows how another group of students mapped the word *moat* after reading the material about the Middle Ages. The diagram in Figure 7.2, following the format suggested by Schwartz and Raphael, is a record of their collaborative thinking.

Marc: So let's take the word *moat*. What is it?

Mario: Well, it is like a ditch that goes around.

Marc: It is, but can we think of a more general word?

Mario: *Barrier*?

Liz: That's it. That will work.

Summer: So it is a barrier. Now what are its properties?

Don: Well . . . It goes all the way around.

Maureen: It has water in it, I think.

Marc: And sides that are really steep.

Liz: And it is deep, usually.

Mario: So people can't cross it, without a bridge.

Marc: Is it just people?

Don: It could be animals, too.

Summer: That's true. I hadn't thought about animals.

Liz: So what are examples?

Marc: Well, around a fort to keep the enemy out.

Summer: Or maybe a village or settlement.

Mario: It could keep out people or wild animals maybe.

Don: I know. How about a zoo moat?

Maureen: What is a zoo moat?

Don: Sometimes zoos don't have cages. They keep the wild animals away from you with a moat.

Maureen: Does the moat have water in it?

Don: It could, but. . . .

Figure 7.2

Student-Created Word Map to Define *Moat*

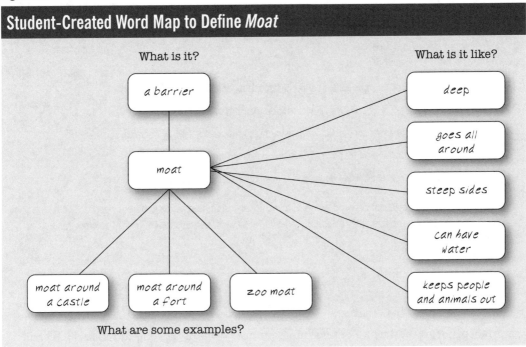

The conversation continued for a short period of time. Students were not merely defining a word but, more importantly, through conversation they were coming to understand what constitutes a definition of a word or term.

Conversations like this can seldom occur before reading. Students need the text as a foundation for concentrating on individual words. Focusing on a word within a now-familiar context is easier and more meaningful than learning the word before the context is known. Consequently, vocabulary is almost always addressed more effectively *after* reading than taught before reading. However, there are occasional exceptions. The criteria in Figure 7.3 can be used in making decisions about when to address vocabulary.

Using these criteria, a teacher can usually dramatically reduce prereading vocabulary instruction and engage students quickly with the text—much earlier than has traditionally been the case. This frees up time for students to access prior knowledge and

> **V**ocabulary is almost always addressed more effectively after reading than taught before reading.

Figure 7.3

Vocabulary: When to Teach (Hammond 1984)

The word is:

___ 1. Necessary for text comprehension and not defined by context

___ 2. Necessary for text comprehension and defined explicitly in text

___ 3. Necessary for text comprehension and defined implicitly or partially by context

___ 4. Not necessary for overall text comprehension but an interesting word

___ 5. Not necessary for text comprehension and has little interest or relevance at this time.

If condition 1 prevails, discuss the word before reading and revisit it after reading. If condition 2, 3, or 4 prevails, address the word after the reading. If condition 5 prevails, perhaps teach or discuss after the lesson or at a more opportune time.

use it for predicting or hypothesizing. Moreover, the teacher allows students to encounter new words independently and figure out meanings on their own. In the long run, this is preferable to being dependent on the teacher for word learning or on exercises that do not build independence. Of course, if students are unable to figure out a critical word on their own during reading, the teacher can always step in and provide timely help. The intention of the guidelines is not to force students to founder but simply to build independence.

Some students believe that unless they know the meaning of each word in a text, they cannot continue, and they shut down intellectually, to their own detriment. They can be greatly helped by realizing that although knowing the words is useful and important, it is often possible to solve problems, enjoy a story, or acquire new information without knowing all the words. For example, consider this story problem:

Mr. McCallister had received a letter from the Environmental Protection Agency that there was evidence that the roof on his shed contained asbestos shingles. He would be required to replace the roof. He would need six pallets of new shingles. Each pallet would cost $120.00. The labor for tearing off the old shingles and applying the new shingles would be $920.00. What will be the total cost for Mr. McCallister to replace his roof?

Now read the passage without the underlined words that might flummox many students. As you can see, the student who perseveres will probably be able to do the problem correctly because the underlined words are not essential to solving it. Imagine that this student is taking a high-stakes mathematics examination and each correct response is critical to reaching an acceptable performance level. Confident perseverance is an asset in this situation.

To read well independently, students cannot be intimidated by new words and unfamiliar language usage. Neither should they merely disregard them when they encounter them. Students need to believe they can figure things out on their own, and they must have the inclination to do so. Equally important, they need to see word learning as an interesting and enjoyable endeavor. The more engaging vocabulary learning is, the more attracted students will be to exploring word meanings with the teacher and on their own.

To celebrate vocabulary growth at any level, we offer the guidelines in Figure 7.4.

Students, and even some teachers, view vocabulary as a barrier to wide independent reading. After all, the thinking goes: *How can children read unless they know all of the words?* However,

Figure 7.4

Guidelines for Vocabulary Development (Hammond 1994)

1. Promote words. Talk about words. Discuss new words and old words with new meanings.

2. Have a word wall of interesting and unusual words.

3. Think not only in terms of words but also interesting phrases and sentences.

4. Teach in context, within real stories and texts.

5. Talk about how authors use words to convey just the right idea or meaning.

6. Encourage and compliment students when they show versatility with their oral and written language.

7. Make students aware of words. Help them understand that sometimes we encounter an unusual word, we think for the first time, then we see or hear that same word again and again. Chances are it has been there all along. We just haven't been attending.

8. Map words as recommended by Schwartz and Raphael (1985) or Frayer et al. (1969).

9. Play with words on occasion. For example, select a word such as *hit* or *run* and see how many ways the word can be used meaningfully: hit play, hit the ceiling, hit and run, take a hit, or run of luck, run a race, run for office, rerun, run down, and so on.

10. Remember that words are not just learned or unlearned. Vocabulary growth is always a work in progress.

when we examine what readers do when they read independently in real life, they seem to fare quite well and do not allow the presence of some unknown words to stand in their way. Just as importantly, teachers and students need to celebrate the opportunity to learn new words and phrases while becoming more attuned to the interesting ways that language can be used to convey meaning.

In summary, independent readers are best developed and nurtured when the instructional program includes these elements:

- guided reading procedures that promote independent reading and thinking
- a variety of independent and individualized reading activities that feature student-selected materials, student-directed inquiries, and student-led discussions and projects
- opportunities for students to think about their own thinking in ways that build a metacognitive disposition
- instruction that helps students navigate successfully through the challenging vocabulary and language conventions of texts on their own

A Framework for Rethinking Comprehension Instruction

Children's natural capacity for meaning making requires continual nurturing to flourish. The optimal conditions for growth include a balance of teacher-directed and self-directed activities that involve students in having real conversations about real texts and using what they know to learn more. Their classroom experiences greatly influence the behaviors and dispositions that they carry with them from one grade to the next and beyond the classroom into the world outside of school. They need more than assignments to complete. They need teachers who ask fruitful questions, provide useful feedback, promote investigation and discovery, stimulate metacognition, and encourage critical reflection. Also important is teacher timing: knowing when to intervene and when to allow students to proceed on their own; when to extend thinking and when to narrow the focus; when to change conversational direction and when to stay the course. The choices teachers make—from week to week, day to day, moment to moment—have a strong, cumulative effect on what students learn.

What we have proposed in this book is a rethinking of how we go about teaching children to read. Whether we can teach reading comprehension directly or explicitly is not a question that particularly interests us because we believe it to be the wrong question. The central question is: *What can teachers do on a day-to-day basis to enhance students' existing propensity for comprehension and high-level thinking?*

> *The central question is: What can teachers do on a day-to-day basis to enhance students' existing propensity for comprehension and high-level thinking?*

We know that effective daily instruction goes far beyond the mere teaching of skills or modeling strategies. We know it is based on a view of student strengths, not a deficit model of student weaknesses. We know that it begins not with what the teacher knows but with what the learners already know and can already do. We know that it is based on the premise that comprehension is first and always the priority, not on the premise that "first we learn to read and then we read to learn." We know that comprehension experiences must not be delayed until decoding skills are accurate and rapid. We know that students must read real texts that stimulate their interests and satisfy their curiosities and that they must *engage in* reading, not *learn about* reading. We know that effective instruction begins with a belief in the capacity of children to think critically and creatively: all children, whatever race, ethnicity, socioeconomic level, age, gender, or past levels of achievement.

Over many years of working in classrooms, we are continually amazed by the capacity of students to think, persevere, and engage in meaning making. The students clearly have what it takes. So if we are to promote the highest quality of reading and thinking in classrooms, we must look to our own beliefs and actions as teachers. We must reflect on the type, tone, and timeliness of our language. We must listen carefully to our learners and take our cues from what they are saying and what they already know. We must refrain from so much telling and performing and shift to facilitating inquiry and discovery. We must learn to ask the right questions at the right time: questions that promote deeper thinking and reflection. We must not view teaching merely as the daily selection of strategies or activities to do with students, and we must be wary of routines and rituals that lead students, and ourselves, to respond mechanically. We must be tolerant of errors and confusion and the wonderful messiness of teaching and learning. And finally, we must constantly work at our own craft. We need regularly to rethink what we are doing and why we are doing it so as to provide the best possible experiences for learners.

We conclude this chapter and the book with our thoughts about the kind of learning and teaching we would like to see in the classrooms of the future. Our vision is based on our view that reading instruction must consistently aim to build self-directed learners and thinkers.

- We would like comprehension to be seen as an extension of the meaning making in which students engage long before they start school, not something that occurs only after so-called prerequisite skills are taught and mastered. We would like to see the concept of "skill mastery" replaced with the concept of masterly, skillful reading.

- We would like to see reading instruction reoriented to the high-level thinking that most effectively engages learners intellectually and emotionally. When we teach in the way we have described in this book, learners are challenged to think critically and creatively, and they have a great time doing it. We would like all students to have the same kinds of exhilarating experiences daily.

- We would like to see students raise their own questions, search for answers, and use information instead of simply recall it. We would like to see the practice of asking comprehension questions replaced with thoughtful exchanges among students and teachers that develop the disposition to comprehend.

- We would like to see the power of curiosity unleashed, whether students are involved in guided reading or are pursuing self-selected materials for their own purposes. We would like to see students asking the questions more often than the teacher. When curiosity is the motivating force, finding answers brings the kind of satisfaction that sustains and enriches learning for all students.

- We would like to see students learning from teachers and enjoying their interactions with teachers but not becoming dependent on teachers. We would also like to see teachers genuinely value independence and self-direction in their students and neither want nor need them as dependents.

- We would like teachers to see themselves not as fonts of knowledge, examiners, entertainers, or managers but as orchestrators of satisfying comprehension experiences and facilitators of important conversations.

- We would like to see the K–12 community of teachers work together on the design of comprehension experiences so that consistent threads run from the primary grades through high school and beyond and so that teachers at all grade levels in all subjects have the same commitment to developing thinking readers.

Teaching children to read and think effectively is very likely the most challenging and yet most satisfying dimension of teaching, one that yields great benefits. Reading is a prime medium for developing the discerning, critical, and creative thinkers that are so essential for a productive life in a sustainable democratic society. Contributing to that effort and to conversations about the effort is a privilege as well as a great pleasure.

Now What Do You Think?

A Follow-up Invitation to Our Readers

Here are the statements you thought about before reading this book. We invite you now to consider them again and decide again if you agree or disagree. You may want to compare your earlier responses with your responses now. Under each statement, we have expressed our own views.

_____ 1. Much of what we know about reading comprehension has been discovered within the past two or three decades.

The history of thinking about comprehension includes the work of Huey and Thorndike in the early part of the twentieth century, Bartlett's seminal work in the 1930s, and the important work done at the Center for the Study of Reading in the 1970s and early 1980s. Our current knowledge is based on extensive historical foundations.

_____ 2. Classroom observation studies indicate that teachers in grades 1–6 spend a significant amount of time teaching students how to comprehend texts.

Durkin's classic study is sobering. However, she did her research in the late 1970s. Since then, to a large extent in response to her work, teachers have given more attention to teaching comprehension. However, Durkin's real message is that assessing comprehension is not the same as teaching comprehension. That caveat is as pertinent today as ever, especially given the current heavy emphasis on assessment. A related issue is whether teaching comprehension strategies is synonymous with comprehension instruction.

_____ 3. Young children are predisposed to make sense of their world, including understanding the texts they read in school.

Young children have a natural disposition to construct understanding. When literacy curricula are focused primarily on comprehension from the very start, children learn to read and write as easily and smoothly as possible. However, although making sense of the world is a natural process, learners still need effective instruction to become effective readers and thinkers.

_____ 4.   The anticipation or prediction of upcoming story events motivates students and enhances their comprehension.

Prediction arouses curiosity, which motivates students to read. Predicting also engages students' prior knowledge, enhances their comprehension, builds their capacity for critical thinking, and has a positive impact on their overall attitude toward reading. A rich discussion of predictions, and the thinking behind them, is one of the surest ways to engage students in comprehending and enjoying narratives.

_____ 5.   It is normal for several students to read the same story and generate different interpretations.

Not only is this normal, but such differences should be expected and encouraged. Because readers are different, they will legitimately construct various interpretations. Discussing these variations encourages students to consider their own ideas in light of others' ideas, a key element of critical thinking.

_____ 6.   Extensive preparation before reading enhances students' understanding of a narrative text.

We find it unnecessary to teach vocabulary, provide an overview of the story, or invite students to share their personal experiences before reading. Too many of these activities build dependencies in students. We prefer inviting predictions and then moving into the story quickly. We have each done this successfully for many years.

_____ 7.   It is a good technique to teach a skill or strategy before reading a story so that students can immediately practice it as they read.

Beginning a reading experience with skill or strategy instruction has serious disadvantages. First, the likely message is that learning to read is about learning a technique and the purpose of the reading is to practice that technique. Second, focusing on a skill or strategy while reading may distract students from constructing meaning. Finally, strategy or skill instruction before reading is usually done out of context for learners and thus is not as effective as it could be. It is better to use the experience of reading and the context of the story as a basis for discussing selected skills or strategies.

_____ 8. A strong emphasis on explicit instruction in skills and strategies is a major priority when the goal is developing critical and thoughtful readers.

We have reservations about what has become a mantra for the literacy profession. We see many examples of so-called explicit instruction that are not helpful or productive for students. The term itself is difficult to define and means different things to different people. Explicitness should not be a criterion for gauging what constitutes instructional effectiveness. Perhaps as a profession we are confusing strategy instruction with comprehension instruction. They are not the same.

_____ 9. Prior knowledge is a critical factor in the successful reading of informational texts.

We view prior knowledge as the most critical factor in the reading of informational texts. Of course, some ways of accessing and using prior knowledge are more effective than others. It's important for teachers to become skilled at having students use their preconceptions to generate hypotheses about what they are going to be learning.

_____ 10. A student's misconceptions about a topic should be minimized or corrected before the student reads an informational text about the topic.

Students bring to their learning a host of preconceptions. The key is to get them out in the open, whatever they are. The act of reading for students then becomes a dynamic process of confirming what they already know and, more importantly, discovering new ideas and information. We cannot emphasize too strongly that teachers and students should not be afraid of misconceptions. In order to teach well, we have to understand what students know and how they think. That is really the essence of teaching.

____ 11. Allowing students to share their misconceptions with peers may inhibit the comprehension and learning of the other students.

If students are going to share their preconceptions in class, their peers will inevitably hear misconceptions. There is absolutely no evidence, empirical or otherwise, that this is detrimental to learning. When students see their teacher actually encouraging them to be tentative, to risk being wrong, they can relax and explore their thinking fully. Of course, initial misconceptions can be addressed in substantive postreading discussions.

____ 12. The process of reading informational texts tends to be similar across the various subject areas (e.g., science, social studies, math, health).

The process of acquiring information in different subject areas is very similar. We begin with what we already know and move from there to explore what we don't know. We read with hypotheses in mind and ask ourselves questions as we read. We often reread for clarification and deeper understanding. These are common cognitive practices that facilitate comprehension in any subject.

____ 13. Talking is a primary vehicle for constructing meaning.

Talking is indeed a medium for constructing meaning. Often we say that we need to "talk it through" when we have an issue to understand or a knotty problem to solve. We can talk with others or with ourselves. It is through talking that we clarify and negotiate meaning. For the talk among learners to be effective, it must be focused and thoughtful.

____ 14. One of the most effective ways to improve the quality of student talk is to change the nature of teacher talk.

We cannot emphasize too strongly that the nature of teacher talk in classrooms determines the quality of student talk, as the dialogues in this book illustrate. When teachers give up the floor, so to speak, and ask the right kinds of questions, they invite students to converse with each other in more productive and beneficial ways. Teachers who use talk merely to tell, explain, or elicit correct answers will restrict student thinking and learning.

_____ 15. Writing is a major means of fostering comprehension and learning.

Writing leads writers to examine and clarify their own thinking and thus is a major aid to comprehension and learning. Writing involves constructing meanings and reflects the writer's thinking. Writing about a text enhances comprehension because the writers must reflect on the ideas and state them in their own words. Doing so puts the writer's attention firmly on the information in the text, and that enhances comprehension.

_____ 16. First students learn to write, and then they write to learn.

Students should be writing to learn from the very beginning. Even preschool children who engage in scribbling are stating their ideas and their understanding of the world. Their inclination to communicate understandings needs to be encouraged and nurtured. Delaying an early focus on content (usually to concentrate on spelling or other mechanics) deprives children of the opportunity to engage in meaningful written expression. Imagine discouraging very young children from talking until they can articulate well and speak in complete sentences. No one would argue for that, and it's the same with writing. It's important for parents and teachers to celebrate first attempts at both speech and writing to focus children's attention on meaning.

_____ 17. Writing models and frames can develop student dependency.

These aids to writing provide useful illustrations of how to organize and convey ideas, and reluctant writers may write more easily when using them, but students can become dependent on them if they are used too frequently or for too long a period of time. Students need many opportunities to organize and state their ideas as they wish, without feeling they need to stay within boundaries specified by others.

_____ 18. At any grade level, the primary focus of writing should be on the quality of the content.

The content is indeed the most important aspect of student writing at all grade levels. In the earliest grades, it is paramount because it is at this time that young writers are developing their confidence as writers and their attitudes toward writing. Too much emphasis on mechanics can reduce students' confidence and lessen their interest in writing. As they develop confidence, they can pay more attention to language usage, sentence structure, spelling, and so on.

____ 19. The long-held view that first children learn to read and then read to learn is still viable in today's schools. This is contrary to what we know about reading comprehension. Young children are reading to learn from the very beginning. Even preschool children are curious about what is happening in a story. They ask questions, they interpret pictures, and they want to turn the page to find out what happens next. They are also eager to learn from informational texts. Reversing the mantra yields a statement that is a much better guide: Read to learn and you will learn to read.

____ 20. Word recognition must be accurate and rapid before sufficient attention can be directed to comprehension.
We reject this argument as applied to reading. The relationship between decoding and comprehension is not either/or; nor is it sequential in nature. When students are making sense of what they are reading, their word processing (decoding) is actually enhanced. At the same time, skillful word recognition helps to increase the potential for understanding. Readers fare best when comprehension is their priority from their earliest reading experiences and when their teachers understand the complementary relationship between comprehension and decoding.

____ 21. When students read text orally to a teacher or classmates, their comprehension is usually enhanced. For more than a hundred years, the best scholars in our profession have asserted that students need to read silently when the goal is comprehension, so it is a mystery why round-robin oral reading continues to flourish in many classrooms and schools. When we want children to think about what they are reading, they should not be worrying about performing flawlessly in front of their teacher or classmates. Oral reading can be used for sharing ideas or reflecting on the craft of an author, but in those situations learners have read the text silently first and are rereading it orally to support what they are saying about the text. "Silent reading precedes oral reading" used to be a standard guideline and should again be embraced. Students at the earliest stages of literacy development are the exception. Their reading aloud serves as a kind of feedback mechanism. This behavior disappears as they mature.

____ 22. An effective way of enhancing vocabulary growth is to address vocabulary after the reading of the text.

Attending to vocabulary after reading allows students to use the context of the text to talk about words in the text. Vocabulary instruction before reading is almost always out of context for the learner and makes word learning more difficult and less interesting. We have embraced this principle for many years and are pleased to see a trend beginning to develop in this direction.

____ 23. Effective comprehension instruction usually begins with teacher modeling.

We think effective comprehension instruction begins with what the learners already know and can do. Modeling is most effective after students have engaged in some learning experiences and want to observe someone else demonstrate a relevant behavior. So we view with skepticism the advice: "Begin by modeling. . . ."

____ 24. Thinking about one's own thinking is critical to effective independent reading.

Students' understanding of what good readers and writers do, their awareness of their own reading and writing behaviors, and their reflections on their own thinking all lead to self-sufficiency. Metacognitive awareness empowers learners, helping them think for themselves and gain control over their own learning. Engaging students in metacognition is important at all ages and grade levels.

____ 25. An important measure of effective literacy instruction is how readers perform when the teacher is not present.

Some students perform quite well in the presence of a teacher but seem lost when the teacher is not there to provide directions and make decisions for them. Students cannot be considered fully skillful readers and writers until they have developed the capacity to sustain their reading and writing independently. Excellent teachers cultivate independence, taking pride in students who can think for themselves and perform responsibly and productively on their own. It is not simply a case of turning students loose to proceed on their own, however. Instruction must have features that encourage and support independence. This is an important, though often overlooked, goal of teaching.

References

Aaronson, E., N. Blaney, C. Stephen, J. Sikes, and M. Snapp. 1978. *The Jigsaw Classroom.* Beverly Hills, CA: Sage.

Adler, M. 1940. *How to Read a Book: The Art of Getting a Liberal Education.* New York: Simon & Schuster.

Adler, M. J. 1982. *The Paideia Proposal: An Educational Manifesto.* New York: Macmillan.

Allington, R. L. 2007. "Proven Programs, Profits, and Practice." Keynote presentation at the National Reading Recovery & K–6 Classroom Literacy Conference, Columbus, OH, February 3–6.

Allington, R., and P. Johnston. 2002. *Reading to Learn: Lessons from Exemplary Fourth-Grade Classrooms.* New York: Guilford.

Anderson, R. C., E. H. Hiebert, J. A. Scott, and I. A. G. Wilkinson. 1985. *Becoming a Nation of Readers: The Report of the Commission on Reading.* Washington, DC: National Academy of Education, Commission on Education and Public Policy.

Anderson, R. C., R. E. Reynolds, D. L. Schallert, and E. T. Goetz. 1977. "Frameworks for Comprehending Discourse." *American Educational Research Journal* 14: 367–81.

Applebee, A. N. 2000. "Alternative Models of Writing Development." In *Writing: Research/Theory/Practice*, edited by R. Indrisano and J. R. Squire. Newark, DE: International Reading Association.

Applebee, A. N., R. Burroughs, and A. S. Stevens. 1994. *Shaping Conversations: A Study of Continuity and Coherence in High School Literature Curriculum.* Report Series 1.11. Albany, NY: National Research Center on Literature Teaching and Learning, State University of New York at Albany.

———. 2000. "Creating Continuity and Coherence in High School Literature Curricula." *Research in the Teaching of English* 34: 396–429.

Applebee, A. N., J. A. Langer, M. Nystrand, and A. Gamoran. 2003. "Discussion-Based Approaches to Developing Understanding." *American Educational Research Journal* 40 (3): 685–730.

Atwell, N. 1989. *Coming to Know: Writing to Learn in the Intermediate Grades.* Portsmouth, NH: Heinemann.

Bakhtin, M. M. 1986. *Speech Genres & Other Late Essays.* Translated by V. M. McGee. Edited by C. Emerson and M. Holquist. Austin, TX: University of Texas Press.

Barbe, W. 1961. *Educator's Guide to Personalized Reading Instruction.* Englewood Cliffs, NJ: Prentice Hall.

Barbe, W., and J. L. Abbott. 1975. *Personalized Reading Instruction.* West Nyack, NJ: Parker Publishing.

Bartlett, F. C. 1932. *Remembering: A Study in Experimental and Social Psychology.* Cambridge, U.K.: Cambridge University Press.

Bear, D. R., M. R. Invernizzi, S. Templeton, and F. Johnston. 2007. *Words Their Way: Word Study for Phonics, Vocabulary, and Spelling Instruction*, 4th ed. Upper Saddle River, NJ: Prentice Hall.

Beck, I., and M. McKeown. 1991. "Conditions of Vocabulary Acquisition." In *Handbook of Reading Research*, Vol. II, edited by R. Barr, M. Kamil, P. Mosenthal, and P. D. Pearson, pp. 789–814. White Plains, NY: Longman.

Beck, I. L., M. G. McKeown, and L. Kucan. 2002. *Bringing Words to Life*. New York: The Guilford Press.

Beck, I. L., C. A. Perfetti, and M. G. McKeown. 1982. "Effects of Long-Term Vocabulary Instruction on Lexical Access and Reading Comprehension." *Journal of Educational Psychology* 74: 506–21.

Betts, E. A. 1946. *Foundations of Reading Instruction*. New York: American Book.

Bingham, N. 2000. Creative Disequilibration. Paper presented at the annual conference of the Association for General and Liberal Studies, Chicago, IL, November 2, 2000.

Bomer, R. 1995. *Time for Meaning: Crafting Literate Lives in Middle & High School*. Portsmouth, NH: Heinemann.

Brady, M. 2008. "Cover the Material—or Teach Students to Think?" *Educational Leadership* 65 (5): 64–67.

Bransford, J. D., A. L. Brown, and R. R. Cocking (Eds.). 2000. *How People Learn: Brain, Mind, Experience, and School*. Washington, DC: National Academy Press.

Britton, J. 1967. "The Speaker." In *Talking and Writing: A Handbook for English Teachers*, edited by J. Britton. London: Methuen Educational.

———. 1970. *Language and Learning*. Harmondsworth, England: Penguin.

———. 1982. "A Reader's Expectations." In *Prospect and Retrospect: Selected Essays of James Britton*, edited by G. M. Pradl. Montclair, NJ: Boynton/Cook.

Brown, A. 1980. "Metacognitive Development and Reading." In *Theoretical Issues in Reading Comprehension*, edited by R. J. Spiro, B. Bruce and W. F. Weaver. Hillsdale, NJ: Lawrence Erlbaum Associates.

Brown, J., K. S. Goodman, and A. M. Marek. 1996. *Studies in Miscue Analysis: An Annotated Bibliography*. Newark, DE: International Reading Association.

Brown, M. W. 1949. *The Important Book*. New York: HarperCollins.

Brown, R. 1973. *A First Language*. Cambridge, MA: Harvard University Press.

Bruner, J. 1960. *The Process of Education*. Cambridge, MA: The President and Fellows of Harvard College.

Bruner, J., J. Goodnow, and A. Austin. 1956. *A Study of Thinking*. New York: Wiley.

Butler, P. 2002. "Imitation as Freedom: (Re)forming Student Writing." *The Quarterly* 24 (2). Available at: www.nwp.org/cs/public/print/resource/361. Accessed June 4, 2011.

Buzan, T., and B. Buzan. 1993. *The Mind Map Book: How to Use Radiant Thinking to Maximize Your Brain's Untapped Potential*. New York: Penguin.

Byars, B. 1981. *The Midnight Fox*. New York: Penguin.

Campbell, R., and D. Green. 2006. *Literacies and Learners: Current Perspectives*, 3d ed. Frenchs Forest, NSW, Australia: Pearson.

Carle, E. 1969. *The Very Hungry Caterpillar.* New York: World.

Cazden, C. 2001. *Classroom Discourse: The Language of Teaching and Learning*, 2d ed. Portsmouth, NH: Heinemann.

Chall, J. S. 1983. *Stages of Reading Development.* Chapter 4. New York: McGraw-Hill.

Chall, J. S., and V. A. Jacobs. 2003. "The Classic Study on Poor Children's Fourth-Grade Slump." *American Educator* 27 (1): 14–15, 44.

Chall, J. S., V. A. Jacobs, and L. E. Baldwin. 1990. *The Reading Crisis: Why Poor Children Fall Behind.* Boston, MA: Harvard University Press.

Costa, A., and B. Kallick. (Eds.). 2000. *Discovering and Exploring Habits of Mind.* Alexandria, VA: Association for Supervision and Curriculum Development.

Courlander, H., and W. Leslau. 1950. "The Fire on the Mountain." In *The Fire on the Mountain and Other Ethiopian Stories*, by H. Courlander and W. Leslau. New York: Holt, Rinehart & Winston.

Covey, S. 1989. *The Seven Habits of Highly Successful People.* New York: Simon & Schuster.

Cowley, J. 1999. *Mrs. Wishy Washy.* New York: McGraw-Hill Wright Group.

Cox, T., Jr. 2001. *Creating the Multicultural Organization: A Strategy for Capturing the Power of Diversity.* San Francisco: Jossey-Bass.

Cramer, R. L. 1968. An Investigation of the Spelling Achievement of Two Groups of First Grade Classes on Phonetically Regular and Irregular Words and in Written Composition. Unpublished doctoral dissertation. Newark, DE: University of Delaware.

———. 2001. *Creative Power: The Nature and Nurture of Children's Writing.* Boston: Addison-Wesley Longman.

———. 2004. *The Language Arts: A Balanced Approach to Teaching Reading, Writing, Listening, Talking and Thinking.* Boston, MA: Pearson.

Daniels, H. 1994. *Literature Circles: Voice and Choice in the Student-Centered Classroom.* Portland, ME: Stenhouse.

Davis, F. 1944. "Fundamental Factors of Comprehension in Reading." *Psychometrika* 9 (3): 185–97.

Dewey, J. 1910. *How We Think.* Boston: D. C. Heath.

Dewitz, P., J. Jones, and S. Leahy. 2009. "Comprehension Strategy Instruction in Core Reading Programs." *Reading Research Quarterly* 44 (2): 102–26.

Dixon, C. N., and D. D. Nessel. 1992. *Meaning Making: Directed Reading & Thinking Activities for Second-Language Students.* Englewood Cliffs, NJ: Alemany Press.

Dorros, A. 1994. *Elephant Families.* New York: HarperCollins.

Duckworth, E. 1996a. "Teaching as Research." In *The Having of Wonderful Ideas and Other Essays on Teaching and Learning*, 2d ed., by E. Duckworth. New York: Teachers College Press.

———. 1996b. "The Having of Wonderful Ideas." In *The Having of Wonderful Ideas and Other Essays on Teaching and Learning*, 2d ed., by E. Duckworth. New York: Teachers College Press.

———. 1996c. "Twenty-Four, Forty-two, and I Love You: Keeping It Complex." In *The Having of Wonderful Ideas and Other Essays on Teaching and Learning*, 2d ed., by E. Duckworth. New York: Teachers College Press.

Durkin, D. 1978–1979. "What Classroom Observations Reveal About Reading Comprehension Instruction." *Reading Research Quarterly* 14 (4): 481–533.

Dykstra, D. I. 2005. "Against Realist Instruction: Superficial Success Masking Catastrophic Failure and an Alternative." *Constructivist Foundations* 1 (1): 49–60.

Eisner, E. W. 2002. "What Can Education Learn from the Arts About the Practice of Education?" In *The Encyclopedia of Informal Education*. Available at: www.infed.org/biblio/eisner_arts_and_the_practice_of_education.htm. Accessed June 4, 2011.

Elbow, P. 1994. *Writing for Learning—Not Just for Demonstrating Learning*. Amherst, MA: University of Massachusetts.

———. 2004. "Write First: Putting Writing Before Reading Is an Effective Approach to Teaching and Learning." *Educational Leadership* 16 (2): 8–14.

Elkind, D., S. Dick, and C. Brown. 1974. *Evaluation of World of Inquiry School, Final Report*. Rochester, NY: University of Rochester.

Fader, D., and M. H. Shaevitz. 1966. *Hooked on Books*. New York: Berkley.

Festinger, L. 1957. *A Theory of Cognitive Dissonance*. Stanford, CA: Stanford University Press.

Flavell, J. H. 1976. "Metacognitive Aspects of Problem Solving." In *The Nature of Intelligence*, edited by L. B. Resnick, 231–36. Hillsdale, NJ: Erlbaum.

Flynn, R. M. 2007. *Dramatizing the Content with Curriculum-Based Readers Theatre, Grades 6–12*. Newark, DE: International Reading Association.

Frayer, D., W. C. Frederick, and H. J. Klausmeier. 1969. *A Schema for Testing the Level of Cognitive Mastery*. Madison, WI: Wisconsin Center for Education Research.

Freebody, P., C. Ludwig, and S. Gunn. 1995. *Everyday Literacy Practices in and out of Schools in Low Socio-Economic Urban Communities*. Brisbane, Australia: Centre for Literacy Education Research, Griffith University.

Freeman, E. B. 1991. "Informational Books: Models for Student Writing." *Language Arts* 68 (6): 470–73.

Fulwiler, T., and A. Young (Eds.). 2000. *Language Connections: Writing and Reading Across the Curriculum*. WAC Clearinghouse Landmark Publications in Writing Studies. Available at: http://wac.colostate.edu/books/language_connections/. Accessed June 4, 2011. Originally published in print in 1982 by National Council of Teachers of English, Urbana, Illinois.

Gagne, R. M. 1965. *The Conditions of Learning*. New York: Holt, Rinehart & Winston.

Gardner, H. 1993. *Multiple Intelligences: The Theory in Practice*. New York: Basic Books.

Gentry, J. R. 1981. "Learning to Spell Developmentally." *The Reading Teacher* 34: 378–81.

Gick, M. L., and K. J. Holyoak. 1980. "Analogical Problem Solving." *Cognitive Psychology* 12: 306–55.

Glasser, W. 1992. *The Quality School: Managing Children Without Coercion*, 2d ed. New York: HarperCollins.

Goodman, K. 1967. "Reading: A Psycholinguistic Guessing Game." *Journal of the Reading Specialist* 6: 126–35.

———. 1969. "Analysis of Oral Reading Miscues: Applied Psycholinguistics." *Reading Research Quarterly* 5: 9–30.

Goodman K., and C. Burke. 1973. *Theoretically Based Studies of Patterns of Miscues in Oral Reading Performance*. Final report. Project No. 9-0375, Grant No. OEG-0-9-323075-4269. Washington, DC: U.S. Department of Health, Education, and Welfare.

Gough, P. B., and W. E. Tunmer. 1986. "Decoding, Reading and Reading Disability." *Remedial and Special Education* 7: 6–10.

Graham, S., and M. Hebert. 2010. *Writing to Read: Evidence for How Writing Can Improve Reading. A Carnegie Corporation Time to Act Report*. Washington, DC: Alliance for Excellent Education.

Graham, S., and D. Perin. 2007. *Writing Next: Effective Strategies to Improve Writing of Adolescents in Middle and High Schools*. New York: Carnegie Corporation.

Hamel, G. 2009. "The Facebook Generation vs. the Fortune 500." *Wall Street Journal Blogs*. March 24. Available at: http://blogs.wsj.com/management/2009/03/24/the-facebook-generation-vs-the-fortune-500. Accessed June 4, 2011.

Hammond, W. D. 1984. "Vocabulary: When to Teach." In *Reading Comprehension: Make Every Child a Winner*, edited by D. Hammond, D. Nessel, and J. Thelen. A Learning Institute Coursebook. Belmont, CA: Learning Institute.

———. 1994. "Often Asked Questions About Vocabulary Development." In *Treasury of Literature Staff Development Guide—Intermediate*, 44–47. Orlando, FL: Harcourt Brace.

———. 1999. "A Balanced Early Literacy Curriculum: An Ecological Perspective." In *Early Literacy for the New Millennium*, edited by D. Hammond and T. Raphael. Ann Arbor, MI: Center for the Improvement of Early Reading Achievement.

Hart, B., and R. T. Risley. 1995. *Meaningful Differences in the Everyday Experience of Young American Children*. Baltimore: Paul H. Brookes.

Harvey, S., and H. Daniels. 2009. *Comprehension & Collaboration: Inquiry Circles in Action*. Portsmouth, NH: Heinemann.

Hattie, J. 2009. *Visible Learning: A Synthesis of Over 800 Meta-Analyses Relating to Achievement*. New York: Routledge.

Henderson, E. H., and J. W. Beers (Eds.). 1980. *Developmental & Cognitive Aspects of Learning to Spell: A Reflection of Word Knowledge*. Newark, DE: International Reading Association.

Herber, H. 1978. "Teaching Reading in the Content Areas." Englewood Cliffs, NJ: Prentice Hall.

Hillebrand, R. 2004. "Beyond Primer Prose: Two Ways to Imitate the Masters." *The Quarterly* 26 (2). Available at: www.nwp.org/cs/public/print/resource/1792. Accessed June 4, 2011

Hillocks, G., Jr. 1986. *Research on Written Composition: New Directions for Teaching.* Urbana, IL: ERIC Clearinghouse on Reading and Communication Skills and the National Conference on Research in English. ED 265 552.

Hogrogrian, N. 1971. *One Fine Day.* New York: Macmillan.

Hoguet, S. 1983. *I Unpacked My Grandmother's Trunk.* New York: Dutton.

Holdaway, D. 1979. *Foundations of Literacy.* Portsmouth, NH: Heinemann.

Holt, J. 1964. *How Children Fail.* New York: Dell

Huey, E. B. 1908. *The Psychology and Pedagogy of Reading.* New York: Macmillan. Reissued in 1968 by MIT Press in Cambridge, MA.

Hullfish, H. G., and P. G. Smith. 1961. *Reflective Thinking: The Method of Education.* New York: Dodd, Mead & Company.

Hunt, L. 1970. "Effect of Self-Selection, Interest, and Motivation upon Independent, Instructional, and Frustrational Levels." *Reading Teacher* 24 (2): 146–51.

Hyerle, D. 1993. Thinking Maps as Tools for Multiple Modes of Understanding. Unpublished doctoral dissertation. University of California, Berkeley.

Jensen, E. 2005. *Teaching with the Brain in Mind*, 2d ed. Alexandria, VA: Association for Supervision and Curriculum Development.

Johnston, P. H. 2004. *Choice Words: How Our Language Affects Children's Learning.* Portland, ME: Stenhouse.

Kelley, E. 1947. *Education for What Is Real.* New York: Harper & Bros.

Keene, E. O., and S. Zimmerman. 1997. *Mosaic of Thought.* Portsmouth, NH: Heinemann.

———. 2007. *Mosaic of Thought*, 2d ed. Portsmouth, NH: Heinemann.

LaBerge, D., and S. J. Samuels. 1974. "Toward a Theory of Automatic Information Processing in Reading." *Cognitive Psychology* 6: 293–323.

Langer, J. A. 2001. "Beating the Odds: Teaching Middle and High School Students to Read and Write Well." *American Educational Research Journal* 38: 837–80.

Langer, J. A., and A. N. Applebee. 1987. *How Writing Shapes Thinking: A Study of Teaching and Learning.* Urbana, IL: National Council of Teachers of English.

Latrobe, K. 1996. "Encouraging Reading and Writing Through Readers Theatre." *Emergency Librarian* 23 (3): 16–20.

Leuf, B., and W. Cunningham. 2001. *The Wiki Way: Collaboration and Sharing on the Internet.* Upper Saddle River, NJ: Pearson/Addison Wesley.

Lewis, M., and D. Wray. 1995. *Developing Children's Non-Fiction Writing.* New York: Scholastic.

Lindfors, J. W. 1999. *Children's Inquiry: Using Language to Make Sense of the World.* New York: Teachers College Press and the National Council of Teachers of English.

Lunsford, S. H. 1997. "And They Wrote Happily Ever After: Literature-Based Mini-Lessons in Writing." *Language Arts* 74 (1): 42–48.

MacLachlan, P. 1985 *Sarah, Plain and Tall.* New York: HarperCollins.

Macrorie, K. 1988. *The I-Search Paper: Revised Edition of Searching Writing.* Portsmouth, NH: Heinemann.

Markham, J. C. 2005. "Inquiry Versus Naïve Relativism: James, Dewey, and Teaching the Ethics of Pragmatism." In *Reflective Teaching, Reflective Learning: How to Develop Critically Engaged Readers, Writers, and Speakers*, edited by T. M. McCann, L. R. Johannessen, E. Kahn, P. Smagorinsky, and M. W. Smith. Portsmouth, NH: Heinemann.

Martin, B., Jr. 1996. *Brown Bear, Brown Bear, What Do You See?* New York: Henry Holt and Co.

Marzano, R. J., D. J. Pickering, and J. E. Pollock. 2001. *Classroom Instruction That Works: Research-Based Strategies for Increasing Student Achievement.* Alexandria, CA: Association for Supervision and Curriculum Development.

Mayer, M. 1969. *Frog, Where Are You?* New York: Dial.

McCann, T. M., L. R. Johannessen, E. Kahn, P. Smagorinsky, and M. W. Smith. 2005. *Reflective Teaching, Reflective Learning: How to Develop Critically Engaged Readers, Writers, and Speakers.* Portsmouth, NH: Heinemann.

McCrindle, A. R., and C. Christensen. 1995. "The Impact of Learning Journals on Metacognitive and Cognitive Processes and Learning Performance." *Learning and Instruction* 5 (2): 167–85.

McDonald, J. P., N. Mohr, A. Dichter, and E. C. McDonald. 2007. *The Power of Protocols: An Educator's Guide to Better Practice*, 2d ed. New York: Teachers College Press.

McGovern, A. 1967. *Too Much Noise.* Boston: Houghton Mifflin.

McMahon, S. I., T. E. Raphael, V. J. Goatley, and L. S. Pardo (Eds.). 1997. *The Book Club Connection: Literacy Learning and Classroom Talk.* New York: Teachers College Press.

McNeil, J. D. 1984. *Reading Comprehension: New Directions for Classroom Practice.* Glenview, IL: Scott, Foresman.

McPhail, D. M. 1990. *Lost!* Boston: Little, Brown and Company.

McTighe, J., and F. T. Lyman. 1988. "Cueing Thinking in the Classroom: The Promise of Theory-Embedded Tools." *Educational Leadership* 45 (7): 18–24.

Moffett, J. 1968a. *A Student-Centered Language Arts Curriculum, K–13: A Handbook for Teachers.* Boston: Houghton Mifflin.

———. 1968b. *Teaching the Universe of Discourse.* Boston: Houghton Mifflin.

Moffett, J., and B. J. Wagner. 1991. *Student-Centered Language Arts, K–12*, 4th ed. Portsmouth, NH: Heinemann.

Moguel, D. 2003. "Effective Classroom Discussions: Getting Teachers to Talk Less and Students to Talk More." *Social Studies Review* 42 (2): 96–99.

Nagy, W., R. C. Anderson, and P. Herman. 1987. "Learning Word Meanings from Context During Normal Reading." *American Educational Research Journal* 24: 237–70.

Nagy, W., P. A. Herman, and R. C. Anderson. 1985. "Learning Words from Context." *Reading Research Quarterly* 20: 233–53.

National Institute for Literacy and the Center for the Improvement of Early Reading Achievement (CIERA). 2006. *Put Reading First: Kindergarten Through Grade 3*, 3rd ed. Washington, DC: National Institute for Literacy and the Center for the Improvement of Early Reading Achievement.

National Reading Panel. 2000. *Teaching Children to Read: An Evidence-Based Assessment of the Scientific Research Literature on Reading and Its Implications for Reading Instruction.* Washington, DC: National Reading Panel.

Naughton, V. M. 2008. "Picture It!" *The Reading Teacher* 62 (1): 65–68.

Nemeth, C. 1986. "Differential Contributions of Majority and Minority Influence." *Psychological Review* 93: 23–32.

Nessel, D. 1987. "Reading Comprehension: Asking the Right Questions." *Phi Delta Kappan* 68 (6): 442–45.

Nessel, D., and C. Dixon. 2008. *Using the Language Experience Approach with English Language Learners: Strategies for Engaging Students and Developing Literacy.* Thousand Oaks, CA: Corwin.

Nessel, D., and J. Graham. 2007. *Thinking Strategies for Student Achievement: Improving Learning Across the Curriculum, K–12,* 2d ed. Thousand Oaks, CA: Corwin.

Nessel, D., and M. Jones. 1981. *The Language-Experience Approach to Reading: A Handbook for Teachers.* New York: Teachers College Press.

Nystrand, M., A. Gamoran, R. Kachur, and C. Prendergast. 1997. *Opening Dialogue: Understanding the Dynamics of Language and Learning in the Classroom.* New York: Teachers College Press.

Ogden, C. K., and I. A. Richards. 1923. *The Meaning of Meaning.* New York: Harcourt, Brace and World.

Ogle, D. 1986. "K-W-L: A Teaching Model That Develops Active Reading of Expository Text." *The Reading Teacher* 39 (February): 564–70.

Palincsar, A. S., and A. E. Brown. 1984. "Reciprocal Teaching of Comprehension-Fostering and Comprehension-Monitoring Activities." *Cognition and Instruction* 1 (2): 117–75.

Paris, S. G. 2005. "Reinterpreting the Development of Reading Skills." *Reading Research Quarterly* 40 (2): 184–202.

Paris, S. G., and J. Jacobs. 1984. "The Benefits of Informed Instruction for Children's Reading Awareness and Comprehension Skills." *Child Development* 55: 2083–93.

Parsons, L. T. 2006. "Visualizing Worlds from Words on a Page." *Language Arts* 83 (6): 492–500.

Paul, R. W. 1987. "Dialogical Thinking: Critical Thought Essential to Acquisition of Rational Knowledge and Passions." In *Teaching Thinking Skills: Theory & Practice,* edited by J. B. Baron and R. J. Sternberg, 127–48. New York, Freeman.

Paulsen, G. 1987. *Hatchet.* New York: Bradbury Press.

Pearson, P. D. 2010. "The Roots of Reading Comprehension Instruction." In *Comprehension Across the Curriculum: Perspectives and Practices K–12,* edited by K. Ganske and D. Fisher. New York: The Guilford Press.

Perkins, D., and T. Blythe. 1994. "Putting Understanding Up Front." *Educational Leadership* 51 (5): 11–13.

Piaget, J. 1953. "How Children Learn from Mathematics Concepts." *Scientific American* 189: 74–79.

———. 1973. *Human Intelligence.* New York: Basic Books.

Pichert J. W., and R. C. Anderson, R. C. 1977. "Taking Different Perspectives on a Story." *Journal of Educational Psychology* 69: 309–15.

Postman, N., and C. Weingartner. 1969. *Teaching as a Subversive Activity.* New York: Dell.

Purcell-Gates, V. 1988. "Lexical and Syntactic Knowledge of Written Narrative Held by Well-Read-to Kindergartners and Second Graders." *Research in the Teaching of English* 22: 128–60.

Raphael, T. E., S. Floria-Ruane, and M. George. 2001. *Book Club Plus: A Conceptual Framework to Organize Literacy Instruction.* CIERA Report. Ann Arbor, MI: CIERA/University of Michigan.

Raphael, T. E., L. S. Pardo, and K. Highfield. 2002. *Book Club: A Literature-Based Curriculum.* Littleton, MA: Small Planet Communications.

Raths, L. E., 1961. *Teaching for Thinking.* Columbus, OH: Charles Merrill.

Ritchhart, R. 2002. *Intellectual Character: What It Is, Why It Matters, and How to Get It.* San Francisco: Jossey-Bass.

Roberts, T., and L. Billings. 2008. "Thinking is Literacy, Literacy Thinking." *Educational Leadership* 65 (5): 32–36.

Robinson, A. 1993. *What Smart Students Know.* New York: Crown.

Robinson, F. P. 1970. *Effective Study*, 4th ed. New York: Harper & Row.

Rosenblatt, L. M. 1938. *Literature as Exploration.* New York: Appleton-Century.

———. 1978. *The Reader, the Text, the Poem: The Transactional Theory of the Literary Work.* Carbondale, IL: Southern Illinois University Press.

Ross, L. Q. 1989. "Cemetery Path." In *Goodman's Five-Star Stories: Sudden Twists*, edited by B. Goodman. Providence, RI: Jamestown.

Routman, R. 2002. *Reading Essentials: The Specifics You Need to Teach Reading Well.* Portsmouth, NH: Heinemann.

Rowe, M. B. 1987. "Wait Time: Slowing Down May Be a Way of Speeding Up." *American Educator* 11 (Spring): 38–43, 47.

Russell, D. 1956. *Children's Thinking.* Boston: Ginn and Company.

Rylant, C. 1985 *The Relatives Came.* New York: Simon & Schuster.

Schwartz, B., and P. Gallant. 2009. "Literacy Learning and Instruction: In Search of Complexity." *The Journal of Reading Recovery* 8 (2): 61–65.

Schwartz, R. M., and T. E. Raphael. 1985. "Concept of Definition: A Key to Improving Students' Vocabulary." *The Reading Teacher* 39 (2): 198–205.

Senge, P. 1990. *The Fifth Discipline: The Art and Practice of the Learning Organization.* New York: Doubleday.

Shah, I. 1972. "Cooking by Candle." In *The Exploits of the Incomparable Mulla Nasrudin*, by I. Shah. New York: E. P. Dutton.

Skinner, B. F. 1938. *The Behavior of Organisms.* New York: Appleton-Century-Crofts.

Smagorinsky, P. 2007. "Vygotsky and the Social Dynamics of Classrooms." *English Journal* 97 (2): 61–66.

Smith, F. 1973. "Twelve Easy Ways to Make Learning to Read Difficult." In *Psycholinguistics and Reading*, edited by F. Smith. New York: Holt, Rinehart & Winston.

———. 1998. *The Book of Learning and Forgetting.* New York: Teachers College Press.

Snow, C. 2002. *Reading for Understanding: Toward an R&D Program in Reading Comprehension.* Santa Monica, CA: RAND Science and Technology Policy Institute.

Spache, G. D., and P. C. Berg. 1955. *The Art of Efficient Reading.* New York: Macmillan.

Stahl, R. 1994. "Using 'Think-Time' and 'Wait-Time' Skillfully in the Classroom." ERIC Digest. ED 370 885.

Stauffer, R. G. 1969. *Teaching Reading as a Thinking Process.* New York: Harper & Row.

———. 1970. *The Language-Experience Approach to the Teaching of Reading.* New York: Harper & Row.

———. 1975. *Directing the Reading-Thinking Process.* New York: Harper & Row.

Stauffer, R. G., and A. Burrows. 1960. *The Winston Basic Readers.* New York: Holt, Rinehart & Winston.

Stauffer, R. G., and W. D. Hammond 1965. *Effectiveness of Language Arts and Basic-Reader Approaches to First Grade Reading Instruction.* Final Report, Cooperative Research Project. U.S.O.E. 1769. Newark, DE: University of Delaware.

Taba, H. 1962. *Curriculum Development: Theory and Practice.* New York: Harcourt, Brace & World.

Tatum, A. 2009. *Reading for Their Life: (Re)building the Textual Lineages of African American Adolescent Males.* Portsmouth, NH: Heinemann.

Taylor, B. M., D. S. Peterson, P. D. Pearson, and M. C. Rodriguez. 2002. "Looking Inside Classrooms: Reflecting on the 'How' as Well as the 'What' in Effective Reading Instruction." *The Reading Teacher* 56 (3): 270–79.

Tharp, R. G., and R. Gallimore. 1988. *Rousing Minds to Life: Teaching, Learning, and Schooling in Social Context.* Cambridge: Cambridge University Press.

Thorndike, E. 1917. "Reading as Reasoning: A Study of Mistakes in Paragraph Reading." *The Journal of Educational Psychology* 8 (6): 323–32. Reprinted in 1971 in *Reading Research Quarterly* 6 (4): 425–32.

Torbe, M., and P. Medway. 1981. *The Climate for Learning.* Portsmouth, NH: Boynton/Cook.

Tresselt, A. 1964. *The Mitten: An Old Ukranian Folktale.* New York: Lothrop, Lee & Shepard.

Veatch, J. 1959. *Individualizing Your Reading Program.* New York: Putnam's Sons.

Vogt, E. E., J. Brown, and D. Isaacs. 2003. *The Art of Powerful Questions: Catalyzing Insight, Innovation, and Action.* Mill Valley, CA: Whole Systems Associates.

Vygotsky, L. S. 1962. *Thought and Language.* Cambridge, MA: MIT Press. Originally published in 1934 in Russia.

———. 1978. *Mind in Society: Development of Higher Psychological Processes.* Cambridge, MA: Harvard University Press.

Wallace, L. 2010. "Multicultural Critical Theory. At B-School?" *The New York Times* January 10: BU1.

Watson, J. 1925. *Behaviorism.* New York: W. W. Norton.

Wells, G. 1986. *The Meaning Makers: Children Learning Language and Using Language to Learn.* Portsmouth, NH: Heinemann.

Wells, G., and G. L. Chang-Wells. 1992. *Constructing Knowledge Together: Classrooms as Centers of Inquiry and Literacy.* Portsmouth, NH: Heinemann.

Wink, J., and L. Putney. 2002. *A Vision of Vygotsky.* Boston: Allyn & Bacon.

Wolf, D. P. 1987. "The Art of Questioning." In *Academic Connections, Winter 1987*, edited by R. Orill. New York: College Entrance Examination Board.

Wood, K. D. 1988. "Guiding Students Through Informational Text." *The Reading Teacher* 41: 912–20.

Wood, K. D., D. Lapp, J. Flood, and D. B. Taylor. 2008. *Guiding Readers Through Text: Strategy Guides for New Times*, 2d ed. Newark, DE: International Reading Association.

Zinsser, W. 1988. *Writing to Learn: How to Write—and Think—Clearly About Any Subject at All.* New York: Harper & Row.

———. 2006. *On Writing Well.* 30th anniversary ed. New York: HarperCollins.